BOXL

The Story of an English Parish

by
Daevid Hook and Robin Ambrose

"A time there was, ere England's grief's began,
When every rood of ground maintained its man;
For him light labour spread her wholesome store,
Just gave what life required, but gave no more;
His best companions, innocence and health;
And his best riches, ignorance of wealth".

'The Deserted Village' by Oliver Goldsmith.

Copyright © Daevid Hook
and Robin Ambrose

First published in Great Britain 1999
Reprinted 2009

ISBN 0 9537430 0 4

The rights of Daevid Hook and Robin Ambrose to be identified as the Authors of the work has been asserted by them in accordance with the Copyright, Designs and Patents Act 1988.

All rights reserved. No part of this publication may be reproduced, stored in a retrieval system, or transmitted in any form or by any means without the prior written permission of the authors, nor be otherwise circulated in any form of binding or cover other than that in which it is published and without a similar condition being imposed on the subsequent purchaser.

Printed in Great Britain by Modern Press Ltd., Maidstone, Kent

Dedication

To our wives, Carole and Pat,
for their patience and support.

CONTENTS

Preface
Chapter 1   In The Beginning
Chapter 2   Boxley Abbey and its Dissolution
Chapter 3   The Wyatts
Chapter 4   Boxley Church
Chapter 5   Penenden Heath
Chapter 6   Crime and Punishment
Chapter 7   Community Life
Chapter 8   The Whatmans
Chapter 9   Boxley House
Chapter 10   Park House, Boxley
Chapter 11   Victorian Times
Chapter 12   Boxley School
Chapter 13   The Great War
Chapter 14   The Best-Dalisons
Chapter 15   The Lushingtons
Chapter 16   The Decline and Fall of Vinters
Chapter 17   The Second World War
Chapter 18   The Balstons and The Trousdells
Chapter 19   Boxley Village
Chapter 20   Weavering and Grove Green
Chapter 21   Sandling, Boarley and Tyland
Chapter 22   Down by the River
Chapter 23   Over the Hill
Chapter 24   The Countryside
Chapter 25   Harvesting the Earth
Chapter 26   Boxley Paper Mills
Chapter 27   Famous Connections
Chapter 28   Places of Refreshment
Chapter 29   Odds and Ends

PREFACE

It is over 100 years since Rev. Cave-Browne published his "History of Boxley Parish" in 1892. We have felt it time to up-date and expand upon his book, and in doing so we have adopted the scope of the old Boxley parish, which was larger than today's. This gives us the opportunity to include the stories of Penenden Heath, the Whatmans and Vinters, the Lushingtons, and the areas westwards to the river, north over the Downs, and east to Weavering and Grove Green. All this is set against the changing worlds of agriculture, education, employment, the Church, and society in general.

Our sources are the rich archive material available at County Hall and at Strood, and also at Maidstone Museum. We refer frequently to Cave-Browne and to Edward Hasted who published his History of Kent around 1800. Also to William Coles-Finch who included Boxley subjects in many of his writings and to J.M. Russell's "History of Maidstone" of 1881. A Maidstone local historian Mr J.W. Bridge left much material behind, as well as leaving his own impact as a personality and builder. The annual volumes of the Kent Archaeological Society (Arch. Cant) have been another fruitful source, together with the Smythe Manuscripts and the E.R. Hughes sketches and history held in the Maidstone Museum Library. May it not be thought arrogant if we presume to have found some inaccuracies in these earlier writings and to have tried to correct them.

We have looked to the memories imparted to us by very many people who knew Boxley in the old days. Their kindness and patience in letting us into their homes to reminisce and to show us around is much appreciated. There are too many to thank them all by name, but we are particularly grateful to the Best-Shaw family who have made available photos and memorabilia of Park House in the times of Major Best and later the Best-Dalisons. To Marc Cummins, who with some friends had the foresight to talk to Wally Gosling in his twilight years and record memories going back to 1900. To Mrs Marjorie Lyle for making available the memories of her parents Helen Watt and Rev. John Watt. To Hugh Balston and his family for their memories of Louisa Whatman, Vinters, the Trousdells and much besides. Not least to Rev. Malcolm Bradshaw, who came across the Wallis memoirs and has put us in touch with many interesting people.

Finally, thanks to Michael Carter, Fran Wilson and the staff at both local Archives, to Richard Stutely and Veronica Tong at Maidstone Museum who have all aided our researches, and to Tim Wakelin for his photographic assistance.

CHAPTER 1
In the Beginning

Outwardly, the village of Boxley displays an air of timelessness, remaining, almost uniquely for this part of Kent, virtually untouched by the ravages of twentieth century 'progress'. How long this can be maintained is questionable with the M20 now bisecting the southern borders of the parish and the High Speed Rail Link planned to decimate its western flanks, and The Street, Boxley under siege by the motor car.

Almost unaltered for the past two centuries, the village probably first became established somewhere after 825 A.D., in the years of comparative peace that followed the termination of the independent Kingdom of Kent by the successful invasion of Egbert of Wessex. Prior to this the inhabitants dwelt in a collection of isolated farms, as their forbears had done for centuries.

The Domesday Book of 1086 first names Boxley as a village, but the history of the land covered by the old parish of Boxley is as old as time itself. The neighbouring village of Aylesford justifiably lays claim to being one of the oldest continuously inhabited villages in the country. When our earliest ancestors first decided to cease their nomadic lives and put down roots, rivers were the highways that gave access through the impenetrable forests that cloaked the interior of Britain. They settled the fertile river banks and evidence of their occupation remains in the splendid group of Neolithic megaliths in the Medway valley, the most famous of which, Kits Coty, is less than a thousand metres outside Boxley's boundary. The historian Hasted mentions a group of standing stones which he says stood in 'Goddards Hill' within Boxley parish, but this is almost certainly a reference to Gottes Hill which was the old name for Blue Bell Hill. The stones were either an avenue of stones that bordered the old Roman road below the crest of the hill, or a chambered tomb that stood in the field behind Cossington Service Station, looking very much like Kits Coty and about 400 metres outside the parish. Incidentally, Gottes Hill became known as Boxley Hill and then later, probably to avoid confusion with the road we now know as Boxley Hill, it took its current appellation from the Old Blew Bell Inn which stood upon the slope overlooking Kits Coty.

Utilising the high ridges of the Downs to orientate themselves, the early Britons created a trackway, which today is closely followed by the North Downs Way. They spread outwards, hacking clearings from the dense vegetation. A

BOXLEY PARISH

Neolithic axe from Boxley Warren chalk quarry and later Bronze Age artefacts from Boarley, Tyland and behind the Chiltern Hundreds stand witness to those first to dwell in what became Boxley Parish.

The Romans came and brought with them their technological skills. Their mastery of stone ensured that their presence would be remembered as never before, their buildings being the first which did not rot away with time, and most importantly enabled them to create the outstanding legacy of their wonderful network of roads. Their first great highway of Watling Street traversed the far side of the Downs from Canterbury to Rochester and on to London, and another ran from Rochester down Blue Bell Hill (some 100 yards nearer to Boxley than the present road), then via Week Street and Stone Street where Maidstone later evolved, to Amber Green near Staplehurst, and on to the coast. A lesser road ran beneath the southern slopes of the Downs from Wouldham and Burham, crossing near Cossington Service Station and on through Boxley, Detling and Thurnham. At the western end of Boxley parish it remains as just a line of trees before becoming a farm track alongside Boarley Farm, then a footpath through the cornfields to Forge Lane, in the village, then close by the church and on to Harpole Farm and Detling.

On examining the map one discovers that the site of St Stephen's chapel at Cossington, below Kits Coty, and the churches of Boxley, Detling and Thurnham lie on an exact straight line. It is fascinating to conjecture whether these buildings arose alongside the Roman road, or did the Romans improve on an earlier straight track which had sacred sites along its way? It is amazing just how many churches lie along 'ley lines', which are said to plot the course of ancient energy, which our 'civilisation' no longer allows us to feel.

Yet another road ran from Wrotham crossing the Medway near Springfield and Moncktons Lane at a point later known as Radford, possibly referring to the ford where Saxons crossed to attend the 'Raed' or meeting place on Penenden Heath. Early historians believed that near where this road meets today's Sandling Road, was the site of the 'lost' Roman station of Vagniacae. However this has not been substantiated by hard archaeological evidence. Around this time also, the country's first great trade route evolved along the lower slopes of the Downs, which we now refer to as the Pilgrim's Way. Cornwall sent her tin for trade and many a poor soul trod the way en route to slavery in Europe.

Although no definite evidence of Roman villas has been found unlike those nearby at Eccles and the Mount by the High Level Bridge in Maidstone, Roman building material has been observed incorporated in the construction of Boxley Abbey, and coins, brooches and even a pair of tweezers have been unearthed to the north of the Abbey, indicating that a Roman farmhouse probably stood near the road in the vicinity of Boarley Farm. Which site is probably the longest continually inhabited in the parish. Roman interments at Harp Farm and Vinters and at the new A229 roundabout near Tyland, bottles and pottery at Cobtree, and artefacts from near Harbourland show that Roman settlement extended throughout the parish. Harbourland possibly takes its name from the remains of an ancient stone building (i.e. a Roman farmstead or villa), which provided shelter for later pilgrims or travellers.

The removal of troops from Britain to defend Rome against the barbarian hordes, left the Britons to face the marauding raiders and Picts alone. King Vortigern sought military aid from the low lands of Europe, the best known of which mercenaries were the Jutish chieftains Hengist and Horsa. (Although historians are undecided whether these were their real names). With their new allies, the Britons crushed the Picts and Hengist was awarded the governership of Kent. Gradually however, the Britons came to regret allowing foreigners to colonise their lands, and deposing Vortigern they elected his son Vortimer and engaged the Jutes in battle at what became known as 'The Battle of Aylesford'. Certainly this battle was fought in the vicinity, but the Anglo Saxon Chronicle records it as at Aegelsthrep, which does not translate as Aylesford. Interestingly, the 1611 description of the boundary of Boxley, places an Aglesfield on the borders of Boxley and Bredhurst, suggesting that the battle was not contested at the ford but fought on higher ground in Boxley. Tradition has it that the Jutes' Kentish standard of white horse tails was raised at a large sarsen stone thereafter known as The White Horse Stone. This stone lay by the road in a field known as Standard field, opposite Cossington Service Station, but was destroyed in 1823. The stone now bearing its name, which lies on Boxley's boundary, is probably one of the stones from the previously mentioned chambered tomb on Gottes Hill which was removed to the field edge when the tomb was destroyed by a well known wrecker of ancient monuments, Farmer Green. If the stone had been in its present position in 1611 it would almost certainly have been incorporated as a significant marker of the Boxley boundary.

Although it is probable that the Britons won the battle of Aylesford, driving the Jutes back into their stronghold of the Isle of Thanet, just two years later they were themselves crushed at Crecganford (possibly Crayford) and abandoned Kent which for more than 350 years became the Jutish/Saxon Kingdom of Kent.

In 695, Wihtred, one of the greatest Kings, is recorded as holding a council of his nobles and clergy at Bearsted, to draw up a code of laws. It is quite possible that this actually took place on Penenden Heath, the traditional meeting place for the people of Kent, which covered a far larger area than it does today. As there does not appear to have been an actual settlement at Boxley at that time, it was recorded as at the nearest village of Bearsted.

Peace never lasted long in our part of Kent, and the Danes were the next invaders. Tradition has it that they raided up the Medway and sacked a Saxon fort near where Allington Lock now stands. Although this could have stood near St Lawrence's church, Allington, it is just as likely to have been in Boxley on the high ground now occupied by the Museum of Rural Life at Sandling. The discovery of a Viking bearded axe in Sandling Lane lends weight to this theory.

In 894 King Alfred's troops under his son Edward, routed the Danes at the battle of Farnham, which many historians have incorrectly sited at Farnham in Surrey, but which almost certainly was the now defunct and little known settlement of Farnham which stood on the borders of Boxley and Aylesford, south of the crematorium on Blue Bell Hill.

Yet again, in 1016 blood soaked Boxley's fields when Edmund Ironside defeated a Danish force at Otford and drove it in flight across the ford at Aylesford and through the streets of the village, their pursuit taking them probably along the Roman road, down Forge Lane and through the village of Boxley.

History next impinges itself on Boxley in 1066 when King Harold having repulsed Harold Hardrada, the Norwegian claimant to the throne, at Stamford Bridge near York, force-marched his troops south following the news that William of Normandy had landed at Pevensey. He rested for four days at London to allow the local militia, or 'fyrd', to gather, then probably via Watling Street he marched south through Rochester and down Blue Bell Hill to where his Kentish reinforcements awaited him, gathered in their customary meeting place on Penenden Heath. So the men of Boxley marched off to death and defeat at Senlac Hill and surrended their freedom to the Norman yoke.

England was shared out under Norman overlords. William's half-brother Bishop Odo was granted the Earldom of Kent as a reward for his valour at Hastings where, despite being a cleric and thus restrained by his vows from bearing edged weapons or drawing blood, he was always in the thick of the action. He must have been a fearsome sight, with his large frame encased in chain mail, laying about him with a stout iron mace. Most historians paint Odo as a greedy man who began encroaching on the lands belonging to the church, including Maidstone hundred, and thus Boxley. However, it is now commonly agreed that the lands concerned had been illegally taken over by King Harold and his brothers prior to the conquest, and only inherited by Odo. In 1076, Lanfranc the Archbishop of Canterbury, sued for restoration of his property and a huge concourse of both Saxon and Norman nobility and the local populace, gathered on Penenden Heath for the trial. After three days of wrangling over the nuances of Anglo Saxon law, there was a finding in favour of Lanfranc and Odo was forced to relinquish a number of his holdings, including Boxley.

Penenden Heath, being the place where the 'shiremote' met three times a year, conducted by the King's sheriff, and attended by all the local dignitaries, was again the venue in 1086 when the landowners were called to meet there to provide full particulars of all their landholdings for the Domesday survey. This is the first real insight we have as to the Boxley we know today.

"In Maidstone Hundred in the Lathe of Aylesford, Robert Latimer holds Boseleu (Boxley). Before 1066 it answered for 7 sulungs (1400 acres) and now for 5 sulungs (1000 acres). Land for 20 ploughs. The lordship has 3 ploughs. 47 villagers with 11 smallholders have 16 ploughs. 3 mills at 36 shillings and 8 pence. 16 slaves. 20 acres of meadows. Woodland for 50 pigs. Value before 1066 – £25, now £30 but Robert pays £55. Previously young Alnoth held it (this was the brother of King Harold). Helto the steward holds $^1/_2$ sulung (100 acres) of this manor. He has 1 plough, 1 smallholder and a Frenchman, 2 acres of meadow and woodland to graze 6 pigs – value 40 shillings".

Thus the recorded population of Boxley was 76 (60 freedmen plus 16 slaves) compared to 108 in Maidstone. Boxley however appears to have been a valuable property with its 3 mills and quite possibly having a Church even at that early date.

CHAPTER 2

Boxley Abbey and its Dissolution

jFollowing Odo's disgrace, the Boxley lands remained the property of The Crown for many years. As a reward for his support in helping him usurp the throne from The Conqueror's granddaughter Matilda, King Stephen granted William of Ypres much land in Kent, including the Manor of Boxley. Apparently a somewhat unpleasant character who had been heavily involved in suppressing the anarchy which followed Stephen's enthronement, William later began to regret his misdeeds. Doubtless to curry favour for himself in the after-life he, like a number of his contemporaries, decided to support the fledgeling Cistercian Order. Founded in Burgundy in 1098, they built their first British Abbey at Waverley in Surrey in 1128 and by the end of that century their holdings had blossomed to over 100 religious houses.

In 1146 William constructed the Abbey of Boxley, and brought over monks from Clairvaux in France, granting them the Manor of Boxley in exchange for absolution, and their prayers for his eternal soul. The Cistercians were known as 'White Monks' because of their white dress, although outside of the Abbey walls they covered themselves with a black cloak. Originally called 'St. Mary's', it later took the name of 'The Abbey of The Holy Cross of Grace'.

All Cistercian Abbeys were built to a standard plan and one need only look at the imposing ruins of Rievaulx or Fountains Abbeys to appreciate Boxley Abbey's impact upon the neighbourhood and local people. It stood and dominated the area for 400 years, gradually gaining in prosperity as gifts of land and money were thrust its way. Included in these were the Manors of Hoo, Chessington and Yarmouth, Stoke Church, Eastchurch and Chingley. Also the head of the Boarley spring waters, the corn mill (whose remains still stand close to The Running Horse hostelry), Fairmeadow in Maidstone, the right to catch and keep rabbits on the downs at Boarley and Boxley Warrens, the right to fish the Medway opposite Allington Castle, and the right to hold a fair. This fair was in the locality, close by the present Yew Tree Inn, still known by the name of 'Farthings', and one supposes that the fair was used to trade horses, cattle and the like.

On his accession to the throne in 1189, Richard I granted the monks a charter confirming their possessions, which was later renewed on at least two occasions. Perhaps in gratitude, it was Abbot Robert of Boxley, together with the Abbot of Robertsbridge, who in 1193, travelled to Bavaria to find and ultimately arrange the release of King Richard, after his capture and imprisonment by Saladin. (Popular history has chosen to record incorrectly a more colourful tale of the minstrel Blondel). Another Abbot, Walter, was present in Canterbury at the murder of Thomas Becket, and as Becket was himself a Cistercian, Walter undertook his hurried burial at the risk of the King's displeasure. As it was the dominating edifice in the area, Edward II chose to reside at Boxley Abbey in October 1321. He was laying siege to Leeds Castle, following the refusal of its guardian to provide lodgings for Queen Isabella en-route for pilgrimage to Canterbury. The Abbey also served as a haven for those who temporarily, or sometimes permanently, required to slip from the public's eye. One of the former, was Haymo, Bishop of Rochester who in 1326 was summoned to London with the other ecclesiastic hierarchy, to help effect a reconciliation between King Edward II and his Queen. The populace supported the Queen, and a plan was hatched by the citizens to seize the Bishop of London and attack those supporting the King. The Bishop of Exeter fell into the hands of the mob and was beheaded at Cheapside, and his contemporaries were forced to flee for their lives. The Archbishop of Canterbury escaped by the expediency of 'borrowing' Haymo's horse, causing the hapless prelate to flee on foot. Two days later the footsore Haymo finally found refuge in Boxley Abbey. The weak and inept King Edward was murdered the following year. Abbey life was not all peace and harmony as illustrated by Abbot John's appeal to the crown in 1512 for the arrest of four monks, who were said to be rebellious and apostate.

Although it is a subject so well aired in most writings on Boxley, brief mention must be made of the "Rood of Grace". This was a wooden figure of Christ which, to those who made pilgrimage to come and see it, seemed miraculously to move. The story is that the image was made by a carpenter whilst serving as a prisoner in France. Upon his escape or release he made his way back to England with the image carried on the back of a horse. Close by Boxley the horse suddenly bolted and made its way to the Abbey, at the last galloping inside. From this story comes the name of the hostelry, "The Running Horse". The image remained at the Abbey, which also offered at least one other, namely a stone image of St Rumbold which only the pure of heart could lift. The many pilgrims who received the right signs from these images showered the monks with gifts of money. So it was that the Abbey became very rich indeed, both in money and in land.

By the time of Henry VIII the Abbey lands covered a considerable area, the better part of the old Boxley Parish. East to the village and beyond; west beyond Tyland; south to the Sandling Water Mill and north over the Downs, where names such as Upper Grange Farm and Monkdown Wood tell their own story. The name 'Grange' is worth considering. A dictionary definition is an outlying farmhouse belonging to a Monastery or feudal lord. As well as Upper Grange Farm there is Lower Grange Farm (sometimes called the Nether

Grange) which lies to the south of the Abbey and is now divided from it by the Motorway. This connection will be where the name Grange Lane comes from. Several farms would have served the Abbey. Hasted mentions Abbey Farm lying "nearer the hills". This is probably what we now know as Boarley Farm and not the present Abbey Farm which is close by the road which leads to the Abbey.

The Cistercians were exempted from paying tithes on the lands they occupied. This was later to be the subject of an argument in 1846 when the then owner of the Abbey Lands, Lord Romney, clashed with the Vicar of Boxley. The latter insisted that tithes were due to him from the tenants of Upper Grange Farm and Harps Farm. Romney succeeded in proving that these had been part of the Abbey lands and that at the time of the dissolution Henry VIII had conferred the tithe exemption on the lands for all time. The Best family were able to use the same argument to cease paying tithes on Court Lodge Farm.

Only two of the Abbey buildings remain. The massive barn-like structure, which mercifully still stands brooding in sight of the motorway, is normally described as a barn or granary. However, the evidence of an original upper floor, with the existing windows which would have given it light, and the lack of an original large door to allow the entry of a high-laden wagon, both suggest another purpose. The better opinion is that this was the "hospitum" to the Abbey where travellers would have found shelter without impinging on the quiet contemplation of the monks. It is quite awe-inspiring to step inside this ancient building. Its length is 197 feet and its width 36 feet. There are massive beams, believed to be made of durmast oak, and the timbers supporting the roof are set in a scissor truss. The main structure is of local ragstone, whose durability has aided its survival. Architectural historians have dated half of the roof to about 1280, with the other half, which has more elaborate joints and a king post, being a little later. It would therefore appear likely that the building was at some time doubled in size to become one of the largest such structures in England. Adaptability has also ensured its long life. Although not designed as a barn, the passing centuries have seen it pass to agricultural use for storage and the like. In the 1840's and 1850's John Millen and a partner set up Millen and George's Brewery there. One outlet was James Bath's beerhouse in one of the Abbey Gate Cottages nearby, probably the one at the western end. Another outlet was a beerhouse built by George Fowle at the Forstal near Aylesford, which became the Pottery Arms. After all, Millen and George were only reviving that English tradition of brewing which first began in her Abbeys.

The other remaining Abbey building stands just below the present Abbey Farm on the corner with Grange Lane. This is the old St. Andrew's chapel, which contained a holy relic, said to be the little finger of St. Andrew, encased in silver. It has had a mixed history, probably being first built in the late 1400's for pilgrims to hear Mass before proceeding to the Abbey and its images, or continuing their journey to Becket's shrine at Canterbury. It seems that there was once accommodation for a priest to live there as well, one such being John Personne in 1490. After the dissolution and the Reformation, and during the centuries which followed, it was to become entirely a dwelling, then in part a shop and at one time a Post Office. It is a very important survival. There are local legends that a tunnel connects the Chapel to the Abbey, and indeed of tunnels shooting off from the Abbey in all directions. A memory persists also that the monks would travel by boat up the Medway to Allington and make their way to the Abbey by way of footpaths which survive today. These include the stretch which runs between Sandling Place and Invicta Lines to link the Chatham Road with Sandling Lane, known by some as "cut-throat" alley.

And so to the Dissolution. By the 1500's the Abbey seems not to have been

A private sketch from the Best-Shaw collection, showing the abbey Gateway and a building to the right, long ago demolished.

managed too well. Perhaps they had grown complacent with their riches. Certainly the Abbot was not setting a very good example. In 1508 the Abbot was a constant visitor to Allington Castle where he was wont to flirt with Lady Wyatt's maids. One day he went too far and the spirited Lady Wyatt had him carried out of the main gateway and placed in stocks in front of the castle. He complained to the King, and Sir Henry Wyatt was called in front of the Privy Council to explain his wife's action. Wyatt told them that if any of them had done what the Abbot did then she would have clapped them in the stocks as well! This induced much laughter and Lady Wyatt was quite properly forgiven.

Even before the Dissolution the Crown had become jealous of the incomes of all Abbeys, and a tax was raised. Boxley had to ask for time to pay, and an inspection took place which found various shortcomings. The pot was now boiling. As well as his matrimonial problems and quarrels with the Pope, Henry VIII was short of money. His seizure of the Monasteries of England swung into action and was irresistible. In Boxley's case Abbot John Dobbes went quietly and surrendered the Abbey to the Crown in 1537. Legends persist that the monks buried there treasure somewhere in Boxley and that it still waits to be found.

It was during the seizure of the Abbey's possessions that the "Rood of Grace" was found to be a fraud, its miraculous movements having been achieved by artful parts which were manipulated by the Monks themselves. Similarly the pure of heart had been helped to lift St Rumbold's image by hidden hands or devices. And yet when questioned the old Monks disclaimed any knowledge of these malpractices. Considering the mood of the time it seems strange that neither Abbot nor Monks were punished. Indeed, the Abbot and senior monks were granted pensions. The images were ceremoniously destroyed. The anti-Catholic mood is well captured by the words of a contemporary who wrote that the "silly lambs of God's flock were seduced by the false Romish foxes at this Abbey".

By a mixture of desecration, robbing of stone by local people, and the ravages of time and nature, the Abbey fell into ruins. In their time the Puritans wrought some more destruction. What now remains is part of a gateway, a not inconsiderable run and height of outer walling and the previously noted Barn and chapel. The sale particulars for the Abbey in 1890 included the information that in the Abbey wall on the west side of the kitchen garden are said to be two entrances to underground passages, leading to Boxley Church in the east and Allington Castle in the south west. Interestingly, the antiquarian Thomas Charles made a sketch of the north west tower of Allington Castle showing a door described as 'the entrance to the secret passage'. A projection of both passages would put them in exact alignment. Did the Wyatts who once owned both properties, construct a bolt-hole along the 1200 yards between them? More realistically, photographs exist showing an underground conduit at the Abbey, of ragstone construction and some 5 foot to 6 foot high. Above this would have been the 'neccessarium' or row of privies, which could be 'flushed' via a system of sluices directing water from the stream which arose to the north of the Abbey, through the conduit and on to the cess-pit. In place of the Abbey there was to arise a Tudor mansion built by the Wyatt family, though much altered over the centuries.

Anyone seeking detail about the Abbey's layout and facilities is best referred to the 1973 volume of Archaeologia Cantiana.

Sir Henry Wyatt.

CHAPTER 3

The Wyatts

Having seized the Abbey, Henry VIII exchanged most it its lands and those of the vicarage of Boxley with one if his favourites Sir Thomas Wyatt in 1540. Because the lands given by Henry were granted to Sir Thomas for his lifetime only, on his death in 1542 they reverted to the Crown. However, it was not long before his son, Sir Thomas Wyatt the Younger, again took possession of the Boxley lands. A grant probably earned by his valour at the Siege of Landrecies and at Boulogne.

The Wyatts tend to be better known for their association with Allington Castle, which lies across the Medway from the western boundary of Boxley parish. In fact Boxley has just as great a claim to the family, as the memorial tablet in the chancel of the Church testifies. The first Wyatt of note was a Yorkshire man, Sir Henry Wyatt. He is the subject of the story that whilst imprisoned in Scotland by Richard III during the Wars of the Roses, he was left unfed, but befriended a cat who gave him warmth and brought pigeons to his cell. Henry persuaded his jailer to cook them for him, and thus sustained, survived his ordeal. After the Battle of Bosworth, the victorious Earl of Richmond, now crowned as Henry VII, and the first Tudor King, freed him and seven years later in 1492 Henry Wyatt purchased Allington Castle.

Sir Henry also found favour with Henry VIII who when he visited Wyatt at Allington Castle would have his bedroom door drywalled up each night behind himself and his manservant, for extra security. Sir Henry's wife, Anne, was a formidable woman according to anecdotes in the family records. The previous chapter told of how she clapped an Abbot of Boxley in the castle stocks.

Sir Henry's son, Sir Thomas Wyatt the Elder, was born at Allington in 1503. He was a talented poet famed for introducing the sonnet into English poetry; and like his father spent much time at the Royal Court. In his youth, Thomas was reputedly the lover of Ann Boleyn who often visited from her father's neighbouring castle of Hever. Many of his love sonnets are believed to be inspired by her and by the beauty of the fields, woods and river around Allington and Boxley. Following his early estrangement from his young wife Elizabeth, daughter of Lord Cobham, court gossip claimed the rekindling of the affair. Whilst awaiting execution, Queen Anne comforted herself by reading a book of his poems, and was attended on the scaffold by Thomas's sister Margaret Wyatt, by whom she sent to Thomas a jewel with the single word

'Remember'. Thomas surreptitiously removed her body and arranged for its burial. Despite the rumours connecting him to Ann, and his brief arrest at the time of her trial, he managed to escape Henry VIII's notorious wrath, and indeed went on to exchange lands with the King and become the owner of what became known as the Boxley Manor and Boxley Abbey Estates, including the Manor of Newnham Court.

Sir Thomas Wyatt the Younger was very different from his more cerebral father. He is well recorded as a youthful hell-raiser, especially his feats of window-breaking on the streets of London, for which he spent a month in The Tower, and his love of 'sport'. He installed a bull-ring at Allington Castle where bulls would be savaged by dogs whilst his cronies bet on which dog would prove bravest.

In 1553, when Queen Mary decided to marry Philip of Spain, he became involved with the dissidents who were fearful of the Catholic influence on their religion. Thomas's descendants claimed that he mistrusted the empire building ambitions of the Spanish and their penchant for slavery, but it is possible that he was most influenced by his fear that the vast Boxley Abbey lands which he held, might be returned to the Church. Originally he had planned to move abroad prior to the marriage, but the imminent confinement of his wife with his son George, delayed him, and he was induced by his associates to become the figurehead of the rebellion.

He instigated meetings on Penenden Heath where the cause was espoused, and on 25th January 1554 in Maidstone High Street he proclaimed the start of the uprising. Most of the common men of Boxley marched with him, behind the banners of their respective lords, which between them controlled almost all of the lands in the parish. Sir Henry Isley of Sundridge, owned the Vinters Estate, occupied by his brother Thomas; the Knyvett family held the Park House, Sandling Estate, and Wyatt himself was Lord of the Abbey and Manor Estates. About five years earlier, the West-Kent lords had set up a militia scheme to support the Duke of Northumberland's government following his overthrow of Protector Somerset. (England was governed by 'Protectors' throughout the six year reign of Edward VI, who was only ten at his accession). The existence of these 'trained bands', provided a ready means of mobilisation, and a nucleus of fighting men.

First securing Rochester, they marched on London, picking up support along the way. The failures of the planned uprisings in Devon and the Midlands through betrayal and lack of organisation, and the withdrawal of the promised support of the Londoners, coupled with Wyatt's hesitancy to seize his opportunities, were fatal to the success of the revolt. Gradually his followers dwindled and he was arrested and charged with treason. Refusing to implicate Mary's sister (later Queen) Elizabeth in the uprising, he was executed and hung on a gibbet on Hay Hill, near where now stands Berkeley Square. Later his body was drawn and quartered and his head set on a pole. Ironically many of his local supporters, whilst awaiting trial, were imprisoned at Allington Castle, where earlier they had gathered to plan the rebellion. Sir Henry and Thomas Isley were hung upon Penenden Heath and their heads set on poles at Maidstone bridge, whilst the Knyvett brothers were hanged at Sevenoaks. Their lands and Wyatt's, and thus almost the entire parish of Boxley, were seized by The Crown. It was not only the landowners of Boxley who suffered. For example, John Warcoppe a tenant farmer of land near the Great Lake of Boxley, was attainted for high treason. Subsequently pardoned and fined, he lost his tile kiln and tenancy. Alexander Fisher tenant of Harpole Farm was also fined. How many Boxley men lost their lives following their lords is not known, but it is perhaps significant that the valuation of Wyatt's estates following their seizure shows that more than 10% of the 53 farms were occupied by widows.

With their enormous wealth and possessions stripped from them, including their Allington Castle home, Sir Thomas's widow Jane and her 5 children found themselves virtually penniless and homeless. Probably as a result of petitioning by Jane's half-sister Mary Finch, a member of the Queens Privy Chamber, Queen Mary granted Jane a small residue of her estate and an annuity of 200 marks. The majority of the lands were distributed to local dignitaries who had opposed the insurrection, such as Sir Robert Southwell sheriff of Kent, Sir Thomas Cheney and George Clarke of Wrotham. The latter of whom received the Nether Grange Estate (Lower Grange) and the Park House, Sandling Estate. Mary Finch also received a grant of some of Sir Thomas's lands and throughout the following reign of Queen Elizabeth various favourites received parcels of the estate, notably Sir John Astley who received almost half of the farms in Boxley. In 1567, by which time Sir Thomas's eldest son Arthur had died unmarried, Queen Elizabeth granted to the surviving son George, the manor of Weavering, and intriguingly to his 'brother', Edward the manor of Coptre (Cobtree), Coldblowes and Shires Mead. George had no brother, and it is possible that Edward Wyatt (who died in 1590) was an indiscretion of the juvenile Thomas Wyatt the Younger. However the Royal Historical Society supposed him to be an illegitimate son of Sir Thomas Wyatt the Elder, which would have made him George's uncle. It has even been conjectured that his mother was Ann Boleyn! This separate branch of the Wyatt family continued to live at Cobtree and generations of them were buried at Aylesford rather than with their kinfolk in Boxley. In 1570, by an Act of Parliament, Sir Thomas's children were 'restored in blood', and thus their rights as his legitimate heirs were recognised, and more of the Boxley lands were returned to the family. It is not clear just which lands were given by Queen Mary to Jane and which were granted later by Elizabeth to Jane and George. Various farms and holdings probably came in dribs and drabs as their grants and indentures expired. Certainly by 1622, George, having inherited his mother's estate was living at Boxley Abbey where he died two years later.

BOXLEY PARISH

Whether it was the Wyatts themselves who built the Tudor Mansion amongst the Abbey ruins is not known for certain. The present house, which takes the name Boxley Abbey, includes surviving parts of the original mansion, including just one of the original tall Tudor chimneys. It seems that a new facade was constructed in the 1700's and further alterations took place over the years. An old plan of 1801 shows it originally as a large 'L' shaped building, but a year after purchasing it in 1814, Lord Aylesford pulled down the long wing and sold the material off in lots. William Balston bought some for use in Springfield House.

Only two of George's nine children lived a full span and left children of their own – Hawte and Francis, who both sought to redeem the families fortunes in America. Francis had married Margaret, daughter of Sir Samuel Sandys. Her uncle Sir Edwin Sandys effectively controlled the Virginia Company and in 1620, now knighted, Sir Francis went to America as Governor of Virginia and his brother Hawte accompanied him as preacher. Both returned to Boxley in 1626. In 1632 Hawte succeeded his father's lifelong friend George Case as Vicar of Boxley. His younger brother Henry had been Curate of Boxley for two years prior to his premature death in 1624. Sir Francis returned to the Colonies for a second term as Governor in 1639, accompanied by Hawte's two sons George and Edward. Edward married there and became the ancestor of the Virginia 'Wiats', descendants of which dynasty return frequently to Boxley to trace their roots. It was probably Sir Francis who first altered the spelling of the surname to Wiat or Wiatt.

Boxley Abbey circa 1760. The main wing which was pulled down in 1815.

Sir Francis's uncle by marriage, George Sandys, who at his death in 1643 was described by the then Vicar of Boxley as the premier English poet of this era, spent his final years at the Abbey. He made use of the summerhouse there to produce many of his works, and became a great influence on the poets who followed him. He lies buried in the chancel of Boxley Church, and there is a tablet and window to his memory.

Henry Wiat inherited on the death of his father Sir Francis, and on his own death willed the Estate to his daughter Frances, wife of Sir Thomas Selyard (Seyliard). Henry's surviving brother Edwin, a sergeant-at-law, and later M.P for Maidstone, contested Lady Selyard's title to the Estate. Eventually it was agreed that Boxley Manor would go to Edwin whilst the Selyards would retain Boxley Abbey. It was probably Edwin who built Boxley Manor House, but the Wiat name was not to hold sway in Boxley for much longer. Not one of his seven children produced an heir. At the death of Richard Wiat in 1753, the manor passed to Lord Romney, whose father had married Margaret Bosvile, whose mother Virginia was Edwin's sister, daughter of Sir Francis Wyatt. Boxley House became part of the vast Romney Estate.

BOXLEY PARISH

Boxley Church mid 1800's with the puzzling building on the right mentioned on page 257.

CHAPTER 4
Boxley Church

The traditional view of the ages of the various parts of the Church is that the outer porch was the original Norman Church built about 1100, followed by the present main building of about 1250, with the Tower rising in two stages, latterly in the 1400's. When the "new" Church was built, the original one was relegated to more practical and less holy uses. Mr J.W. Bridge thought that it was probably used as a workshop or store in connection with the later building works, and then left as a meeting room. Mr Bridge also suggested why the outer porch (and others like it) came to be called the Galilee Chamber. It lies outside the main Church building, just as Galilee lay on the edge of Palestine and was none too fertile and of lesser significance. As to the narrow door in the north wall of the porch, some think this would have led to a rood screen in the original Church whilst others think it more likely to have led to an upper chamber which was either later removed or perhaps never completed.

In 1997 Mr David Carder examined the Church building closely and wrote an essay, and he consents to references to his own deductions and opinions. Like many before him he was intrigued by the porch. Viewed externally, the most obvious feature is that the west door is not central, and that original windows have been blocked up, all indicating major alterations over the years. Internally the north wall is a hotch-potch of masonry, with the remains of two arches. On the east wall can be seen the outline of a very steep roof. David Carder believes that the original Church had a tower (upon which the present tower has risen) and presents the following as a possible order of events:-

1. A pre-Conquest Church existed on the site. If this was stone rather than timber, the nave may still be represented in the walling of the porch.

2. A Norman Church was built around 1100, comprising an aisled nave with a central tower, and below that a chancel, and a sanctuary to the east. The nave may have incorporated the Saxon one. An aisle to the north may have been added later in the 1100, only to be demolished by the late 1400's.

3. In the early 1200's the present aisled nave and chancel were built, so relegating the old nave to common use.

4. In the early 1400's the tower was rebuilt on existing foundations. A rood loft may have been added at around this time.

However, there is evidence that the church was in existence earlier than 1100. Our own research has uncovered, amongst the archive papers of The

Dean and Chapter of Rochester, a charter made by Henry I dated 1101. In this, Henry grants to The Cathedral and Priory of St. Andrew the Apostle at Rochester – 'Boxley Church with all appurtenances, lands, tithes customs and liberties, just as and better than ever Giffard, the King's chaplain held it, and Ansfrid the clerk, before that'. Ansfrid is mentioned in the Domesday Book of 1086 as holding many lands in Kent. It would seem probable that Boxley Church existed at the time of Domesday, but possibly was not mentioned in the book, because the church was held separately from the rest of the village. Robert Latimer holding the manor, and Ansfrid, the church.

When we attempt to go back beyond the Conquest we enter realms of guesswork and imagination. How far back do we dare to go? In our opening chapter we pointed out the co-incidence of the Churches of Thurnham, Detling and Boxley laying on a straight line which projected westwards leads to the site of St Stephen's Chapel at Tottington, amongst the ancient stones which lie below Kits Coty. It is believed that around Tottington in ancient times there were stone circles, destroyed over the years by farmers. Was Boxley Church on some processional route to a centre of pagan worship? Indeed, was Boxley Church itself built upon a pagan site? We know that when St Augustine brought Christianity to Kent in 597 AD he was commanded by Pope Gregory to build his churches upon pagan sites. The pagans themselves worshipped close by springs and ponds, which are abundant around neighbouring Court Lodge Farm and Parsonage Farm. If there was a trackway of such antiquity, then one supposes that the Romans incorporated it in their slip-road to the east which ran from their main route down Bluebell Hill, for a Roman track passed by the Church. Maybe they worshipped here as well. The church builders may well have utilised the old Roman road to provide hard foundations for the three churches built along its length.

But enough of conjecture, however romantic the thoughts. We can move forward with some certainty from the 1400's. We can jump to 1588 when a beacon was lit on the Church tower to pass on the warning that the Spanish Armada had been sighted. We can contemplate how the interior of the Church may have appeared from the 1600's. The Reformation and all the changes brought about by Henry VIII would long before have seen the rood screen removed, and with it various images. At some date the outer porch, or Galilee Chamber, had come into the ownership of Vinters Estate. On the north wall is a slate tablet mentioning as a first owner Roger Vinter in the 1400's, and beneath is the burial vault for successive owners. The aisle of the Church itself was not open to the roof as now, but rather had a ceiling. At the western end was a gallery, where, according to George Wallis in the chapter on Victorian Times, the choir sang. It is very hard to imagine that gallery now, for no signs remain. In the Bell-ringing chamber is a recess which must have given access to it, although whether there were stairs down and into the nave is unknown. There was once (and may still be there to be found) an inscription that "This

BOXLEY CHURCH

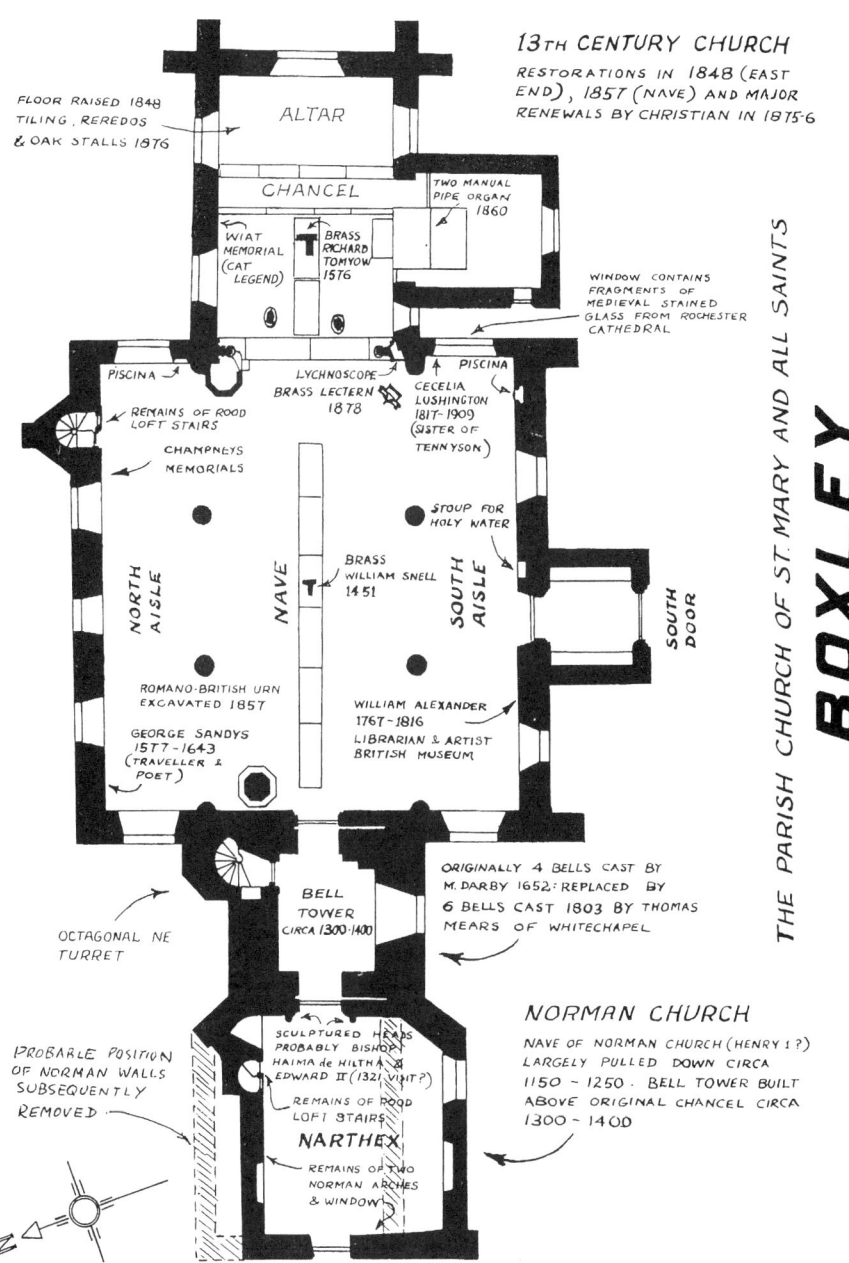

Layout of Boxley Church, by kind permission of Mr. Ron Howard

Church was new pew'd in 1737" and well into Victorian times there were box-pews with doors, whilst there was a large reading desk towards the present choir stalls.

From 1857 drastic alterations took place. The box-pews were removed and replaced with those seen today. The gallery was taken away, and the ceiling removed and the open roof refurbished. The reading desk went, and the choir stalls were built. Pulpit and font and the decoration behind the altar were all added. The floor is said to have been raised rather earlier in 1848, and the floor tiling is clearly Victorian.

But the medieval structure remains, with pillars and arches made of block chalk quarried from the hillside, so that with the ragstone outer walls the whole building grows naturally out of the turf. The pillars slope slightly outwards, to imitate the sides of a ship, or Ark. As the main body of the Church is entered, it will be noted that the chancel turns at an angle to the right. This is called a weeping chancel, and imitates Christ's head falling to one side as he hung on the cross. On the good authority of a curate of some years ago, the Church revealed a ghost. There were two separate occasions when the organist played 'The lost chord' whereupon the figure of a bride appeared at the west door.

Boxley has a proud tradition of bell-ringing and the present peal of six bells was hung in 1803. They made an impression on Lord Tennyson during his family visits, and earned a mention in his "In Memorian".

This is not meant to be an exhaustive description of the Church. Students of stoups and piscinae, squint holes and the lychnoscope may seek elsewhere, such as Cave-Browne and the Church's own guide. Likewise for details of the monuments, the most interesting of which are to the Wyatts and the Lushingtons. The Church takes the title of St Mary and All Saints. Originally it was just All Saints, until it was thought a good idea to add St Mary who was the patron saint of Boxley Abbey. A nice perpetuation, and a reminder of the parish's other ancient religious house.

Finally, to the Churchyard, entered by the lych-gate which is another Victorian addition bearing the date 1875. Here is the inevitable Yew tree, be it a pagan survival, a deterrent to stray cattle, a source of wood for bows, or whatever else. To the left of the Church porch is the grave of John Wallis "late of the 34th Regiment of Foot" who fought under Wellington. He was the father of George Wallis who gives us those memories in the chapter on Victorian Times. As we will see, young George prospered after the humblest of origins, and one can imagine with what love and pride he constructed this tomb from his newly formed building business. Wander round these tombs and grave stones and you can read a roll-call of Boxley history – Athawes, Lushington, Best, Balston, Tyrrwhit-Drake, Mercer. Names of more humble stock who prospered – Blinkhorn, Fowle, Roots. The Whatmans lie beneath the porch, but outside is the grave of Ann Leigh, their "faithful and attached Nurse". Likewise Samuel Lamb, "faithful steward to Lt Col Best". Generations of common folk lie here, several deep, unmarked. But not entirely forgotten, because the Church records tell of some. Many were infants, baptised in haste such as a daughter named "Repent in Tyme" and buried in 1612. Had she not been baptised, then could she have entered the Churchyard at all, or if so must she be buried on the north side of the Church?

From the reign of Henry VIII the registration of baptisms, marriages and burials became compulsory and since then every incumbent has kept a register. Taking deaths, the Boxley Registers may give us food for contemplation in this Churchyard, for here lie such as the following. In 1594 Alice Walter and her illegitimate son Nicholas. Also in 1594 twelve having died of the plague including the wife and two daughters of Christopher Watleman. In 1595 Ellis Gwinne, overseer, "being riotous after drink, he was struck with a hammer by Thomas Kemslye". In 1598 Thomas Weaver, "a young man tossed by a cow and falling down, died". In 1606 William Stocke "killed by a fall of chalk".

Not just parishioners were buried here. In 1630 "an unknown infant, thrown in the river". In 1626 "a certain traveller with a red beard and a blue doublet". He was later found to have come from Durham. In 1641 "a certain wandering old woman".

So they all lie here, the high and the lowly, all cared for by successive clergy. One cleric felt constrained to write in 1646 – "Lest anyone thinks that all the inhabitants of the parish care for order, and obey the canons of the Church, – public prayers are rejected by most, and I am sorry to say it is most difficult to reduce them to order".

'Fintonagh' Penenden Heath circa 1914.

CHAPTER 5

Penenden Heath

The thing to remember when considering the history of the Heath is that its area was originally much greater than the recreation ground which it was to become. For example, Bagshaw's Directory of 1847 described it as "an extensive plain". It would have stretched east to Newnham Court Farm, south to at least a line through the site of the Convent on the brow of Boxley Road, west to Cuckoo Woods, and north towards Boxley village. Its particular historical importance derives from the fact that it lies near enough at the centre of the County. Even before the Norman Conquest it was a meeting place for the people of Kent and it was where justice would be administered and punishment inflicted. Indeed, the name "Penenden" is said to mean in Saxon the "place of penalty" and executions were carried out there over many centuries. Variations in spelling occur, such as Penninton, Piccendene Hothe, Pickenden, Pinnendene and Pittenden. The Saxons are reputed to have held here an Assembly of Wise Men to come to decisions for the good of the community. Long before elections developed in their modern form it was on the Heath that polls were taken for County elections of Members of Parliament. In the early years Kent was allowed just two representatives, an arrangement first introduced by William the Conqueror who referred to them as "Knights of the Shire".

We have previously noted the momentous trial of Bishop Odo in 1076. Cave-Browne and Russell both give detailed accounts, and the event is too well-known to warrant repetition. Down the years other great gatherings either did or are assumed to have happened on the Heath. Numbered amongst these are the Revolts of Wat Tyler in 1381 and Jack Cade in 1450 and Wyatt's Rebellion in 1554. The Civil War saw Royalists assembling there in 1643 and then, after the Battle of Maidstone in 1648, the victorious Roundheads camped there before moving on to Rochester. They stayed long enough to court-martial and shoot some of their own soldiers for looting. In 1828 it is estimated by some commentators that an incredible 40,000 people gathered to petition Parliament in protest against the Catholic Emancipation Bill, they preferring to keep a pure Protestant constitution.

Situated to the east of The Bull public house was the old Shire Hall or County Court, literally the court for the whole County, where all civil matters were dealt with at monthly sittings. Criminal matters would have been dealt

BOXLEY PARISH

with elsewhere, in later years by judges who moved around the County and sat at Assizes in the major towns. Hasted described the Shire Hall as a "poor low shed" and this was replaced in 1830 by a small stone building built by John Goodwin, who was uncle to the famous Maidstone artist Albert E. Goodwin. This stone building was removed in 1877 and re-constructed in the garden of Bleak House in Peel Street and used as a summerhouse, before being finally demolished in 1975. By Victorian times the civil justice system had grown and there developed separate County Courts for the major towns and their districts. Into the 1990's and this process is being reversed with some districts being deprived of local court offices. As the Shire Hall, the building on the Heath was the scene of elections for those two representatives which for many years the wider county was allowed, although Boroughs were allowed separate representatives. All freeholders who had the right to vote had to travel to the Heath from afar. The Reform Bill of 1832 split Kent into two divisions, Eastern and Western, and each could return two members. In 1868 a mid-Kent division was introduced, and each of the three divisions was then allowed one Member of Parliament. There used to be a horse-block outside the Shire Hall, and the story is that successful candidates would use it to mount their horses and then gallop away in triumph.

In terms of justice, what excites people's imagination is the public executions which took place, at first on gallows on the high ground approximately now on the corner of Heathfield Road and Sittingbourne Road. The spot is still shown on some maps as Gallows Hill. For many years Heathfield Road was known as Hangman's Lane. The scale of despatch should not be under-estimated. Even before 1066 criminals were being executed hereabouts and Russell records that when sand was being excavated for use in the building of Maidstone Prison several hundred skeletons were found. More recently still, more bones were allegedly found when the Motorway was being built. Occasionally the bodies were passed to surgeons for dissection. At other times the bodies were returned to their home villages and hung on a gibbet in an iron casing as an awful reminder to others. There the bodies would rot away or be picked clean by wildlife. It is said that women would then steal away a bone or two as a good-luck charm.

The preludes to the hangings made for a public spectacle. In later years the unfortunate criminals would be brought up from Maidstone in chains by cart, or even tied to a rough sledge and dragged along by a horse. For example, in 1769 Susannah Lott being convicted of poisoning her husband was dragged along on a hurdle and first hung and then burnt. Some criminals would join in the "fun" by playing up to the crowd.

By about 1800 these violent scenes were affecting some local people's sensibilities. Ladies and gentleman passing by could not but help see the dangling bodies on such a prominent hillock. In 1813 the under-sheriff reported that he had selected a new site for the erection of the gallows "on the right hand side of the road from Aylesford across Penenden Heath, into the road leading from Maidstone to Detling, nearly opposite the toll of trees which adjoins the public house". This has to be the Bull, as the Chiltern Hundreds did not open for at least another ten years. The gist of the report was that the new site was low enough to keep it more out of sight, particularly from the gentry of Boxley! One can deduce that this site was near the mouth of Faraday Road. But it was still not good enough, witness this letter written in 1819 by local gentry:-

"We the undersigned landowners and inhabitants residing in the immediate vicinity of Penenden Heath, take the liberty of laying our request to you, that the execution of malefactors who have forfeited their lives to the laws of their country, which has been hitherto carried into effect on Penenden Heath, may be removed to the front of the New Gaol at Maidstone as is customary in most gaols in England. Our property, on the days when these unfortunate men are to forfeit their lives is much injured; the mob after the execution, sodden with drink, generally break through the fields, trample down the hedges and crops and in fact instead of the execution operating 'interrorum', it is actually by many of the workmen and apprentices considered a day of pleasure. We beg to submit our request to your favourable consideration ".

Eventually the public executions were moved down into Maidstone, at first outside the prison wall for more public spectacle. The last hanging on the Heath was in 1830 when three young men paid the ultimate penalty for setting fire to some farm buildings. A calmer atmosphere began to pervade the area, with occasional fairs when sheep and cattle were sold.

Just as the area of the Heath was so much larger in earlier years, so was the layout of the roadways quite different. There was no Boxley Road running south from what is now the south-west corner of the Heath. Sittingbourne Road was on a line much further east, surviving as the footpath which comes out opposite the Stakis Hotel. It then continued to Detling.

Coming from Boxley village and passing Grange Lane on your right, there is a fork with Sandy Lane (or Back Lane) going left and now passing under the Motorway. This was the route from Boxley into Maidstone, across the Heath and down what now survives as the Wheeler Street Hedges to the east of the site of the Convent. Then down to Union Street, or Tyler's Lane as that was once called. Is that because Wat Tyler came down that way from his rabble rousing on the Heath? The soil of what are now Boxley Road and Sittingbourne Road was still heathland.

On the subject of Wat Tyler, it seems to be accepted by most historians now that he came from Maidstone rather than Dartford. As a tiler by trade, and given that the local tile industry was centred in Boxley in the area of the old Abbey, might he have been a Boxley man?

As to the route of the road running east to west, this is essentially unchanged, coming from Aylesford, along Sandling Lane and on to the

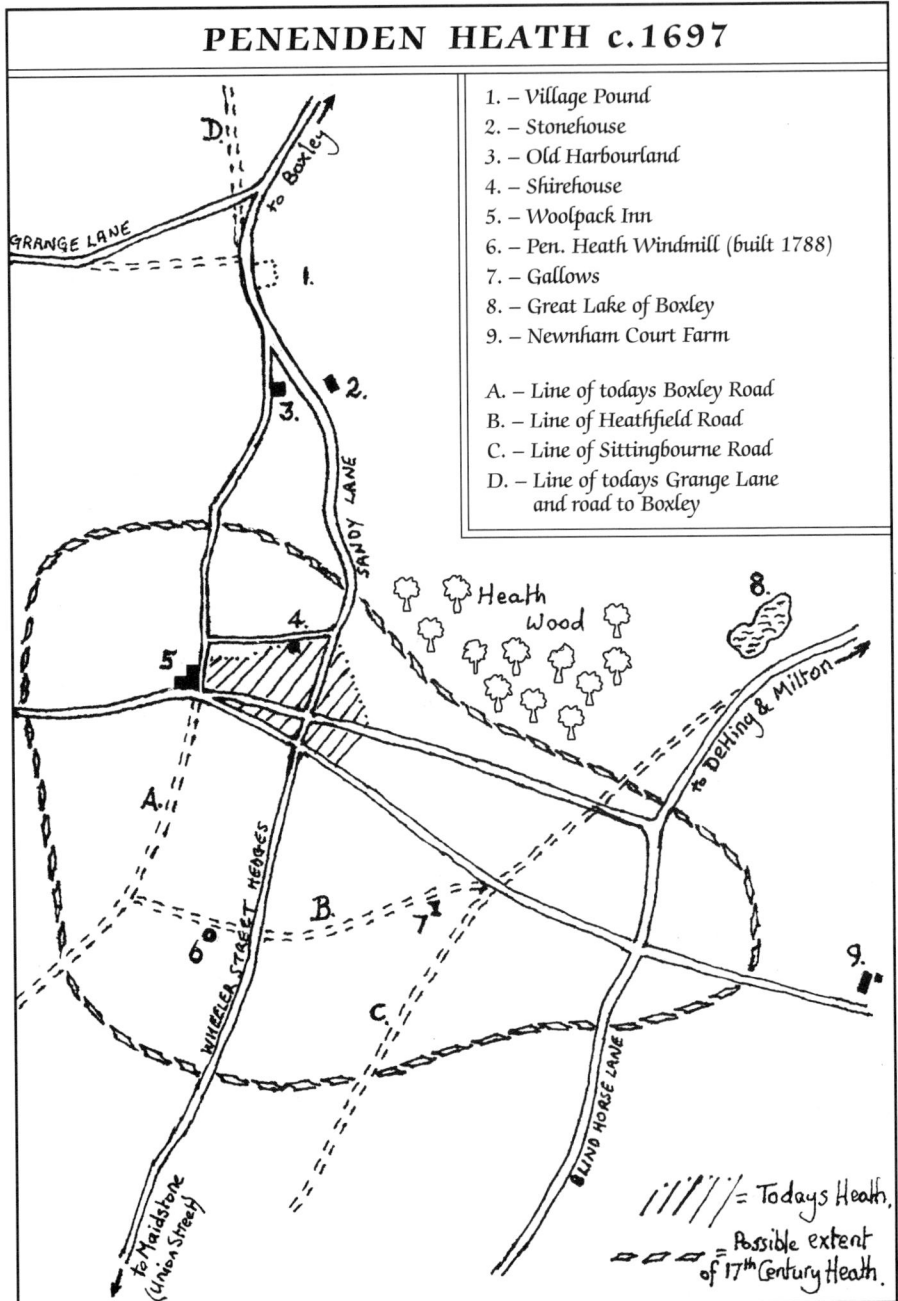

Bearsted Road as we know it today. From there on to Ashford. At the end of the 17th Century a second road forked off at the Harbourland Lane junction, crossing the green just north of the Bearsted Road to join up with the Detling Road about 300 yards north west of Newnham Court.

A brief word now about Enclosures. For centuries the peasantry had been able to cultivate open fields and use common land for grazing their livestock. The landowners acknowledged that the peasants needed land to support their families, and custom and long use established these rights. But as time passed, the landowners began to gradually assume control of these areas of land. For example, in 1543 a Wyatt is recorded as having enclosed "Boxley Park" and some woodland. There is then record of disturbances between 1548 and 1550 when the villagers threw down the fences and sought to claim back their previous land use.

Politicians became divided over the subject. One wrote of the "evil of enclosure for emparcation" – in other words, the landowners were taking essential land away from the villagers to add to their own pleasure grounds. A debate raged, and the counter-argument was that enclosures helped to provide wealth, on the basis that in one man's ownership he would care for the land and improve it, but as common land nobody cared enough. A description in the 1700's of some common land was doubtless true of Penenden Heath, namely "covered with furze, thorns, brakes or heaths". The old house which stood on former heathland down Northdown Close would not have been called Thornhills for nothing. Grassland of the same period was described as being so poor that cattle and sheep grazing there seemed half-starved. Around 1796 the official view was that the "waste lands and impoverished commons of the county" were overdue for enclosure.

It is against this background that changes began to occur in the 1800's. Lord Romney owned and had enclosed almost the whole of the heathland and in 1816 he gave some 27 acres to the Borough of Maidstone with the intention of providing employment for the poor. The idea was to encourage poor people to cultivate the land in question, but it proved a failure. In 1824 the Borough sold to Captain Daniel Tyssen who then constructed Foley House on that part of the land where stood Folly Farm. Incidentally, the money raised was put towards the cost of building Holy Trinity Church in Maidstone which was consecrated in 1826. Thereafter, more of the Heath was sold to individuals. The new owners began planting trees and, as one contemporary wrote, provided "shelter and shade". So the once large area of heathland began to be nibbled away for proper cultivation or house building.

What remained "public" became the haunt of travellers and vagabonds. Boxley Parish records between 1879 and 1881 show the baptisms of a scissor grinder, pedlar, chairmender, tinker, traveller and licensed hawker, all of whose address is simply "Penenden Heath". One imagines the Boxley Vicar or some very keen curate moving amongst them determined to see their humble lives improved.

Even though the public hangings were no more, the sensibilities of the gentry were still upset, as to which consider a letter written in 1867 by the Vicar of Boxley to Lord Romney, in support of a petition against "the disgraceful proceedings which arise from the fairs on Penenden Heath held annually on Good Friday". And complaining that "a number of idle lads have assembled on the Heath on Sundays making a great deal of noise and generally having a donkey with them which they ride and drive about". Lord Romney was asked to try and do something about it, and the petition was signed by worthy Boxley names such as Best, Whatman, Mercer, Foster, Lushington and Rev. Richards himself.

Major Best from neighbouring Park House was annoyed for another reason. Logs kept disappearing from his wood piles, and he suspected the gypsies camping on the Heath. He instructed his gamekeeper to drill holes in one or two logs and fill them with gunpowder, afterwards plugging up the holes. Sure enough, these particular logs found their way onto the camp fire and instead of the gypsy kettle coming cheerfully to the boil, it was blown sky high and the gypsies afrighted. Major Best smugly recorded that no more of his logs disappeared thereafter.

In about 1882 Lord Romney made a further gift to the people of Maidstone of the recreation ground as it is known today. The area was closed in by iron railings and a monument was erected in the south-west corner to record his generosity.

We can now begin to trace the development of the land around the recreation ground, as areas passed into private hands. To the south of Gallows Hill had been built Foley House with its surrounding parkland. The large area opposite the Heath and running back to Heathfield Road came into the ownership of Ralph Fremlin who, until he died in 1910, lived in Heathfield House which stood where the development of Silchester Court is now located. It was Ralph Fremlin who founded the Pale Ale Brewery in Maidstone in 1861, being joined later by his brothers in partnership. He was a deeply Christian man and contributed much money towards the building of St Paul's and St Faith's and St Luke's Churches. The Bull Public House was for many years the only Fremlin's tied pub, and true to his religious beliefs no Fremlin's pub was allowed to open on a Sunday.

Mrs Fremlin continued to live at Heathfield House until she died in 1929. In widowhood she dressed completely in black, and would ride around in a carriage drawn by two black horses. In 1930 a large portion of the Fremlin Estate was bought by the Builders Clarke and Epps, and soon the houses facing the Heath were built and Faraday Road was laid out. Surviving amongst all this 1930's development are two interesting houses in Penenden Heath Road. The first is Heathfield Lodge which bears the date 1870 and is where the gardener lived. The other is Gate Lodge, built in the style of a Swiss Chalet and where

Heathfield House in Heathfield Road, once the house of Mr. R. J. Fremlin. Demolished 1982.

the coachman lived. The Fremlins had been on holiday to Switzerland where they formed the desire to have a chalet of their own back in England. They were presented with the upper framework of one, and back home they commissioned a local builder Mr Bridge to erect the chalet for them as a Lodge House to their northern drive. The result is an exquisite building, with Kentish ragstone below and genuine Swiss timbering above. If you look closely you can see at first floor level at the front the small door giving access to the storage space for skis. Also visible is the pole (now shortened) which such Chalets in Switzerland had to mark their position when they were covered by feet of snow! The interior is equally charming with panelling and secret places.

During the early days of all these happenings Hangman's Lane became known as Fremlin's Lane and then at last Heathfield Road. One particular house built in Heathfield Road in the 1930's is worth a special mention, namely "Avonlea". In the chapter on Victorian times there is included the memories of George Ephraim Wallis who was born in Boxley in 1823 of very humble country stock. He managed to improve himself and climb beyond the normal expectations of his class, and he went on to found the Maidstone Building Company of G.E. Wallis Ltd. Both his son and grandson succeeded him in the business and both became Mayors of Maidstone. The grandson, Leslie Wallis, built "Avonlea" for himself, using old materials that he had been gathering over the years. For example, some of the York slabs came from Chatham Dockyard. The Company had just finished building the Shakespeare Theatre at Stratford-upon-Avon and that gave inspiration for the house name.

At risk of straying from the old Boxley Parish, the land south of Heathfield Road was once part of the heathland, and the Convent was built about 1905. Near that site stood Mr Blinkhorn's windmill "on Penenden Heath" which attracted a newspaper story in 1823 when a child was struck by one of its sails and killed. Built in 1788 by Christopher Fidge, in 1827 the windmill was sold to Captain Tyssen. When Robert Blinkhorn's lease expired in 1839 it was dismantled and some of the workings exported to Australia and the structure moved to Millfield at Folkestone.

On the corner of Heathfield Road and Boxley Road was Penenden Farm which, until the 1930's, was owned by the Whatman family and latterly farmed by Mr Mitchell. This area was not to be developed until the 1950's.

West of Boxley Road and running south from North Way down to Sandling Lane was another large estate associated with a large Victorian house known as "Penenden". This stood approximately behind the parade of shops on the junction of Boxley Road and Sandling Lane. It was built about 1830 by Daniel Scratton and the Sale Particulars of about 1910 describe it as being set in 26 acres of paddocks, woodland, orchard and gardens. The woodland was known as Hook Wood and was later to give its name to Woodland Way. Until she died

"Penenden," Maidstone (View from the Entrance Gate).

in 1899 Mrs Emily Bosanquet lived there, being the widow of James Whatman Bosanquet – a scion of the Whatmans of Vinters, and a sometime partner with Balston at Springfield Mill. Emily and James were the parents of Lily Best-Dalison who is the subject of a later chapter. The last occupiers would appear to have been Mr and Mrs Hugh Scarlett. The Estate was sold in 1935 and the grand old house demolished. The housing development on the western side of Boxley Road was to follow. It is said that this stretch of road was once known as Gallows Hill.

Some Sale Particulars of pre-1914 are well worth dwelling upon for they give the flavour of long lost days. In the language of the time, the residence was approached by a Carriage Drive and you entered a Hall with a fireplace. There were Dining Room and Drawing Room with bay windows, followed by a Morning Room and Library. On the first and second floors were in total 9 bedrooms and a separate Man Servant's Bedroom. There was a Servants Hall, Butler's Pantry and stone paved kitchen and scullery. In the basement was a furnace room, the house being heated by hot water pipes. There were 3 wine cellars and a beer cellar. All the bedrooms had fireplaces, and some had closets. There appeared to be just one bathroom.

Outside was stabling and a double coach house and also a harness room with fireplace, and a groom's bedroom. Over the stable was a hay loft and a fruit room. Further outbuildings included a cow lodge, wood lodge and a range of pig sties. Adding to this the kitchen garden and we can imagine a largely self-sufficient house. There is one survival from those days, namely Bell Cottage in Sandling Lane. This was where the gardener lived. At one time Bell Cottage was a Dame School, where a lady would take in a few pupils for private education.

On the corner opposite the present parade of shops and where the houses of Staplers Court now stand, there stood the house "Staplers" until it was demolished in the 1960's. Here for many years lived Dr Halfpenny whose medical practice was in Maidstone, although he held some consultations at home. He and his wife used to throw many a jolly party there. It is said that the house had probably reached the end of its useful life when it came down. An earlier occupant had been Leslie Caldecott who was to live finally at Boxley Abbey for some years. Behind was a field where sheep would graze. Before "Staplers" and before the Bull were built, an Inn known as "The Woolpack" stood here.

Today's Bull Public House was mainly built in Victorian times and has latterly been much extended, but the Bull has dispensed beer since at least 1715. Amongst the many Licensees was Mr Rague Pettit who died prematurely in the 1890's. The Breweries then were prejudiced against a widow continuing to run the business, but because Mrs Pettit's brother lived on the premises she was allowed to continue. She remained there until 1921, bringing up seven children. As previously mentioned, being a Fremlins Pub it never opened on a Sunday, but Sarah Pettit chose to use part of this day of rest to attend church twice. Her husband had been buried at Boxley and the story is that his coffin was carried on foot from the Bull to the church, the tiring pallbearers having to rest their load at intervals.

Well remembered by older local people was Abnett's Fair, held at Eastertime on the Heath between the two wars. Mr Abnett was a travelling showman who in the winter stored his equipment at Gladstone Road. With the arrival of spring he would be on tour with his roundabouts and side-shows. The fun of the fair continued after dark with paraffin lamps adding to the atmosphere.

The bowling green and tennis courts have been in use since about 1927. Certainly between the Wars, if not earlier, the rough ground then surrounding the recreation areas towards Boxley was known as the "fuzzies". Hereabouts too was the rabbit warren with seemingly hundreds of the creatures scampering about.

Brief mention should be made of cricket on the Heath, for in the early days of the game many important matches were played there, a club having been formed by 1786. For example, in 1807 thirteen men of All England played twenty- three men of Kent for a prize of 1000 guineas. Incidentally, this was probably one of the first matches when round-arm bowling was employed, as opposed to under-arm lobs. A few years later, Yalding village team played a team selected from the Medway Towns for a 200 guinea purse, lunch being laid on at The Bull, where landlord John Craute had to send a cart to The Kings Arms at Boxley for more beer! Both pubs then being owned by The Kings Arms landlord, William Manwaring.

The Chiltern Hundreds Pub will be mentioned in a later chapter. The road close by leading to Detling was once a turn-pike road. Between the Wars this road was surprisingly so busy that P.C. Ted Kirby from Boxley was needed to direct the traffic. Close to the pub and standing high still stand the pair of Chiltern Cottages. They were built about 1805 on land enclosed out of the heathland by the Overseers of the Poor of Boxley, for the use of the poor. In 1821 more land was enclosed and added and Chiltern Hundreds Farm created. Later James Whatman bought the land, selling it to Major Best in 1896. One of the cottages was the boyhood home of Wally Gosling, who will flit in and out of our story as gardener, cricketer, soldier, choirboy, bell-ringer, special constable, verger and much else besides. Down the bank in front of the cottages he would slide. His first job on leaving school at 14 in 1903 was at Bunyard's Nursery. The Bunyard family were Maidstone Nurserymen of national repute and in 1876 they leased land for use as nurseries behind the Chiltern Hundreds. George Bunyard lived at Newnham Court for a while. Wally Gosling's starting wage was the equivalent of about 30 pence per week!.

The 1930's development was to change the character of the locality considerably. The parade of shops arose at the same time to provide for the needs of the householders. Roy Page's Grocery Shop took orders and delivered to the home. Mr Pantony from down the Boxley Road did the rounds with his milk cart. There was a shop not far from the Chiltern Hundreds, which has now become a Hairdressers, and others along Sandling Lane. A new community had been born.

So has the Heath moved on from a Saxon meeting place and wasteland to its present residential area. But what a history!

Foley House built on former heathland early 1800's and demolished 1950's.

CHAPTER 6

Crime & Punishment – Boxley Malefactors

For centuries, executions on the Heath were perhaps the principal form of spectator entertainment. Local people, bringing ale and food to partake of picnics, were treated to a discourse listing in horrible detail the offences of those sentenced to hang, and often the condemned themselves would address the crowd, sometimes with bravado and other times in penitence. One would have thought that the brooding proximity of the Penenden Heath gallows, elevated on its hill, would be a salutary reminder to the inhabitants of Boxley to abide by the somewhat draconian laws of the land. It is therefore strange to find that Boxley malefactors feature quite strongly in the assize records. Today, when people live in fear for their personal safety and that of their possessions, it is interesting to observe that in our 'less civilised past', burglary and petty theft were considered to be far more serious crimes than they are today, and punished accordingly. Examples of different crimes and punishments are detailed here to illustrate this point and provide a small insight into the lives of our forebears.

1579: John Hyder shoemaker was found guilty of burgling the house of Lancelot Stephenson at Boxley, with the intention of stealing goods (nothing actually stolen) – for this he was hanged on the Heath.

1590: George Mendpace a yeoman (and thus an affluent farmer of some substance) was hanged for breaking into a field at Vinters and stealing a gelding belonging to John Cuttes.

1598: John Halsnoth, labourer, stole two cows from Martha Baynham widow at Boxley, for which he too was hanged.

1596: Mercy Moxley a spinster from Boxley stole a petticoat from John Hudesford at Boxley, also 3 neckerchiefs, a hat and a woman's waistcoat. She avoided a death sentence because she was pregnant and was remanded in jail. Three years later she was still there.

Some of these desperate souls paid the ultimate penalty not only for their crimes but also due to their lack of education! Today's laws considers that an educated man with life's advantage, should know better, and he is thus perhaps dealt with more harshly. In the past it was quite the opposite. Apart from the crimes of murder, rape, highway robbery, burglary and horse stealing, one could appeal to have one's sentence set aside by claiming 'benefit of clergy'. This meant that one had been taught to read, and was usually proven by reading a passage from a Latin Psalter. (The passage was known as 'the neck verse' and was usually Psalm 51 verses 1 or 14 which beseech God for mercy or deliverance). The skill of reading was considered too valuable to be thrown away for a misdemeanour, and this practice certainly provided an incentive for learning! The reprieved would be branded on the ball of their thumb, and should a miscreant with two brands on his thumb be convicted of a third capital crime, his pleas for mercy would go unheard.

Thus Thomas Johnson, a weaver of Boxley was granted clergy for stealing two cows, a crime which cost John Halsnoth his life. Likewise Thomas Argo, a husbandman (smaller tenant farmer) of Boxley, who stole 7 silver spoons from George Allen, yeoman at Boxley, had his death sentence set aside by benefit of clergy. Whereas John Thrasher, a Boxley labourer, was hanged for assaulting two gentlemen at Boxley. Edward Peirce a yeoman of Boxley, claimed clergy after stabbing and killing Nicholas Younge at Maidstone. Ignorance was definitely not bliss!

Another popular punishment was whipping. John Willard and William Morgan, labourers of Boxley, stole 12 hop poles from Thomas Brewer, who in 1625 owned most of Sandling and the Nether Grange. For this they were tied to the back of a cart and whipped constantly whilst the horse travelled a distance of fifty paces. 1629 saw William Mershe, a Boxley labourer whipped for stealing 12 cheeses worth the princely sum of 9 pence, from Mathew Hudsford at Boxley. In 1594 Eglantine Grymsditch, spinster of Boxley was found guilty of speaking slanderous words for which she was set in the pillory at market time, with a paper above her head detailing her crime, and whipped.

Six years later, Thomas Santesilleon, gentleman of Boxley, fell foul of the law for not attending Church for 3 months. Summoned for his default and found guilty, the court placed him in the service of the Archbishop of Canterbury.

Television and the Cinema have glamorised the highwayman, but the records show that gold and jewels could be hard to come by, and in reality the plunder was far more mundane. In 1620 John Harrison, a notorious Boxley highwayman was apprehended and convicted of 3 charges of highway robbery. The first charge was that he stole 3 shirtbands and 12 shillings from Christopher Lamb in the Queen's highway at Chatham. On the second occasion he assaulted Augustine Smith on Boxley Hill (now Bluebell Hill) and stole a threepenny knife, a dagger also worth three pence and a 5 shilling pair of gloves. Finally at Birchen Green (where now is Cobtree Golf Course) he and Christopher Broome, a Boxley labourer were said to have waylaid John Ewell and stole a 10 shilling cloak, 24 table napkins and 2 tablecloths, two shirts and just 14 pence in coin. Broome was at home when the constable arrived and was thus presumed innocent as he 'did not flee', and found not guilty. The incorrigible Harrison was hanged, amidst much merriment, on the Heath. Another highwayman to end his days on the Heath's gallows was a former bricklayer Edward Wilkins, found guilty of holding up and assaulting John Pyend in the highway at Boxley and stealing 10 shillings.

Nowadays, newspapers are full of tales of feuds between neighbours, but in the second half of the 16th Century it was essential to be on good terms with your neighbours, especially if you were old and poor. Otherwise you were liable to be accused of using witchcraft to cause any misfortunes that might befall them. In 1573, Alice Day, wife of a Boxley tanner, was accused of bewitching to death Thomas Chylde, husbandman of Boxley, his daughter Isobel, and Alice Goodwyn a widow who lived at Upper Grange Farm. She was found guilty of murder by witchcraft, but as she was pregnant she was remanded in custody. Somehow she engineered her release (perhaps more witchcraft?). Four years later she was found guilty of bewitching John Collyns (of Boarley Farm) so that he lay gravely ill for a year, and bewitching to death two heifers belonging to Frances Waynewright who lived in the venerable Boarley Cottage. Her punishment is not recorded but a year later, after poor John Collyns having suffered a relapse and a further 13 months of languishing, finally died, she was once again found guilty and reaped her apparently just reward on Penenden Heath gallows. Twelve years on, Alice White, a Boxley spinster was fortunate to be found not guilty of bewitching to death a cow, and also bewitching Alice Whittingham so that she died.

Even in the 19th Century, felons were fearful of facing the courts. In 1819, Charles Beauman, formerly a miller of Sandling corn mill, whose family milled there for generations, and his accomplice Valentine Soper, who had been hop-picking together, broke into the laundry of James Ellis in Barming and stole two large bundles of clothing. They were pursued by the landlord of The Bull and on being intercepted at St Mary Cray, Soper cut his own throat. Beauman was later arrested and spent many years in jail awaiting trial, but his ultimate fate is not known.

It is understandable that Boxley men should have been involved in all the Kentish uprisings, as the gatherings invariably took place in Penenden Heath. Local hotheads and adventurers would have been easily swayed by 'fighting talk', but of those seventeen Boxley men charged with involvement in Jack Cade's Rebellion, no less than seven were yeomen (i.e. prosperous farmers). In 1382 Boxley also left its mark on the annals of Wat Tylers's Rebellion, when one of its inhabitants became one of the few rebels actually called to task for his actions. William Brown of Boxley and John Webbe of Maidstone were hanged on Penenden Heath for having risen against their lawful King and feloniously slain John Stonehelde of Maidstone and John Godnot of Borden.

CHAPTER 7
Community Life

For much of its existence, Boxley has epitomised the class divide of the 'haves and the have nots'. The ordinary man first bent his knee to the Saxon Kings of Kent, and then the Norman overlords, through the Cistercian abbots to the Wyatts, who owned almost every acre of Boxley's soil. After their demise, the Parish became fragmented under several large landowners, such as the Astleys, Brewers & Grimstones, and eventually the Knatchbulls, Sedleys, Banks and the resurgent Wiats. With Lord Romney's succession to the Wiat lands and Lord Aylesford's purchases from the Sedleys, together with his own inheritance from the Banks family, almost the whole of Boxley was owned by these two great lords with most of the residue held by The Dean & Chapter of Rochester. Later still came the era of the Whatmans and The Bests.

Those not fortunate enough to be born with a silver spoon were reliant on obtaining leases of land from their Lord. Sometimes they were able to obtain indentures, which guaranteed them the land for a specified number of years, with a reasonable chance of extending the lease, or of passing it on to their descendants. Otherwise, they held the land 'at will', which as it suggests meant by the will or whim of the Lord, without the security of a lease. The 1554 Wyatt attainder survey shows that just 43 tenants held a total of 53 'farms' ranging from 2 acres to 300 acres, and of these only 19 had the security of an indenture. The total acreage in use was 2073 acres of which the Wyatts utilised just 152 acres. In addition there were many more acres designated as 'waste', which was common land, such as Penenden Heath, or land unfit for use.

Over the next 300 years, the inhabitants gradually cleared the land, enclosed it and put it to use. As well as paying rents to the big landowners, each yeoman, husbandman and cottager paid a tithe to The Church. This was literally a tenth of his hops or corn or whatever he cultivated on his land, or the tenth pail of milk. Later this was changed to a money payment. The 1844 Boxley Tithe Map records 5782 acres, 2 roods, 3 perches of land as cultivated or in use. This breaks down to 2136 acres of arable land, 1575 acres of meadow or pasture land, 1505 acres of woodland, 146 acres of hop grounds, 94 acres of orchards and fruit plantations, 58 acres of common or waste land, and 70 acres of Rectorial glebe lands. 91 acres were covered by river and roads, with 100 acres being sites of buildings.

In 1871, a return of owners of land, reproduced as 'The Second Domesday

BOXLEY PARISH

Book', records all those who owned land of one acre or more. What is immediately striking is how little we had advanced in sharing out the land. Although we are talking of a time almost within living memory, only 13 families, together with a few organisations, such as The Company of Vintners and The Company of Saddlers, are recorded as owning land in Boxley Parish. Of these, the Lords Romney and Aylesford held the most, followed by the Bests, James Whatman and the Staceys.

The relatively poor nature of the soil, coupled with so much land being owned by so few, was probably responsible for the sparse population in earlier years. In 1676 Boxley only had 15 inhabitants over 16 years of age, per square mile, compared to 35 per square mile in neighbouring Parishes with richer soil. However, to obtain a true picture of population, you would virtually have to double this as the average life expectancy at birth was only about 35, with between 40% and 50% dying before the age of 16. Among the Boxley Parish Records we are lucky to have a record of the names of all males who in 1757 were aged between 18 and 50, and qualified to serve in the militia – some 143 in total. This would equate to a population of approximately 640 men, women and children. By 1821, there were 201 dwellings in the Parish, sheltering 1166 souls, of which 577 were male and 589 female. The 1841 census records 262 inhabited houses with 1398 inhabitants. By 1851 this had swelled to 1508, of whom 248 lived 'over-the-hill', in Dunn Street, Westfield Sole and Grange.

The villages along the North Downs were long renowned for the longevity of their inhabitants. None more so than Boxley. The Maidstone Journal of May 1802 records that, "within the last month, four people died in the Parish of Boxley whose ages totalled 337, viz., 77, 85, 87 and 88. The salubrity of the air of this Parish may be considered not only from the above list but from several left at advanced ages". The following week's paper announced that, "Another Boxley Parishioner has fallen victim to the late unfavourable season, which has proved so formidable to the ancient veterans of that Parish; and died aged 82. There are still sixteen left whose ages amount to 1268". An average of 79.25, and this when life expectancy averaged only 40 to 50 years! The Parish burial register contains numerous octogenarians and older, culminating in the 1759 recording of the death of Edward Roberts at the fabulous age of 106. The register also provides proof that the much vaunted Boxley air left its veterans with a lust for life. One startling entry of 1700 records the marriage of Mary Wollet aged 73 years and her beau, Richard Lewis, who worked as a shepherd and was 92 years young!

Although the Parish was somewhat sparsely populated, out of necessity there was a strong community spirit. Upkeep of the roads was the responsibility of all inhabitants, thus helping to instil a feeling of communal responsibility. It was economically more viable for neighbours in an agricultural community such as Boxley, to toil together to harvest their fields. Thus family units were not inward looking. They did not contain several generations, nor additional relatives, living together under one roof. A normal household would comprise a husband and wife and just the youngest of their children, plus perhaps a servant. In fact, surprisingly, up to a third of all households contained servants. As soon as they reached their teens, children would leave their homes to take up apprenticeships or to go into service. In exchange, their parents would take in someone else's offspring. Apprenticeships were normally of 7 years duration. The child's parents would pay a premium to the master who would in turn provide board and lodging, and training in a skill. The Smythe Manuscripts in Maidstone Museum contain lists of apprenticeships providing a wealth of information about our Boxley forefathers. Thus we have in 1698, John Gouldsmith, whose father Nicholas was a husbandman farming at Harbourland, becoming apprentice to David Springett, blacksmith. (This is probably the earliest reference to the smithy that was attached to the Springate family's cottage at Abbey Gate Cottages). In 1704, William Kempston, son of William Kempston who worked the tannery at Sandling, was apprenticed to Thomas Hughes a Boxley tallow chandler. The year 1725 saw Thomas Alexander, whose father Edmund was a weaver in Boxley Street, taking an apprenticeship with John Baptista, a barber and musician, "to play on a violin". In 1710 stamp duty became payable to the crown on indentures of apprenticeship. Although this was not payable where apprentices were bonded to their own fathers, this does not appear to have made this practice popular. In 1756, William Alexander, a carpenter of Boxley Street preferring to send his son George as apprentice to fellow carpenter John Stonehouse. Likewise Edward Cozens, son of Edward a cordwainer, went to learn the ancient art of shoemaking and making leather articles from John Munn, cordwainer. Those children going into service did not send money home to their parents. Instead, what little they received they saved in order to take on a tenancy of their own, effectively ceasing at a very early age to be a part of their own family. Thus when people fell on hard times, they did not look to their families for aid, but rather to their neighbours, the community and The Overseers of the Poor.

From the start of the 17th century, The Poor Law Acts required each Parish to elect an overseer who were answerable to the Parish vestry, and had the power to raise revenue from local rates – the Poor Tax. Each householder paid a varying amount, dependent on the value of the property they held. The Boxley Registers are available for perusal at The County Archives Office. The first surviving register runs from 1690, and apart from a couple of short breaks, they contain records of all income and expenditure up to the setting up of a new system in 1834. Some inhabitants were in need of weekly aid, mainly through age or infirmity. Examples from 1700, when some 21 inhabitants received regular payments, included George Champion aged 80 and blind, Richard Lewis aged 92, George Dan aged 78 and lame, Jane Newman aged 40 but lame. Also widow Bewley aged 50 and distracted (mad), widow Hyland with a bastard male child aged 4, Mary Golden an orphan aged 9, and Jane Fox with two children aged 17 months and 5 years, and no man. In addition, the overseers would provide money for clothing for poor or orphaned children. These unfortunates would normally be taken in by neighbours who would receive regular remuneration from the overseer. It also fell to him to pay for burial of the destitute on behalf of the Parish. A 1693 register entry (hopefully not a reflection of Boxley hospitality), records the burial of one Robert Rowland, a stranger, stabbed in the eye with a pitchfork. Payment would also be made for transferring itinerants to the Parish of their birth or to that in which they had been domiciled, so that they were not a burden on strangers, but rather upon their home community.

The overseer would also pay the apprenticeship costs for a poor child to give him a start in life. In 1732, Daniel Medhurst a poor child of Boxley was apprenticed to Thomas Collins grocer. The Allington Poor rate register of 1817 shows that William Peters, a papermaker at one of the Sandling mills was paid "for Joseph Winter as per agreement when he had served a year as his apprentice". Although not all apprenticeships were happy affairs and frequently youths did not see out the terms of their apprenticeships to become freemen, young Thomas Newman struck lucky. In 1689, Thomas, a poor child of the neighbouring Parish of Aylesford was provided with a long-term apprenticeship through the Overseers of the Poor, who placed him with George Gill of Boxley. Gill had just converted Boxley's Turkey Mill to papermaking, as well as producing paper at Forstal Mill. He was to dwell with Gill's family until attaining the age of 24, and Gill would instruct him in the mysteries of papermaking. In 1700, in the manner of fairy tales, Thomas married George Gill's daughter Elizabeth. She would have been aged 9 to Thomas's 13 when first he came to live with the family, and now, his apprenticeship served, he was free to marry his sweetheart, the daughter of one of the most important and wealthy men in the area. For Gill was the 'father' of the Maidstone papermaking industry. Their happiness was however to be shattered. That same year, the Parish register records the burial of their baby son, also a Thomas, and just two short years later in 1702 the premature death of Thomas himself. The Lord giveth, and the Lord taketh away.

A further provision for the poor was The Poor House, which provided accommodation for those homeless of the Parish who could not be taken into the households of other Parishioners. A Poor House was first authorised in Boxley as early as 1634. Unfortunately, the Boxley records have not survived, but we do know that at its enforced enclosure in 1834, the Poor House then stood where now is The Hermitage in Boxley Street. In 1805, The Master of The Poor House was John Brigg, and from 1827-32, Walter Hickmott held the post at an annual salary of £30. In 1833, the part of Assistant Overseer of the Poor was abolished and his work taken over by the new master of the Poor House, William Merrall, who also operated his wheelwright's shop in Boxley

Street, and was the church organist. The Poor Law Amendment Act of 1834 required Parishioners to group together in a union to provide a workhouse. Boxley became part of the Hollingbourne Union, and the Poor House was closed and finally sold in 1836. Thereafter the Overseer of the Poor, or 'Retrieving Officer' as he was now known, was instructed to attend in future at the old school room.

The Overseer of the Poor was also able to supplement the income of the poor parishioners, by paying a 'bounty' for the trapping of those wild creatures perceived to be 'vermin'. In 1834, John Martin received 2/- for 2 foxes, 6 pence for 9 cuckoos and 2 stoats and 3/4D (3 shillings and 4 pence) for 10 hedgehogs. William Smith was paid 4/10D for 117 sparrows and £1-13/- for 12 thrushes. The high remuneration for the latter presumably reflects their culinary usage.

Other occasions upon which neighbours were required to gather together were for the Manorial Courts - the Court Leet and Court Baron of the Manor of Boxley. The courts were presided over by the Lord of the Manor's steward. However all decisions were taken by twelve of the chief tenants who were elected to the post of 'homagers', who together formed a manorial jury who oversaw the Lord's financial interests in the Manor. Originally they appointed a Parish Constable, although this power was later taken on by the Maidstone Court Baron. Boxley's Court Baron was concerned with the transfer of copyhold land upon inheritance or sale. It also made decisions on manorial customs and arranged for enforcement of the tithes and quit rents due to the Lord. (Originally, tenants of a Manor were required to provide various services to their Lord, such as accompanying him to war. Later they were released from such responsibilities by the payment of a small fixed annual rent called a 'quit rent'). Under the Court Leet, the homagers were empowered to deal with petty misdemeanours, and administer the communal agriculture. Community spirit was further engendered by the system of 'frankpledge', under which every household formed part of a group of ten, each responsible for the good behaviour of his fellows and the bringing of malefactors to the court to face charges. Occasionally a 'view of frankpledge' would be taken at the Court Leet, where ostensibly every male over the age of 12 would be listed, and thus ensure that they were assigned to a 'tithing', (group of ten). Courts Baron were normally held every 3 weeks and Courts Leet every 6 weeks. However, from the available records, it would seem that in Boxley they originally only met annually, and later this became every 3 years and then 4 years. Presumably because they were the only premises of sufficient size to accommodate large gatherings, the courts were held at the main local hostelries. However, it is possible that psychology was in use here, as being compelled to spend a day at the Inn was probably a great attraction to most Boxley men! The earlier records show that The Red Lion, The Gibraltar Inn, The Bull and the King's Arms hosted the courts alternately. However, by 1847 Melville's Directory shows it being held every 4 years at The Gibraltar Inn. As a reward for allowing this service, (not particularly onerous, as one imagines beer sales must have been most profitable), the landlord was allowed to hold his premises in 'free socage tenure', which meant that he was absolved from paying a rent on his land to the Lord of the Manor.

Down the ages, the inhabitants of Boxley fought and died alongside their neighbours, following their lords into battle against the Saxons and the Normans, and periodically rising against their rulers at perceived injustice. It was Boxley men who helped to swell the ranks of those earliest militia bands raised by Sir Thomas Wyatt and his neighbouring lords. Those same bands who were later to march in the rebellion of 1554 which was ultimately to fracture forever the single unit of Boxley under one powerful Lord, into smaller groups of lesser masters. Under the 1757 Act of Parliament that re-established the militia as a local defence force, every Parish submitted its list of qualified men, and a ballot was then held to determine who would represent each Parish. Those selected had the option of paying for someone to take their place, and if they were too poor to do so, the Overseers of the Poor on behalf of the other Parishioners could be persuaded to pay for such a replacement. This made economic common sense, especially where the selected man was a married man with a large family, and the replacement a single man. Whilst the former was away from home his family would have to be provided for out of the Poor Rates. Thus from at least 1791 to 1799 the Overseer of the Poor for Allington made regular payments to his Boxley counterpart for the upkeep of the wife and child of William Constable of Boxley, who had volunteered to replace an Allington Parishioner selected for the militia. William was perhaps somewhat unfortunate in joining the militia at a time of unrest. Throughout these years he served abroad, certainly in the latter years in Ireland where his militia helped to quell the Vinegar Hill uprising. Often its members were just on standby, but this could cause problems when they were eventually called upon to muster. The Maidstone Journal of 1798 reported the names of Supplementary Militia members who had failed to report for duty, and thus faced the penalty of execution for desertion. They included William Steer of Plaxtol who had been paid as a substitute for John Bridgland of Weavering Street, and William Hilder, a substitute for Benjamin Baffet of Boxley. The journal also reports the commissioning of Boxley volunteers as officers in the Kent Supplementary Militia. Thomas Best was commissioned as major, Lewis Cage as captain, Lewis Cage junior as a lieutenant and the Reverend Charles Cage as an ensign. John Coker, who resided at Boxley House, running the estate for the three spinster Marsham sisters, was appointed Colonel of the Regiment of Volunteers of Oxford, and James Best was captain of The Rochester & Chatham Volunteers.

CHAPTER 8

The Whatmans

At the southern extremity of the old Boxley Parish lies Turkey Court, set on the River Len whose northern bank marked the Parish boundary. The Len powered a mill, latterly called Turkey Mill, which was to become one of the greatest paper-making mills in the country.

The Whatman involvement in the mill began in 1736 when Richard Harris took over its tenancy, purchasing the freehold two years later. Harris had learnt his paper-making skills in the village of Loose, where his papermaker father ran Gurney's Mill. His father's brother-in-law James Whatman, a tanner, lived a hundred yards away and had a son also called James, and the two boys grew up together.

In 1773, having earlier inherited the tannery, the young James Whatman built a new paper mill known as Old Mill, at Hollingbourne. here he installed his friend Richard Harris to run it for the next five years. In 1738, Richard Harris bought the freehold of Turkey Mill, and began a programme of improvement which involved almost the entire reconstruction of the mill. Unfortunately for him, but perhaps fortunately for the history of Boxley, Richard Harris died the following year, leaving the uncompleted mill to his widow Ann. In 1740 Ann Harris married James Whatman, and a great story began.

James and Ann lived by the mill in the residence there, still known as Turkey Court, which Harris had managed to build. During the 19 years of their marriage they continuously improved the mill and soon the writing and drawing papers which they produced were acknowledged to be not only the best in Britain but probably the best in Europe. Testimonials to quality came from such diverse celebrities as the artists Gainsborough and Turner, the writer Blake, and both Napoleon and later still Queen Victoria amongst letter writers. As early as 1753 Whatman writing paper was being exported to America.

After James's death in 1759 his son James took over. To the confusion of researchers and readers alike, the name James was bestowed upon all succeeding Whatman sons. This young James was arguably the most famous Whatman, both for his business skills and social standing. When only 26 he became High Sheriff of Kent. He not only drove the business onwards and upwards but mastered the actual skills of paper-making. He improved Turkey Court itself, which remains today a fine example of a William and Mary house.

This younger James's first wife was Sarah whom he married in 1762. Her father had very good social connections, particularly in London, and he "opened doors" for his son-in-law so that the growth and reputation of the business accelerated rapidly. Sadly Sarah died in 1774 leaving James a widower with two surviving daughters. But he did not remain a widower for long. In 1776 he made another advantageous marriage, to Susanna Bosanquet, who came from a wealthy Huguenot family, her father having been a director of the East India Company. She was 23 to James's 35 and was quite a beauty. She wasted no time in producing a son for her husband, inevitably to be named James. Susanna settled very happily into life at Turkey Court where she began writing her "Housekeeping Book". This has been re-printed in recent years and gives charming insights into how a Big House of the period was run.

By 1782 James Whatman was a very wealthy man and he purchased Vinters Estate to the north, with its old manor house. One Roger de Vinters had bought this estate from the Abbot of Boxley, and by 1343 he had built a manor house there. Ownership duly passed to Ralph Fremingham of Loose and then to Sir Henry Isley. Unfortunately for him, Isley had to forfeit his life and the estate to the Crown as a penalty for supporting Wyatt's rebellion. Queen Mary then granted ownership to Henry Cuttes and it passed through other hands, including Sir Samuel Ongley who was a director of the infamous South Sea Company which ruined many families when the value of its shares collapsed in the "South Sea Bubble". Ongley was obviously spared ruin himself as Vinters remained in his family, and it was his heirs who sold it to Whatman, "lately in tenancy of Henry Champneys". Most of the owners did not live at Vinters and in fact it was several generations of the Champneys family who were tenants there and to whom there is a memorial tablet in Boxley Church. This family were prominent in Boxley for centuries. In 1613 one, Walter Champnes, husbandman was indicted for keeping – "a common tippling-house at Boxley and sold ale and beere" – without a licence.

James set about re-constructing the old building and, after spending some £5000, a grand country house was the result. He employed Humphrey Repton to re-design the parkland, and the family moved to their new home in 1787. Three years later James suffered a stroke, an event which probably sowed the seeds of his decision in 1794 to sell his paper-making empire and retire, at the comparatively early age of 53. During the four years of life left to him, James threw all his energies into improving still more the house and estate lands. Succeeding generations of Whatmans continued the good work. Susanna's Huguenot origins added a French flavour to some of the interiors.

It was the final James Whatman (1813-1887) who made the biggest impact on the house. Incidentally, in his time he was M.P. for Maidstone. Between 1849 and 1852 an already impressive house was still further enlarged, and even the description Mansion would not have done it justice. It was a truly remarkable building. Vinters became one of the social high spots of the county. James would hold tree-archery meetings attended by the elite of Kent. These were followed by a Ball, usually held at the Assembly Rooms in Sandling Road, in order to accommodate the large number of guests. In 1868, following his re-election to the second of his three terms as M.P., he held a celebration fete at Vinters. A hot-air balloon ascended, laden with gas piped from the works at St Peter's Street in Maidstone, and when darkness fell there was a memorable display of fireworks. About 1860, when the first Kent Rifle Volunteers were formed, the park became the venue for their twice weekly drills.

It is interesting to note that despite the enormous wealth garnered from their paper-making industry, and their delightful estate, the Whatmans could not make that final step into the higher echelons of society. In 1838, the final James Whatman wrote to Lord Romney, his friend, requesting permission to court his daughter Charlotte. Romney replied that Charlotte was upset about Whatman's conduct at dinner, and it would be better if he did not see her again. Reading between the lines, Whatman wrote back saying that he understood that the gulf in rank between them was too great, and he should not have aspired so high, but hoped they would remain friends. Although heavily impoverished, the Romneys were 'aristocracy' whereas the Whatmans would never be anything other than 'trade'!

Following the death of this James in 1887 there were to be no more James Whatmans, for he sired four daughters but no son. We shall take up their story and tell of the decline and fall of Vinters in a later chapter.

The south frontage of Boxley House showing the Tudor chimneys.

CHAPTER 9

Boxley House

The earliest origins of Boxley House are not known. Certainly the interior of the present house shows evidence of early seventeenth century style, possibly having been built around a courtyard plan. The cellars are very old and are constructed of chalk. Legend has it that a tunnel connects them to Boxley Church.

We know that Sir Thomas Wyatt the Elder exchanged land with Henry VIII, thus becoming owner of what would later be known as the Boxley House and Boxley Abbey Estates. These lands, having been forfeited to the Crown following the Wyatt rebellion of 1554, were restored to them gradually . Elizabeth I regranting Boxley House to George Wyatt.

For such a splendidly sited and important focal point of the village, it is surprising that this always imposing Mansion never gained great favour with its owners, who for some three hundred years preferred to reside mainly elsewhere. At the beginning of the seventeenth century the house was leased by the Grymstones, an eminent family in Kent, and it is possible that they were responsible for commencing its construction. When Henry Grymstone, vicar of Aylesford, died in 1654, his will included Boxley House. In 1692, Doctor DeLangley succeeded Captain Zachary Browne as tenant, until 1703 when Elizabeth Wiat, widow of Edwin Wiat the Younger moved in. The house remained the residence of various Wiat widows for the next 40 years. Francis Wiat, and then his brother Richard, successive Lords of the Manor of Boxley, preferred to reside at Quex Park in the Isle of Thanet, which had been inherited through their mother Frances. In 1744 Boxley House reverted to a Manor possession and was leased to William Gore.

After the Marsham family inherited the Wyatt lands, in 1753, they became part of the Romney Estate, Lord Romney's seat was at Mote House, and the successive Lords Romney continued to let Boxley House to tenants, dwelling there occasionally themselves. During restoration in the 1960's the inscription "His Lordship's Bedroom" was found.

At the end of the 18th Century, Romney let the house to his three spinster sisters, – Priscilla, Frances and Elizabeth Marsham. When Frances died in 1821, her extensive will detailed stables and coachhouse, brewhouse with brewing copper, washhouse, dairy with barrel churns, laundry, bakehouse and beer and wine cellars. John Coker was the estate manager and his daughter

Boxley House

acted as a companion to the old ladies. He had married Charlotte Marsham, daughter of Charles, 1st Earl of Romney in about 1790.

The next occupant was George James Cholmondeley, whose wife was The Honourable Mary Elizabeth, daughter of the 2nd Viscount Sidney, and the heroine of a remarkable love story. As a young woman, Mary Elizabeth Townsend became the mistress of the 2nd Earl of Romney, and subsequently gave birth to an illegitimate son. Known as Henry Senneck, the boy was raised at Romney's Mote House, believing himself to be the son of a sister of the housekeeper, and later told that the housekeeper was in fact his mother. Finally his lineage was revealed to him, and he was granted an annual allowance, "provided he does not molest the Earl or his family". Whether Lord Romney's dalliance with Mrs Cholmondeley carried on during her marriage is unknown, but after his wife Sophia died in 1812, he remained unmarried. Following the death of her husband, the widow Cholmondeley remained ensconced in Boxley House, now widely acknowledged as His Lordship's mistress. In 1832 the marriage was arranged between Romney's son and heir Lord Charles Marsham, and Lady Margaret Scott. Boxley House being eminently suitable for the proposed newly-weds, Mrs Cholmondeley was given notice to quit. "But where can I go?", she exclaimed. "To the Mote, madam, as Countess", replied Lord Romney, and she accepted this unusual proposal of marriage. Father and son were married the same year, and Mary provided her Lord with another son who became The Honourable Robert Marsham. The 2nd Earl died in 1845, and Mary, now The Dowager Countess of Romney, returned to Boxley House where she lived just two more lonely years, before following her great love to the grave.

It was the 2nd Earl who planted the beautiful hanger wood on the face of the hill above Boxley and also built the summerhouse which enjoys such a spectacular position high on the Downs overlooking the church. The current building incorporates a very old flint wall, said to be part of a very ancient building, dating back perhaps as far as the twelfth century. It was probably a huntsman's lodge or the dwelling of the man designated to oversee the coney warren. Was this a trysting place for Mary Elizabeth? Major alterations and extensions to Boxley House took place during the reign of Queen Anne and again in Georgian times, to give the building its present appearance.

The Boxley House estate was very extensive, stretching from the Chatham Road to the West, as far as Warren Farm to the East, where for a while the family's coachman lived. From Grange Lane in the South, Northwards over the Downs to Bredhurst and Westfield Sole. Several farms were included, and these were mostly let to tenant farmers.

Mr George Wallis, whose Victorian memories are set out in another chapter, knew Boxley House as the "Great House" and wrote of the old Earl residing there himself for a while. This would be about 1830 and the local boys used to watch for his approach in a "low four-wheeled chariot" whereupon they would rush to open the gate at the bottom of the park by the Church and receive sixpence for their trouble.

In about 1890 the then Lord Romney sold Boxley Abbey House and its surrounding land to Major Best of Park House, the part sold off becoming known as the Boxley Abbey Estate. In 1899 Lord Romney sold the remainder of the Boxley House Estate to the Style family, well known local Brewers of the firm Style & Winch. By then the grounds had shrunk to just $14^1/_2$ acres, which included the sites and gardens of twelve cottages in The Street, and the wheelwrights shop, in tenure of Thomas Oxley. In 1903 Robert Henry Style became the owner and he lived at Boxley House until his death in 1945. Bob Style and his wife brought up their daughters Betty and Ursula and son David, and the family joined whole-heartedly in the life of the village for all those years, playing prominent parts in the Church and in activities such as Guides and Cubs. At least two of his Estate workers agree in their opinion that he was a "very nice gentleman", and his wife a "dear soul".

Boxley House during the Style era continued to maintain a full range of servants. The Summerhouse was now home to the Gamekeeper Jesse Hodge, and two of his daughters were maids at Boxley House. The wife of Mr Cripps the village wheelwright was Nanny to the young children. For some years the kitchen was run by a Chef, Mr Hill. The house itself had two halls, drawing and dining rooms, library, gun room and billiard room and eleven or more family bedrooms. For the servants there was a servants hall, butler's pantry, housekeeper's room, kitchen, scullery, their own bedrooms up in the attics, and the cellars. There were enough farms on the estate to provide for many of the family's needs, but for convenience there were close to the house greenhouses and walled gardens and a Dairy. Also stables for the family's horses. Jersey and Guernsey cows were kept to provide milk for the house, and a few favoured villagers could call and take away a jug of warm milk.

For the servants the day began at 6.30 a.m. and lasted into the late evening. There were open fires to clean out, fuelled by all the timber growing on the slopes of the Downs. There was morning tea to take into the various family bedrooms, following which the maids laid out the clothes for the day. Hot water had to be carried upstairs and then the whole house swept and cleaned. Particularly during the shooting season there were house guests to wait upon and their suit-cases to struggle upstairs with. Dinner parties were frequent, with all the extra work that these entailed. There was also many a dance and party. In the hall, from November to March, a log fire burnt both day and night. Beech-wood from the Downs was used specifically, which never flew sparks.

At one time noisy peacocks strutted about outside, and Bob Styles made his grounds available for all manner of village functions. These included large celebrations for Peace after the Great War, the 1935 Silver Jubilee and the 1937 Coronation. At the latter event hundreds of people attended, there were marquees and swings and roundabouts. A Band played and races were run and there were games and a fancy dress pageant by the children.

In the south-east corner of the grounds and towards the Churchyard was a cricket pitch where on alternate Saturdays the Boxley Village Team and Style & Winch Brewery played their home games. Boxley had a flourishing side from well before the Great War and were well supported by the villagers. The pitch was lovingly tended by Wally Gosling, who also played for many years. A pavilion was built (to be burnt down about 1964) and Bob Style's patronage extended to arranging for a wagon to appear at a strategic moment laden with barrels of beer. Boxley cricket effectively ended with the Second War, although some people recall the odd game after 1945.

Sport of a different kind also centred upon Boxley House. Bob Styles was renowned for his Shooting Parties, as was his father Albert, who had leased the right to hunt and shoot over all Romney's lands in 1874, prior to leasing Boxley House itself from 1879. In October there would be Partridge Shoots out at Boarley. In November the pheasants which had been reared were released near the house and beaters drove them westwards all the way across the Estate lands to the Chatham Road. There would be as many as thirty beaters, mostly Estate workers plus the odd man or boy from the village, and they enjoyed a lunch of cheese and corned beef sandwiches washed down by the inevitable Style and Winch beer. These shoots were great social occasions, attended by prominent local people and county dignitaries. Even the Rev. Hale joined in, together with the local policeman Ted Kirby, both being good shots. Reputedly even better shots were the two Style daughters Betty and Ursula who were usually in attendance. For her part Mrs Styles would follow up behind in a pony and trap to collect the fallen birds. If the beaters came across a nest they would be rewarded with up to a shilling, and a broody hen would be found to hatch the eggs for the following season.

On Boxing Day there would be a rabbit shoot, and one year 350 were shot. Bob Style's gun grew so hot that he took his cap off and used it to cradle the barrel in his hand. This may have been the day when it is recalled that the dead rabbits were stacked outside Boxley House in a pile feet high. At this festive time of year the beaters had some gin ladled out to them.

The gamekeeper Jesse Hodge was in time succeeded by Tom Hill, and their job included chasing off poachers. As well as shooting rabbits, a rabbit catcher was also employed, because they were an infestation. The Normans had set up the Warrens on the Downs to supplement their food supply but time and nature had seen an unwelcome increase.

Shoots were also held over the hill at Grange Farm and Harp Farm. Pigeons were another target for Bob Styles, and when the shooting season was over he was minded to pack his bags and set off for fishing in Ireland! His fellow Director Leslie Caldecot lived at Boxley Abbey for some years, and like Bob was prominent in local life. If any village lads were unemployed they both did their best to try and find work for them at the Brewery.

The Style era ended with Robert's sudden death in 1945. The estate was sold, and his widow lived for a while at Parsonage Farm before moving to Wateringbury. The new owners, the Marr-Johnson family, stayed until 1960 when they sold the house to a development company. Thankfully it was unable to obtain permission to demolish it. In 1961, Mr J.D Davies bought and ran it for three years as a private school known as St. Andrew's College, when rugby posts were to be seen. Whilst standing empty for a year there was an exciting period when Planning Permission was sought for its use as a home for retired circus animals. The prospect of lions roaming about caused concern, especially to the Christian congregation nearby. Following their purchase in 1965, an alternative use was granted to Mr and Mrs Tom Knowlden in 1968 for a Hotel and Country Club and their stewardship of the grand old building continued until 1979. A debt of gratitude is owed to the Knowldens for their extensive repair works, starting with a new roof. They discovered that there was once a Bell-tower and they also came across a secret hiding place, thought to be a Priest-hole. Whether it was used as such would have been dependant on the occupiers being a Catholic family. The culmination of months of work came when the electricity supply was up-graded. Tom Knowlden stood some way from the house and at his signal every light came on in a blaze of glory. It was an emotional moment and the re-birth of Boxley House was proclaimed.

During the restoration the old Butler's pantry was turned into a toilet and Mr and Mrs Knowlden and her father were all together as the works progressed. Unknown to them a Butler named Thomas Sales had shot himself in there in 1898. A figure suddenly appeared, moved a few steps and then disappeared. Mr Knowlden himself saw nothing but the apparition was clearly seen by the other two. This was followed by other sightings, and on one occasion two lady guests were coming down the stairs when they both felt themselves pushed by some unseen force.

A stranger happening was to follow. A Squadron-leader was in his car coming up the drive when a young woman wearing a shawl suddenly appeared in front of him and he felt a bump as he seemed to hit her. But upon getting out he could find no trace of anybody. A shaken Squadron-leader presented himself to Tom Knowlden and ordered a very stiff brandy. More amusingly, the Knowldens used to bring in some waitresses from the Medway Towns, and as they arrived one day a figure in white appeared at an upper window. The response of the girls was to all give a cheery wave, either believing it to be a real person or just as likely accepting it as a natural part of life at Boxley House!

All this was getting a bit too much, and the Knowldens decided to have an exorcism. This duly took place by courtesy of a renowned Exorcist who thought that there were three restless spirits abroad. From that day no other happenings were known to occur.

A very much alive and far from ghostly character was a gardener from before the Great War named Will Kilpatrick – known to his friends as "Killer". He it was who led the one-day strike of the Choir as a protest when the Choirmaster put a stop to Carol signing at all the Big Houses. It was thought that the Choir was undignified in accepting so much drink and hospitality as they staggered around the Parish. More famously, Killer married a widow rather late in life and at the reading of the banns the Church clock unaccountably stopped. The villagers thought that, like the rest of them, the clock was amazed at his late surrender to wedlock! In later years another gardener got annoyed by the piercing shrieks of a peacock and killed it with his spade. But he would not confess his crime. Mrs Style was sure he did it and had the dead creature stuffed and stood in a greenhouse where it cast a reproachful eye on the culprit whenever he entered!

One final event during the Knowlden's time may be worth recording. In about 1970 Mr Northcote Parkinson wrote a book entitled "The Life and Times of Horatio Hornblower" in which he set out to trace the 'true life' story of the old sea-dog. He wrote that Hornblower bought Boxley House in 1819 "in whose family it was to remain until 1953". The book sold well and soon people were calling at the Hotel in pilgrimage and rummaging about in the Churchyard to find the great man's grave. Even as recently as 1998 a foreign visitor has called believing that Hornblower's widow was buried in the Church. The book was most convincingly written.

After the Knowldens left, the Hotel business continued until 1996 when it closed and a new dawn beckoned with use as the European School of Osteopathy. Let us rejoice that unlike Vinters and Park House this fine old building is still with us, in its peerless setting twixt Church and Downs.

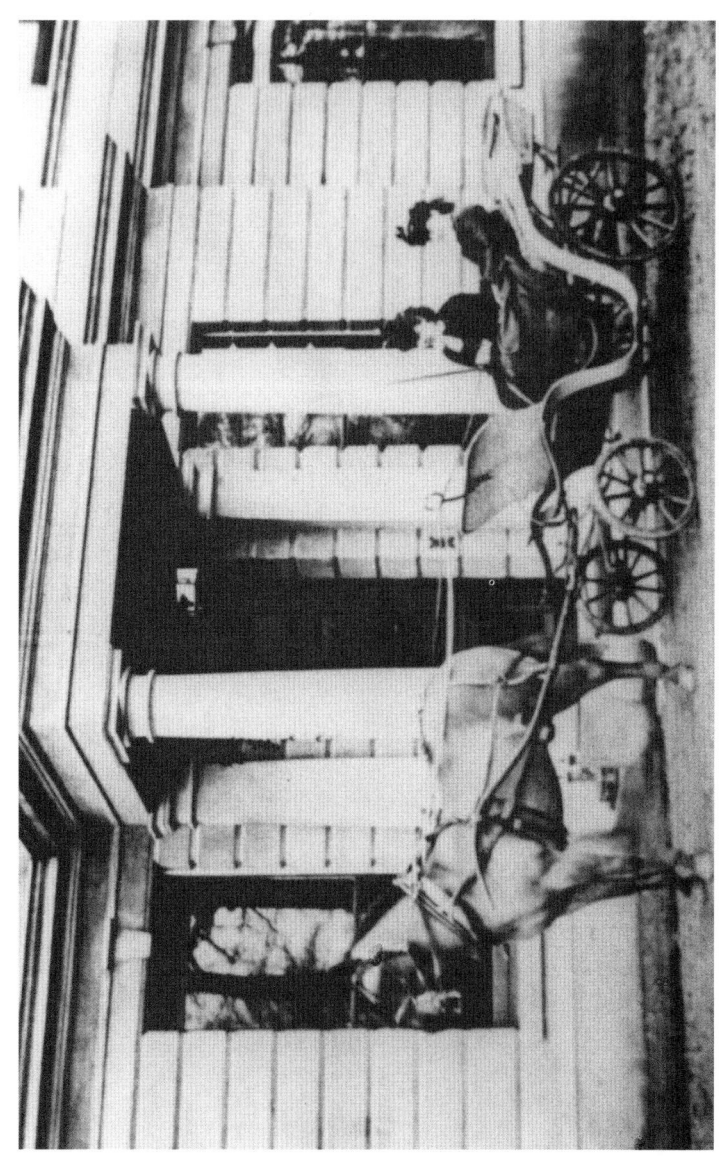

A carriage outside the front porch of the 'new' Park House.

CHAPTER 10

Park House – Boxley

The story of Park House Boxley, is essentially that of two separate houses, each of which bore the name. It cannot be over-emphasised that this Park House, situated in the village, was quite distinct from Park House, Maidstone at Sandling where the Lushingtons were to reside.

The history of Park House is inextricably linked with the Best family under whose ownership it grew to become the dominant house of the village. The Bests first came to prominence as brewers in Chatham in the 1600's. Their business flourished, and with wealth came the rewards, including fine houses such as Rome House and Chatham House. At the start of the 18th Century the patriarch of the family was Thomas Best and he began to extend their lands with various purchases. His eye fell on Boxley, and in 1719 he purchased from Sir Charles Sedley many acres of land in Boxley, including the 120 acre Munkendowne or Monkton Downe Court (which was woodland west of Grange Farm), Walslade (Walderslade), Cherry Croft, Great Cowbeck Wood, and a cottage in Boxley Street divided into two habitations. The following year his son Maudistly purchased Park House and made it his home. From hereon, the family fortunes were derived from a mix of farming and brewing, with Park House acting, for the next century, as their farm and country retreat, whilst their main base remained at Chatham.

The first Park House was constructed within, and took its name from, the Ley or Lea Park that had been enclosed by Sir Thomas Wyatt. It is not known who it was built for, but the Lea Park of 90 acres together with Park Wood formed part of a royal grant by Elizabeth I in 1596, to William Llewyn and Robert Cranmer. Surviving photographs suggest that it probably was of Tudor origin, but the first remaining documentary evidence for it is not until 1672 when a Sarah Smith leased to Richard Ffryer of Boxley – "The Parke House, barn, stable, yard and garden, with a tenement nearby and 9 pieces of land containing 50 acres, late in the tenure of William Hartrupp". The next title deed is dated 1677, when Sarah Higford granted a half share of 'the mansion house and 50 acres', as part of the marriage settlement between her daughter Sarah Coulier and Thomas Oliver (alias Quintine). It is not known whether Sarah Smith and Sarah Higford were one and the same, however one presumes that the latter was either a great beauty, vastly wealthy or both, because she married at least three times. By 1677, she had outlived her first husband

The original Park House, Boxley. Demolished circa 1875. The North Downs in the background. Note the funeral hatchment on the central gable.

Bartholomew Coulier, a merchant, and was then said to be the widow of William Harvey, doctor of Physicke of Islington. She may have been the daughter of (or perhaps the widow of yet another husband) – Henry Higford. The Park House title deeds include a bond of 1670 for £212, which Henry Higford, and William Webb of Stockbury, owed to Philip Bartholomew, the owner of neighbouring Court Lodge.

In 1680, Sarah Oliver, now a widow, married Doctor John St John, and the following year her mother Sarah Higford married yet again to Roger Paine. At Paine's death in 1707 he left everything to his wife Sarah and son Charles. Neither of them appear to have outlived him by much, because by 1712 the property was owned by Sarah St John, widow, and her son Pawlet, who leased Park Farm House and some 81½ acres to John Clark. In 1720 Pawlet St John made John Williams the tenant of the farmhouse before selling his estate to Maudistly Best. However, both tithe and tax documents show that Samuel Athawes farmed the Park House Estate (whilst living at The Parsonage) from the 1690's to at least 1728, and that a Captain Bix had occupied Park House in 1690, but was replaced by William Tuppeny the following year. A map of Park House Estate dated 1697 shows the property as part belonging to John St John, Doctor of Law, and part to Sarah Paine, and farmed by Athawes. Park House retained an acreage of 88½ acres whilst a further 139 acres formed part

PARK HOUSE – BOXLEY

of two farms on the estate. The largest was The Kiln Farm, today known as Stonehouse, and the other was The Little Farm, which stood by the Detling Road, and now lies beneath the M20. The estate was comprised of all the land bordered by the Detling Road, Penenden Heath, Sandy Lane, and the east side of Boxley Street up to where it adjoined Court Lodge lands to the north.

Maudistly's inheritance of the Best empire in 1740 was shortlived, as he died just 4 years later. His eldest son Thomas resided at the beautiful Chilston Park near Lenham, and appears to have been disinterested in either Park House or the brewery. Thomas and his younger brother James, came to an agreement and in 1751 their mother Elizabeth passed Park House to James. His sister Sarah was married to the famous Admiral Edward Vernon, victor of The Portobello Campaign, who endeared himself to the British sailor by introducing the daily ration of rum, diluted with water. Vernon had been given the nickname 'Old Grog', because of the cheap 'grogram' cloak he habitually wore. ('grogram' was a coarse fabric of silk and wool stiffened with gum) – and thus the British tars dubbed their new ration – 'grog'. Admiral Vernon would have visited Park House from time to time, and there is the story that he once brought with him from his travels seeds from which grew two Plane trees. Whether either or both still survive in the old Park House grounds is unknown. Apart from Hornblower (see the Boxley House chapter) this association with Admiral Vernon seems to be the only nautical connection claimed by Boxley.

Major Mawdistly Gaussen Best (1826-1906) and his wife Kitty.

Ownership of Park House came down through two further generations of James Bests, until 1849 when Major Mawdistly Gaussen Best inherited. He was a professional soldier whose adventures would fill a book, and he served both in the Crimean War and the Indian Mutiny. Visitors to Boxley Abbey (which he bought in 1890), may notice some cannon balls piled up by the front door, which are reputed to be relics of those far-off campaigns. Old Park House was not a particularly grand house, having only a drawing room, dining room and library on the ground floor, plus a kitchen, scullery, housekeeper's room, butler's room and a servants hall. Upstairs were 2 main bedrooms with dressing rooms, six other bedrooms (including those for servants), a schoolroom and a sitting room. Major Best found it too draughty and in need of too much repair, but a fortuitous purchase back in 1836, provided the solution. In that year he had been pleased to seize the chance to buy Boxley Lodge, the property which stood just to the north of Park House.

Like its neighbour, this property also had its origins in Tudor times. One imagines that it must have been a source of great annoyance to the occupiers of Park House for many years, because originally it was a tannery. The Boxley, or Marley Stream, rising in the springs around The Parsonage, provided an ideal site for this highly obnoxious but necessary trade. The awful smells emanating from the tanning process must have been most unpleasant to both Park House occupants, and those of the village itself, depending on the direction of the wind.

The 1697 map of Park House Estate shows Mr. Charlton's house and tannery only about 60 yards north of Park House, and the tannery field (where the skins would have been pegged out) immediately to the east. The tannery is probably that mentioned in 1608, for which Cavalier Maycott paid a tithe to Boxley Manor on behalf of his wife, which premises had previously been in the possession of W. Maplisden. The house itself appears to have originally belonged to the Fletcher family, passing to John Cripps on his marriage to Katherine Fletcher. In 1682, Katherine, now a widow, remarried to Thomas Knight, taking the property with her. The Charltons then came into possession, presumably by inheritance. The Parish registers show that, between 1678 and 1705 (two years before his death), George Charlton and his wife Elizabeth produced 17 children! Proof of the high incidence of infant mortality is provided by the fact that no less than 4 were baptised George (3 of whom died), and 3 were named Jane. If the register for the years immediately prior to 1678 were not missing, it might provide evidence of their having even more children.

In 1729, when The Reverend George Charlton married Ann Barrell, daughter of Edmund Barrell, prebendary of Rochester Cathedrial, and vicar of Boxley, his property included, – "a mansion house, barns, stables, outhouses, yard garden and several pieces of land containing 12 acres, heretofore in occupation of Thomas Knatchbull and late of John Wyvell". Wyvell, who was vicar of Boxley between 1690 and 1703, married Christian Charlton and, presumably because the vicarage was becoming dilapidated, he took the opportunity of residing in his brother-in-law's property. One presumes that the tannery was no longer in operation by this time. George Charlton left all his property, which included the forge on Boxley Green and other Boxley lands, to his brother John, who dying childless in 1770 passed it to his nephew,

PARK HOUSE — BOXLEY

Park House servants in 1906. The footmen dressed in mourning following Major Best's death. Seated left is the butler Mr. Prince.

A wedding party outside Park House in 1893. The bridegroom is Rev. Charles Shaw and the bride Elizabeth Louisa Bosanquet.

the Reverend George Burville. It is probable that George Burville had been living in the property since at least 1757, when he became curate of Boxley. He effectively ran the parish on behalf of the non-resident vicars Edmund Barrell and then Dr. William Markham, both of whom had other posts of higher importance. (The latter only gave up the incumbency of Boxley in 1771 when he was made Archbishop of York).

At Burville's death in 1798, the house, by then known as Boxley Lodge, was the venue of a sale of "its complete household furniture, antique and other china, horses, cows and implements of husbandry, including particularly a very excellent post-chaise (carriage), and a large assortment of handsome plate". Surprisingly, considering that the house and farm contents had been sold-off, the historian W.H. Ireland states that Burville's heir, his daughter Frances, and her husband, the Reverend P. Rashleigh, lived at the house. When Major Best purchased it from George Rashleigh, it also sported a brewhouse, coachhouse and laundry, and was said to have been then or late occupied by the vicar of Boxley, The Reverend John Griffin. Smaller than Park House, it had a drawing room, dining room and breakfast room downstairs, together with the kitchen and butler's pantry. Above were 5 bedrooms and a dressing room plus 2 servants bedrooms. However, unlike Park House there were 5 substantial cellars beneath.

Major Best's mother and sisters lived at Park House, whilst he continued his military career and travelled the world, letting Boxley Lodge to various genteel persons. In 1862 he decided to 'settle down' and began to enlarge Boxley Lodge, adding a housekeeper's room, pantry and servants hall with 3 additional bedrooms. Marrying in 1864, he decided that this would be the new marital home, and whilst building was in progress he rented Boxley Abbey and lived there for a while.

The new Park House in its enlarged form was a fine building of huge dimensions. There was a very striking main hall with a flight of stairs dividing left and right onto balconies above. There were at least eleven bedrooms. Downstairs were dining and drawing rooms, library, billiard room, tea room and study. In Victorian times the House staff numbered at least sixteen, and the domestic quarters included the Butler's and Housekeeper's rooms, a vast kitchen, servants hall and silver room. Below the large cellarage was retained. In one of the passages countless bells to summons the servants to all corners. Close by was a coachhouse and stable block, with a scullery, a servants living room, three more bedrooms and a fruit store, above. Sometime after James Best bought Court Lodge in 1832, a well was bored about 300 yards behind the Church, to provide a water supply for Park House. A cogged capstan, turned by a donkey walking in circles, raised the water, and an octagonal structure was erected around the walkway. Later an engine was installed, which in turn became redundant once The Waterworks were operating, and eventually the building was converted into accommodation.

PARK HOUSE — BOXLEY

An aerial view of the 'new' Park House, Boxley, built circa 1876. Street Farm in in the top right-hand corner, and the line of the old road survives as the tree line running through the picture above the roof of the house.

In 1876 the new House was ready, and Major Best and his wife Katherine (Kitty) took up residence. The Old Park House was pulled down, and Boxley Lodge was renamed Park House. There was immediate celebration with a dance attended by 80 people. Kitty began to keep a diary of the Park House dances, and remarked that for this one they only got the hall floors finished the day before! Kitty died in 1896 and over the years she recorded a succession of dances, servants' parties and other beanfeasts. At another dance in 1876 she recorded the volume of sherry, claret and soda waters drunk, and remarked that they "let the champagne flow too freely". 1877 saw a Fancy Dress Ball attended by 168 people, and she danced until 5.30 a.m. To accommodate this number tarpaulin covers were extended outside. Other dances also went on to 5.00 a.m. and one suspects that the servants never saw their beds on those nights. In 1879 there was a Hunt Ball, whilst in 1882 she records 70 horsemen coming to breakfast before setting off a-hunting. In 1883 she had cause to note that the musicians consumed rather too much sherry. Then in 1888 there was a Ball attended by as many as 200. "Joy was unconfined, and loud were the sounds of revelry by night".

We cannot be sure how keen Major Best himself was of dancing, but for his part he started a pack of Harrier hounds in 1867 with which he hunted for twelve years until "rheumatics" made it too difficult for him. Henry Brassey over at Preston Hall took the hounds off his hands.

Away from the House the Estate lands prospered under his care. They dove-tailed in with the Boxley House Estate to the north and extended east to Detling and the Sittingbourne Road. On the edge of the Estate were East Lodge in Harple Lane and Workhouse Cottage (both still standing) and Keeper's Cottage (which has disappeared with 1990's road improvements). The title of Workhouse Cottage has suggested that the Boxley Workhouse or Poor House may have been in this vicinity, but that location is discussed in the village chapter. Rather was Workhouse Cottage where mending might be done for the Big House as employment for retired servants. One latter-day resident became well-known for her lace-making. Keeper's Cottage speaks for itself, and the Clements family provided a generation or two of Gamekeepers for the Estate. In later years the woodman lived there. Close by was the pheasant rearing field.

A much later member of the family around the 1930's was Bert Clements who was blind, but this did not stop him working as a gardener at Park House. He would feel his way around the kitchen garden pulling out the weeds. He found his own way to work from Keeper's cottage, walking along the landway. But one winter's day the snow completely disorientated him and the poor man got himself lost.

Around the village, Court Lodge Farm, Street Farm and Harbourland Farm formed part of the Estate, and Major Best constructed his own Home Farm close by Park House with milking sheds and the like. Gentry such as he took a delight in building the most up-to-date Home Farms as a measure of their status and as an example to their tenant farmers of how things might be done. Their inspiration was the Prince Consort who had built for himself a model farm on one of the Royal Estates. Park House had a busy dairy to supply the family with butter and cream. Around the village were many cottages for the Estate workers, including Bull Cottages towards Penenden Heath. In Back Lane, now leading to the tunnel beneath the Motorway, still stands Stone House where was the Laundry together with Carpenter's Shed close by.

Over the years Major Best took opportunities to add to his land-holdings, for example buying Street Farm and the Fowle Estate in 1865, The Hermitage in 1890 and soon afterwards Boxley Abbey and the separate Estate which went with it. The latter was bought from Lord Romney and included, as well as the Abbey House, Boarley Farm, Abbey Farm and Tyland Farm.

In 1887 he made a very interesting arrangement concerning the road leading to the village. Up to that time it was very narrow, and heading south from the village it went along the lane which still leads to the Vicarage and then dropped across what are now fields, close by the site of old Park House to join the line of the present road near the junction with Grange Lane. Major Best records that his father always wanted to move the road westwards and to improve it, and now he himself had the opportunity to do so. Cynics might say that the old road was too close to Park House for comfort. Construction of the new road was also interesting in that it was laid on beds of faggots to stop it sinking. Workmen in recent years are surprised when their diggings reveal this "foundation". Similarly it is said that the cobbles of the old road lie beneath the soil which is now part of Park House grounds.

Over the years the Best family had gained a reputation as kind and generous employers, which was not just confined to a daily allowance of free beer. They helped the poor, gave to charity and paid pensions. They supported a range of sporting activities and entered into the social life of the County. Major Best himself became High Sheriff of Kent in 1881. He seems to have been a keen supporter of Kent Cricket in the Club's early days, and to have formed a friendship with Alfred Mynn from nearby Thurnham, he a giant both in size and cricketing prowess for the County.

In 1894 Major Best gave up his interests in the Brewery. Two years later Kitty died. They had no children. His sister Emily (1829 - 1899) had married James Whatman Bosanquet (a scion of the Vinters Whatmans) and amongst their children was Harriet Emily Hardinge Best Bosanquet (known as Lily). During Kitty's later years, Lily was her companion, and after his wife's death Major Best was pleased to have Lily still living at Park House. He died in 1906 and left the Estate to Lily, who in 1899 had married a young clergyman Edmund Dalison. By Royal Licence in 1907 Edmund and Lily took the surname Best-Dalison. A new and long and eventful chapter in the history of Park House and Boxley was about to begin under their influence and patronage.

CHAPTER 11

Victorian Times

Boxley is fortunate in having some reminiscences written in 1894 by a remarkable man named George Ephraim Wallis. Born of humble country stock in 1823, he gained for himself sufficient education and skills to go on and found the Maidstone building firm of G. E. Wallis & Son. Here follows an extract from his reminiscences, paraphrased in part.

"I was born at Boxley in 1823 in a cottage close to the foot of the hills, not many yards from the old Pilgrims Road, but the cottage was pulled down many years ago. My parents were in a humble position in life. I do not recollect much of my school days, indeed there were scarcely any to recollect. What little schooling I had was before I was ten years of age under the old man named Hassell who kept a small boys school in the lane leading from the Kings Arms to the cricket field at the back of the Inn. The old man was at times very violent, he not only used a large stick but at times a short horse whip to chastize the boys with.

At the time I am speaking of a lady named Chumney lived at the house where the present Mrs Style now lives at the top of the street. It was known in the village as the "Great House". I used to go to fetch a dinner which Mrs Chumney used to allow the old man. This was also the seat of the old Earl of Romney and he resided there for a short while. When he was staying at Boxley us boys used to watch for his coming in his low four wheeled chariot. We used to run to open the gate for him at the bottom of the park close to the Church and invariably had sixpence given us, which we used to share.

It was the custom at that time for the Sunday School Children once a year during Lent to say the Church Catechism in Church during Divine Service on Sunday afternoon. Our school was held in a part of the Gallery, and the other part was occupied by the Choir, and it was next to the Belfry. All this was cleared away many years ago. We had to get to our places in the Aisle of the Church, where we were placed in a line for the saying of the Catechism, so that all the congregation could see and hear. It happened on this occasion there were several fellows in the Belfry and I being the head boy led the way and passing out one fellow set me laughing by tickling me a bit. I could not stop, so went laughing to my place in the Aisle. When the first question was put – "What is your name?" I was still laughing whereupon the Minister Dr Griffith took hold of me by the collar and pushed me on one side next to the Clerk's

69

desk. There I continued the same so he took hold of me and pushed me down the Aisle, and away I went giggling out of the Church. I could not help noticing as I passed out that a number of the congregation were smiling.

In my very early days there was a regular choir with different instruments to accompany the singing, such as clarinets, bassoon, violin and cello. There used to be much disagreement among themselves, jealous of each other as to who had the best voice and who was the best singer. I remember they used to frequently adjourn to the "Kings Arms" after the afternoon service to practice for the following Sunday. At last they fell out with the Parson the Rev. Cockburn and one Sunday they declined to a sing at all, much to the surprise of the Parson and congregation. It was not long after this, I think it was when Dr Griffith came to the living, that the choir was broken up and done with and the Barrel organ substituted, and the singing done by the school children.

I learnt to play the fife and used to take it with me in my dinner basket whilst tending the sheep on the hills, and played away lustily on it. I was considered good enough to join the Detling Band before I was twelve years of age. I was told the first thing I had to learn was to drink beer. One Christmas Eve we had been out playing all day at the various houses, and the last house we called at was a Mr William Fowle's at Boxley. He lived in a stone house directly opposite the present Malthouse and nearly close to the Green. After playing a turn or two we were invited in the house. It was then rather late, and he plied us pretty freely with old ale and spirit mixed with it. He would keep making the men drink, but I being a small boy I suppose he did not force the drink on me. Presently we missed first one and then another, so that at last there was only Parks the Serpent Player and I left. Mr Fowle went out to see what had become of them, and I found them all more or less helplessly drunk and laying on the lawn in front of the house. He told us to go out and play the Dead March, which we did to the great delight of old Fowle. How the poor fellows got back to Detling I don't know, but parts of instruments and drumsticks were picked up next day on the road!

I think I was something under ten years of age when I was first sent out to work, but a little previous to that I remember the first sixpence I ever earned was on a Fair day. At that time the Cattle Fair at Michaelmas was held on Penenden Heath. I and another boy found our way there on the first Fair day and were engaged by one of the Welsh drovers to help mind the Bullocks, and I was to have sixpence. I had my sixpence which I took home to my Mother.

There was one event which left a lasting impression on my memory. It was one Christmas Eve and my brothers and I with my sister Jane were out carol singing. When we reached Penenden Heath we found crowds of people there, and we learned that three men were to be hung that morning. Sure enough, there was the Gallows nearby ready to receive the three victims. In a very short time they came from Maidstone in a common Tug or wagon with no sides to it, and their coffins in the wagon with them. I remember seeing the coffins very well. They were preceded by a company of cavalry with drawn swords. It was not long before they were launched into Eternity, and I remember my poor sister Jane nearly fainted. These were the last that were hanged on Penenden Heath. I think this was in the year 1830, if so I was just over seven years old at that time. I think these poor fellows met their doom through setting fire to some stacks of corn. There was a considerable amount of Incendiarism at that period, and the breaking of Threshing machines which had just then been introduced. The poor labourers no doubt thought these would deprive them of work, and this was the reason I believe of the Military forming part of the mournful procession.

I think it was 1833 when I was just approaching ten years of age that I began work with several other boys with a Farmer named Usher who lived at the farm at the foot of the hill on the road to Detling. We had to pull a weed with a yellow flower from the growing corn. I remember we went to our work very merrily the first morning, there was quite a string of us, and we worked in a line pulling these weeds up. The Master followed up close behind us so that we could not stand upright to rest our little backs without his seeing us. I shall never forget how my poor back did ache when six o'clock came. I had to continue on till the weeding season was over. I think my pay was four pence a day.

About this age I used to go with my Mother to the Harvest Field to help her. She was considered a good reaper with the sickle and I soon learned to reap and make the bands to bind the sheaves with. At this time the Parson took his Tithe in kind. We used to put ten sheaves to what we called a shock and when the corn was carried away they left every tenth shock for the Parson. But later on a Tithe Commutation Act was passed so that the farmer had to pay in money. Well, when the corn was all carried away we had to go gleaning, and in some seasons I remember we gathered up enough to make pretty well three bushels of flour. This was when the corn was cut with the sickle and not as now with a scythe, we used to do the threshing ourselves on a large sheet in the garden. The corn was taken over to the windmill which then stood in a field going towards Boxley Abbey. This Mill was pulled down some years ago. This amount of flour was a great help to our family during the winter season. We used to do fairly well in the hop-picking season when I think we used to earn on average pretty well four pounds with which my Mother used to rig us up fairly well for the winter with shoes and clothing.

Other work I did was keeping the birds from devouring the corn. This work included Sundays and I had a rattle or clappers to scare them with. This used to do for the sparrows if you kept on perpetually rattling it, but it was no use for the cunning crows. When they came to make a raid on a cornfield they always had one or two scouts on the look-out. These scouts would perch themselves on a tree or some high point whilst the others were feeding on the corn, ready to give an alarm when they saw me coming. I remember especially one day when I had two fields to mind, and as soon as I disturbed them in one field they would fly off to the other. I got dead beat and laid down and cried! For all this I got sixpence per day making 3/6d per week. I gave my Mother 3/- and had the Sunday pay for myself. With the first 3/6d I saved I had a new green round frock made with a lot of white gathering work in front and on the arms. This was the fashion those days among us rustics and I felt quite proud with it on.

My next step was to look after the sheep on the rubbish banks by the chalk cliffs, when I used to take my fife and play away. On other occasions I would take the sheep to graze on Penenden Heath. One day while there a boy who was originally an inmate of our Work House at Boxley came to me with another boy saying they were very hungry. I gave them part of my dinner and put the remainder away again, and I left them to attend to the sheep. It appears they saw where I put it for when I went expecting to have the rest of it for my dinner, bag and all was gone. I had to be all day without food, a nice reward for my kindness. I at times helped this same boy in the Barn threshing the corn, and at times driving the plough. This went on until I was about 15 years old when my pay was ten pence a day.

My ability with musical instruments was getting me well known and on one occasion I was invited to play at a Private Ball at the Old Palace in Maidstone. It was three o'clock in the morning before we got home to Boxley. At six

George Ephraim Wallis in his maturity, seated centre of a family wedding group.

o'clock I was up and had to drive a plough. I nearly fell asleep, the horses got wrong, and the man at the plough threatened to horsewhip me! On another occasion I was going home to Boxley in the early hours after a musical engagement and ended up walking whilst asleep and I walked bang against a stone wall at Harbourland cutting my nose. I was wide awake after that".

The account of Mr Wallis then moves on to him finding employment away from Boxley and with his marriage, and with the founding of the family Building business. He certainly throws light into some dark corners for us, and some comment is called for. His reference to Mrs Chumney is interesting, for this would have been how he heard pronounced Mrs Cholmondley's name. She became the dowager Countess of Romney as related in the Boxley House chapter. He goes on to mention the gallery in the Church "cleared away many years ago" and nowadays one would look in vain for any signs that it was ever there. It is believed to have been sited over the south aisle only. In 1847 the school committee requested that it be extended into the north aisle to accommodate the school children. This was found to be impractical, and the following year the church wardens are reported to have "made the narrow pews on the north side of the Church for use of the school children".

Note the reference to the Cattle Fair on Penenden Heath, and to Welsh drovers who had presumably driven their beasts all the way from Wales. Mr Wallis's account of that last hanging on the Heath corroborates Russell who gave 1830 as that date.

Above all, the account shows us how hard life was for the farm-labouring class. Wives and children joined in the harvest and other work, the children having scarcely any education. Boxley School was to be built in 1846. One senses the deference to the landowners and employers, born of the fears of eviction and unemployment. One also senses the strong influence of the Church.

George Wallis was an exceptional man and he bettered himself. Most of his contemporaries were condemned (if that is not too harsh a word) to lives of servitude and hardship. In Boxley the chances for employment lay in the fields, mills or potteries, or as servants. The landowners in Victorian times were chiefly Lord Romney, the Bests and the Whatmans. There was probably no common land in the parish beyond what Penenden Heath afforded, and note how Mr Wallis took his master's sheep to graze there. His master was no doubt a tenant farmer, and there would have been many of these throughout the parish. They probably made a fair living, but for the labourers the prospects were poor. Matters were aggravated in the early 1800's, by Parliament interfering with the price of wheat, so that some labourers and their families could scarce afford to eat. These conditions, and the arrival of mechanisation such as threshing machines, led embittered men to protest by burning hay ricks. This was the incendiarism of which Mr Wallis writes, and for which men were hung.

Certain landowners like the Bests were showing paternalism and concern for their employees. The building of Boxley School in 1846 shows that the governing classes were beginning to have a conscience, and a concern to improve the lot of the poor. Charles Dickens, of course, was one who campaigned for more social justice. He doubtless had tongue in cheek when he had the poor proclaim:-

> "O let us love our occupations
> Bless the squire and his relations
> Live upon our daily rations
> And always know our proper stations"

The English have always had this strange "love of the lord" that for the most part inclined them to admire and respect their "masters and betters". The French had their revolution in 1789, but there was never any real threat of a repetition in England. The temptation to sabotage took the form of setting fire to the ricks and barns and smashing threshing machines, but nothing worse. Nevertheless, Thomas Balston's definitive book on the Whatmans tells how a bag of golden guineas was found hidden at Vinters after James Whatman's death in 1798. His wife had explained how James feared that revolution might spread to England, and that he hoped the bag might escape a search by the mob.

Under the Poor Law of 1834, Boxley became part of the Hollingbourne Union and its poor were sent to the Union Workhouse at Hollingbourne. The 1861 census shows that of the 229 pauper inmates there, only 9 came from Boxley. This is a remarkably small amount, and testament to the caring nature of the Boxley community and its landowners. The general attitude was still that it was the fault of the poor if they could not find work. The Workhouses were made deliberately uncomfortable to discourage the inmates from staying too long. Note that George Wallis wrote of "our workhouse at Boxley" and elsewhere we argue with confidence that this stood in the village next to the King's Arms and on the site where now 'The Hermitage' stands.

The Church Register for these times shows the range of work which could be found in Boxley, almost entirely for the landowners, or as tradesmen to supply them. Thus woodcutter, gamekeeper, groom, cowman, shepherd and domestic servants of all descriptions, and plain labourers. And blacksmith, wheelwright, waggoner, hoop-maker, cooper, basket-maker, sawyer and saddler. But there was not work for everybody.

However, one dramatic and extreme escape from hardship and servitude suddenly presented itself. Emigration to the colonies. Thanks to their descendants who have visited Boxley in search of their roots we can make reference to two families in particular. Around 1834 the authorities in South Australia were looking to extend their colony without using convicts. They naturally looked to England, and as an inducement offered free passage to persons under the age of thirty years. So it was that in 1838 two Cleggett brothers from Boxley set sail with their young families. In 1852 Robert Lucas from Warren Farm sailed for Australia with his pregnant wife Sophia and their baby daughter. The route took them via Cape Town, where Sophia landed to await the birth of her baby whilst Robert went on ahead. Sophia, soon with two young children, boarded a later boat. Just imagine the great wrench it must have been for these people to uproot themselves and set off on such a long and arduous journey into the unknown. Certainly it seems that the Cleggetts and the Lucas's prospered in their new lives, as did others. For example, a gravestone has been discovered in New Zealand inscribed "Sacred to the memory of Esther Constable, relict of John Constable, yeoman of Boxley Abbey, Kent, England" who died in 1865. His origins have been traced to the Yew Tree public house at Sandling. John Constable's son Edward had emigrated to New Zealand in 1838, becoming one of the first settlers in Auckland, where he became a farmer. In 1850, realising the commercial potential of Waiuku, which was perfectly positioned to control the trade between the Maoris and the burgeoning settlement of Auckland, he moved there and bought land by the waterfront. Doubtless influenced by the family beerhouse at Boxley, he erected a public house which he called 'The Kentish Hotel', and later opened two stores. He came back to England in 1853, returning to Waiuku with his widowed mother Esther. It was her gravestone which was to provide the link between parishes on opposite sides of the world. Today's residents of Waiuku revere Edward Constable as the founding father of their town.

And so it was that emigration helped some poor and ambitious young people of Boxley to better lives. The vestry committee offered help as well, agreeing to pay monies to "defray the expenses of poor people having settlements in the parish, wishing to emigrate". Thus in 1841 a sum of money was paid to send out William Swinnock's wife and five children to join him in New Zealand. Ironically those emigrating helped indirectly those labourers left behind, for there was a smaller pool of workers in English villages. Despite the advance of mechanisation, the demands for labour increased as the so called "Golden Age" of farming arrived (approximately 1850 to 1880).

As the reign of Queen Victoria drew towards its close, those fortunate enough to have work would typically toil for some 54 hours each week. Half the population died before the age of 65, and those who lived into old age had no pensions. Food and drink took up most of people's income. There was an enormous gulf between the ordinary people and the gentry and landowners whose more glamorous lives are better documented, and thus play a more prominent part in this book.

BOXLEY PARISH

Boxley pupils circa 1900 with the headmaster Albert 'Stubby' Mannering and his wife Ann.

CHAPTER 12
Boxley School

The latter part of the Georgian era saw an increasing awareness of social responsibility, and with it concern that inadequate schooling would help to nurture an underclass of criminally inclined, un-ambitious idlers. Before this, education of the lower classes was restricted to a few charity schools in the larger towns. Basic literacy was often gained at Sunday schools, with more in-depth instruction reserved for those lucky enough to gain a good apprenticeship. Before 1817, only one in seventeen of the population of England was receiving any elementary education. Indeed, the gentry felt that an educated working class would be dangerous, as they would then be able to read seditious pamphlets and be led into rebellion!

The village of Boxley was fortunate in having an enlightened Lord of the Manor, in Lord Romney who, together with the vicar (Mr Griffith) leased a building from William Fowle of Street Farm, in the early part of the nineteenth century, for use as a village school. This was probably the school in Forge Lane run by an old man called Hassell (most likely one of the Boxley family of wheelwrights of that name), which was attended by George Wallis in about 1830. The old man was not averse to using a large stick or even a horse whip to maintain discipline. Probably an educated man fallen on hard times, Mr Hassell would have received little remuneration other than provision of a roof over his head and a thrice weekly dinner that the boys would collect for him from Mrs Cholmondley, the dowager Countess of Romney, who resided at Boxley House. The brightest pupils would be used as unpaid assistants to help instruct their classmates, speed in learning being essential as most children's education only lasted about three years, and by the age of ten, like young George, they would be earning their keep in the fields, or in the households of the privileged classes.

From 1833, The State had been making grants to assist voluntary societies to set up schools. One such society was 'The National Society for the Education of the Poor According to the Principles of the Church of England'. The Vicar, The Reverend John Griffith, who was concerned at ills which might arise from want of a proper school, and that they only currently provided tutelage for boys, suggested an application should be made to 'The National Society' for funds. Lord Romney disagreed, and wrote to The Dean and Chapter of Rochester from whom he leased Parsonage Farm, suggesting that if they allowed him to pull down the malthouse attached to The Rectory House, together with a large barn near the green, he would build a good schoolhouse adjoining a small cottage on the premises. The ecclesiastical landlords were not impressed, considering it highly objectionable to have the entrance to the school in a farmyard! Correspondence flew back and forth with Romney becoming increasingly upset that his suggestion for the provision of a school at no expense to anyone but himself, was being rejected. He in turn, rejected the idea of canvassing for subscribers to raise the cash and believing that any funds available from The Society could be more usefully given to a more needy parish, he determined to take no further part in the matter.

Unable to obtain land to build a school it appears that the trustees rented a larger property in Boxley Street, which building later became The Woodman Public House. It is probable that girls were also enrolled at that time. The 1844 tithe map shows the building as a schoolhouse and playground occupied by John Stedman and the 1841 census records a Mary Stedman school mistress. Unfortunately there appear to be no records of the school at this time. For more that ten years the parish struggled on without a proper school until the schoolhouse became badly in need of repair. The owner, William Sharp Avery who was now farming the late William Fowle's old estate, would not sell the building to the trustees as he planned to let it to someone who wished to open a shop there. In 1845, Lord Romney died, and his son Lord Marsham became the new Earl. He had always been amenable to the idea of obtaining funds from 'The National Society', and was glad to provide part of the orchard in The Parsonage grounds to construct a new schoolhouse. The eminent architect, John Whichcord was hired and drew up plans for a 34 feet by 18 feet schoolroom with a washroom, and a passage for hanging cloaks and bonnets, with a connecting door to an attached two bedroomed house for the school master. Outside there was a yard containing a well and privies plus an 80 feet by 70 feet playground.

1846 saw the opening of the new school, built to cope with a maximum of 200 pupils, but as its first school master George Offord and his wife Isabella were the sole teaching staff one expects that the number of attendees was somewhat less. Children would walk in from over the hill and the other outlying districts such as Sandling and Weavering, at least until 1882 when the infants school was opened at Grove Green. The increase in pupils resulted in a request the following year from the school committee to the Vestry committee that enlarged accommodation be provided in the Church for school children. It was resolved to extend the gallery to the North aisle so as to correspond with that of the South aisle. The Offords were followed by three further husband and wife teaching partnerships – Charles and Jane Southby, William and Emma Smith (William also served as parish clerk and organist), and in 1872, Albert G Mannering and his wife Ann. Mr Mannering was to stay for the next 36 years, ruling his educational domain with a rod of iron. Having warned one boy not to attend school dirty, on finding him still unsatisfactorily grimy on the following day he proceeded to take a scrubbing brush to him. Learning was often quite literally knocked into children's heads. It is recalled that having failed to receive an answer to "Who were the children of Henry VIII?", the question was repeated to one poor child with a blow accompanying each syllable. (One cannot help wondering how many of today's scholars would know the answer – such is progress!).

An 1872 meeting of ratepayers determined that educational requirements for the district should now be met by voluntary contributions of the inhabitants with additional subscriptions to be raised from wherever possible, rather than becoming a 'school board' establishment, under the provisions of the Education Act of 1870. Mrs Ann Burton of Brooklyn left a legacy in 1882 to help support the school, as had the £100 from Edward Hunt's will in 1854. Prior to the 1870 Act, some children from the poorer or less enlightened families were prevented from attending school due to the necessity of the weekly payment of 1 or 2 pennies per child. Also in 1872 it was agreed to make an annual grant of £15, to Bredhurst School, towards the expense of educating children living in Dunn Street, in Boxley parish. By 1891, with an average attendance of 118 pupils, a Frederick Worsfold was Assistant Master, Mr Mannering's daughter Kate helped with the infants, whilst Sam Jeffrey was a 'pupil teacher'.

The era of the independent school was almost at an end and with the County Council having taken over responsibility for education, they set up a board of Managers in 1903, appointing the Reverend W. Snape Cadman, Mrs Whatman, Richard H. Seymour of Boxley Abbey, Randall Mercer of Sandling Place, and Major Best of Park House, whilst the parish council's elected representative was Henry Fuller of Gibraltar House. The Managers set a salary of £150 per annum for Mr Mannering (which included remuneration for his wife and daughter), £65 for the then Assistant Master, William Duckett, and £30 for Miss Prince who was employed as a monitor. In 1907, two teachers who were to be remembered by generations of Boxley children, were appointed in place of the Assistant Master. Eleanor Prince (daughter of the butler at Park House) who for some years lived locally at Park Cottage, and Miss Ellen Peters, who was sister of the long-serving church organist Tom Peters. Miss Peters was engaged primarily to teach art, and Daisy Madeley was additionally employed as a sewing mistress.

When Mr Mannering finally left in 1908, (his wife Ann taking over the running of the post office), William Moore previously of St Faiths School, Maidstone, took over at a salary of £85 increasing by annual increments of £5, plus the schoolhouse, coal and carbolic soap! Greater importance was now placed on hygiene, and on more than one occasion steps were taken to exclude children who attended school in a 'verminous' condition, and Parish Nurse Edwards made regular calls to rummage through the children's hair for unwelcome visitors. The school's water was drawn solely from its own well,

BOXLEY PARISH

Boxley School built 1846. Taken circa 1912 with the schoolmaster William Moore and his wife.

A group of children wearing medals for merit. Flanking Mr. Moore are the two long-serving assistants Miss Prince and Miss Peters.

which was prone to contamination from seepage after heavy rain. Twice during 1912 and 1914 many of the pupils were delighted to accept extended holidays when the school was forced to close for seven weeks and four weeks respectively, due to epidemics of whooping cough. Sewage from the school discharged into the stream running through the vicarage garden, now Parsonage Farm! Following an adverse Inspectors report in 1911, a folding screen was fitted to divide the school room into two classes of 40 and 50 pupils, prior to which all classes were held together. One can only imagine the resultant cacophony of youthful voices! Later an additional small classroom was added.

Inspector's visits themselves could be unsatisfactory. Mr Moore recorded the story of a predecessor posting a boy on a wall to keep a lookout and give advance warning of the expected visit of a school inspector. With everything ship-shape and the pupils working diligently, the inspector rode up, dressed in hunting pink, reined in his horse, and called through the school window – "Government Inspector. Everything alright? Log my visit will you", and with that he galloped away!

Although the numbers of children educated at the school gradually declined, discipline was good, and in 1911 the Kent County Council's annual report stated that together with Thurnham School, Boxley had the highest percentage of attendance in the county. On occasion, particularly able pupils won a scholarship to Maidstone Grammar School, and certainly, by the age of 14 when their education was completed, all children were said to be able to read and write. The provision of in-depth needlework tuition for the girls and woodcarving for the boys gave added stimulus. The influence of the Church was always strong and the vicar would look in once a week to ensure that the children knew the ten commandments and other important tenets of the faith. A dearth of male teachers meant that sport was reliant on the goodwill of the local landowners the Best-Dalisons, who allowed use of their sports field at Park House, and in later years Tom Best-Dalison provided football coaching.

The headmaster's records provide interesting glimpses of life at the turn of this century:– July 1907 School closed for a day to allow scholars to attend a treat given by Mr R. Style at Boxley House. November 1908 – School closed for the day to enable annual distribution of clothes. November 1911 - Parents of the Hart children prosecuted for continuously allowing the children to attend school in a verminous condition. (This does not appear to have had any effect because over a period of twenty years successive members of the same family are regularly recorded as being excluded due to their uncleaniless). In 1913, the name of William Kennedy of Kenwell Farm, Walderslade, is reported a number of times for arriving 15 to 20 minutes late and being sent home. Today, when our roads are constantly choked by the cars of parents 'doing the school run', for children who often only live a short distance from their schools, it is sobering to reflect on the plight of poor William. Rising early each day to tend the livestock on his parent's farm, he then had to walk about 3 miles alone in the dark to school, and on arriving late, had to turn around and face the toil up the steep escarpment of the hill to return home. A return journey of some 7 miles! It is not surprising therefore to find that when a later entry records a visit from the Vicar, who gave a pair of new boots to a boy sorely in need, that the footsore recipient was the same William Kennedy. School closure for the 'holidays' was determined by the 'agricultural clock', with the main break of 5 weeks commencing at the end of August during the period of the hop-picking harvest.

The advent of The Great War brought more disruption to the school. Some of the children, once having obtained a doctor's certificate of their fitness, were granted leave to work on farms to support the war effort. Other reasons were put forward for absenteeism. One mother would keep her daughter at home whenever another child was due to be born, seemingly a regular occurrence in the household. The note to Mr Moore read – "I am keeping Lily at home as oh sir, it has happened again". Perhaps she did not know what caused it! In 1916, Mr Moore enlisted in The Royal West Kents and a Miss Wheeler stood in. During these difficult years, local women began providing mid-day meals for the children. Prior to this, only the generosity of Mr and Mrs Moore, who would share their milk and bread (sometimes at the expense of their own children) relieved the hunger pangs of some of the poorer children. In the 1920's, with support from the Kent County Council, a proper canteen was set up. In November 1914 the children were excited by a visit from an old boy, Albert Neale, looking very smart in his army uniform, together with some of his friends from the Canadian Contingent. Six months later, his two sisters who still attended the school, brought the sorrowful tidings that Albert had fallen in action. Better news came with the announcement that another old boy, Albert Brooker, serving in submarine E.11, had been awarded the Distinguished Conduct Medal for exploits in the Sea of Marmara. Soon after his return in 1920, probably influenced by the decline in pupil numbers to just 54, Mr Moore resigned in order to take over at East Farleigh School where some 250 children attended.

The school was now noticeably in decline, and a succession of head teachers came and went. Mrs Maynard until 1924, constantly plagued by ill-health and deputised for by her husband Captain Maynard. Miss Alice Thompson who stayed for just two years, during which she was twice subjected to alarming attacks. On both occasions an intruder entered the schoolhouse and she had to confront him on her own. Despite showing much pluck and bravery throughout, she decided to take up a post in Africa, whose dangers obviously appeared less fearsome than those of Boxley! The closure of Weavering School in 1924 had helped boost pupil numbers to 84 and despite its problems there were over 50 applicants for the headship, to which a Mr W. Gates of Teynham School was appointed. After viewing the schoolhouse, he found it unsuitable and declined to accept, the post eventually being filled by Mr Percy Willcocks who lasted six years, resigning in 1933 when a Mrs Griffin took over. The long-serving Miss Peters soon fell foul of the new Head, and was twice reported to the managers for bad time-keeping, notwithstanding her having to walk from and back to Maidstone in all weathers. The need for Mrs Griffin to leave the class on occasion to see to her baby in the adjoining schoolhouse provided ample opportunity for mischief by the boys, who amongst other things would delight in using their rulers to flick little balls of paste at the clock. The apparent fall in disciplinary standards was reflected in poor levels of attendance by pupils. Some pupils did gamely struggle in from far corners and in all weathers. One in the late 1930's is particularly remembered, who walked all the way from Bredhurst and back home up Boxley Hill at day's end. In the winter rain he wore a brown overcoat which hung over the stove to dry and was still steaming away when he came to put it on again.

In line with the requirements of The Education Act of 1918, and prompted by the expanding council estates in the Maidstone suburbs, new secondary education facilities were in full swing and in 1938, corresponding with the opening of The Girls Grammar School, it was decided that all Boxley children should be transferred to Maidstone schools from the age of 12. Most of Boxley's senior children attending Eastborough School. An entry in the head teacher's record book dated 21st July 1944 records a glass case being smashed and a gramophone lid damaged when a 'robot plane', (doodlebug) landed a half mile away. The Chairman of Managers, Reverend Hale, had fought to keep the school open even before he left the parish in 1935, but six years of interrupted education during the second world war and the dictates of the 1944 Education Act led inevitably to the final closure of the school on 28th March 1945.

CHAPTER 13

The Great War

Much of this chapter is gleaned from the Parish Magazine of 1914-16.

In the Summer of 1914 all was well in Boxley. The Vicar had visited the School on Empire Day. He praised the children for their religious knowledge and exhorted them to try and grow up with a just pride in the Empire that they would one day be called upon to help to rule.

In the cricket team, Wally Gosling "got going" for the first time. The Sandling Mothers had an outing to Whitstable and enjoyed a tea of shrimps and winkles. Weavering School had a marvellous treat at Vinters courtesy of Sir Reginald and Lady Agnes MacLeod. There were games and swings, presents and prizes, and a strawberry tea under the Cedars.

The Choir had their own outing which was to Margate. A party of sixty travelled by train and enjoyed bathing, boating, concerts and shopping. Robert Style was "at home" at Boxley House to the old ladies and children from the Hollingbourne Union (or Workhouse). There were swings, coconut shies and races in which even the old ladies joined. The following week Robert Style was hosting the Boxley School Treat with invitations extended to mothers and to families of workers on the Boxley House Estate. More games and races, and a magnificent tea which was augmented by fruit given by Mr Foster from Court Lodge Farm.

In August war was declared against Germany. The Vicar Rev. Hale called upon his parishioners to seek how best to serve King and Country. The Boxley cricketers played on, but in subdued mood. The lamps that were going out all over Europe were leaving a gloomy Boxley.

At first the Parish Magazine concentrates upon the men joining the armed forces. Well-known Boxley names appear, for example by November 1914 Godfrey and Cecil Lushington, Frank Balston, Robert Style and Alick Trousdell have all enlisted. But very soon the first casualties are reported, although there is something of a sporting air, with a certain Captain "bagging a good few Germans". At Park House the Best-Dalisons made their billiard room available for some wounded Belgian soldiers to recuperate.

It was felt that every man and boy should learn how to handle a gun, and so a rifle club was formed. Mr Best-Dalison made his sandpit available for an open-air range, whilst there was an indoors range at The Malt House.

85

Shooting matches were held with neighbouring clubs, with competitions for "Attack" and "Defence" and "Disappearing Targets" showing a war-like purpose. Meanwhile the ladies of the parish studied for Home Nursing and First Aid Certificates. A branch of the League of Honour was started for women and girls, who made promises of prayer, purity and temperance. But a few of the ladies chose instead to join the men in the Rifle Club.

The Royal West Kents were camped on Penenden Heath and the Parish arranged a recreation tent for them. In 1915 Rev. Hale joined the forces and went off to serve as an Army Chaplain. In his absence the curate Cecil Hilton led the Church, supported by Edmund Best-Dalison and Rev. T.G. Lushington who was Rural Dean. Mrs Poole from the Forstal received a congratulatory letter from the King for having six sons serving in the Army. By 1916 married men were being called up and the Choir were down to just four male voices. A number of Rifle Club members were now away shooting in deadly earnest. The Vicar himself was at a casualty clearing station in France and writing home about his grim experiences.

Sometimes soldiers marched through the village on their way to the Downs to practice trench digging or to carry out manoeuvres. There was much excitement one day when an Army Band led the troops through, and on their way back excited children fell in behind. Two children were so carried away that they followed the soldiers all the way to Maidstone Barracks, where they suddenly felt very lost and alone.

Occasionally the War seemed not so very far away. It seems remarkable to relate that during particularly heavy bombardments the guns in France could be heard in Boxley. Even nearer were the flights of German Zeppelin Airships overhead on spasmodic bombing raids. They were targeting Chatham Dockyard whose protective Aerial Guns were heard firing at them. Indeed, some of our own shells actually came down around Boxley as well as Aylesford and other areas. When a Zeppelin was hit the result was a spectacular blaze in the sky, and one shot down over Tilbury was seen from the village. England was not used to such happenings and there was understandable concern, with windows being blacked out at night.

And in France, at Gallipoli and at sea the casualties from the Parish grew. Boxley's losses were no greater than anywhere else in the country, but the heartache was the same. Winnie Weekes, whose experiences as a scullery maid at Park House are related elsewhere, was having a day-off at her home in Loose. The dreaded telegram arrived telling that her brother had been killed. As she related, "It was the only time I ever saw my father cry".

In 1916 the schoolmaster William Moore joined the West Kents and was posted to India. A post-card from his wife survives, with a picture of Boxley and reporting an air raid the previous night. She wondered if it would all ever end, and how long before her husband would be walking again "up this dear old road". He was to return, but not until 1920. Also posted to India was Wally

THE GREAT WAR

Gosling. He had at first joined the Kent Cyclists Battalion, and was then transferred to the plain infantry and did his fighting on the North-West frontier. Strange to think that the British Army was still engaged with Afghan tribesmen when there was a war in Europe.

Eventually Peace came. News spread around Boxley by Edmund Best-Dalison's excited cries that "The War is over! The War is over!". But life was never to be quite the same again. The Roll of Honour in the Church lists the names of 34 men from the parish who lost their lives.

Just part of a wide lens photo taken in front of Boxley House recording a Parish party in 1919 to celebrate the end of war.

The hall at Park House.

CHAPTER 14

The Best-Dalisons

The Best-Dalisons were revered by the majority of Boxley people for the generosity of their spirits and of their pockets. And yet viewed from the 1990's their way of life might seem remote and even arrogant. The truth is that they reflected the manners and morals of their early years. They were born into Victorian England and assimilated the cultural heights of the Edwardians. They each had a strong Anglican faith and sought to fulfil the perceived obligations of the squirearchy. As large landowners they were due respect, and by their many kindnesses they earnt much love besides. But let it be said at once that their employees, as opposed to the parishioners, may have viewed them somewhat differently!

Mr Best-Dalison we shall refer to for convenience as Edmund. Born in 1858, his family name was Dalison. His chosen life was the Church and he was ordained in 1885. After serving as a curate at Louth in Lincolnshire and then St Michael's, Maidstone he achieved his own parish as Rector of Bletsoe in Bedfordshire. In 1899 he married Lily Bosanquet, niece of Maudistly Best, and he joined his wife to live at Boxley in Park House. He gave up the full-time life of a cleric, but for the rest of his life he was to be 'honorary curate' at Boxley Church,

Mrs Best-Dalison was born in 1867 and we shall call her Lily. Her family connection with Major Best is set out at the end of the chapter on Park House, and when he died in 1906 Lily inherited the Estate. In 1907 she and Edmund took the name Best-Dalison by Royal Licence and for nearly 50 years they were at the heart of Boxley village life. Their new home was the epitome of an English Country House. In the chapter on Park House we had begun to see the breadth of its facilities, its Home Farm and its self containment. They owned several farms on the Estate, let to tenant farmers, and no doubt benefited from various of their crops. Surrounding Park House were kitchen gardens and a large range of greenhouses, where black grapes, peaches and other delights were grown. Orchards, of course, and a state of the art apple store, frost proof and fitted out with racks. The lakes had trout in them. All these facilities demanded a full complement of servants and gardeners and Estate workers. Here were the two worlds of Upstairs and Downstairs.

Very much Downstairs was a scullery maid Winnie Weekes. She was born in 1901 and left school at 12. She related that "for the likes of us" the choices of

BOXLEY PARISH

Lily Best-Dalison

Rev. Edmund Best-Dalison

employment prior to the Great War lay between domestic service or working on the land. Her father did not want to see her in the fields, although she did go and pick up potatoes just long enough to earn money to buy some decent clothes. Smartly attired, she passed her interview with Lily and began living-in at Park House as a scullery maid. She shared a cold attic room with another girl and was up at 6 a.m. to be about her chores. She recalled the large servants hall, and a very severe cook who was far from kind to her. She thought that there were then about nine servants in the house. The stockman would bring fresh meat to the kitchen. She learnt to pluck and draw a chicken, and would save the feathers until there were enough to sell and buy a present for her mother. She also learnt to make butter in the Dairy and remembered the lovely smells that came from the Bakehouse. In 1905 Edmund and Lily's only child had been born, Tom Best-Dalison, and he was to bring mischievous fun to Park House. More of him later, but one of his early pranks was locking Winnie in the pantry. For her it was all surely better than working in the fields. She moved on to service elsewhere, but there were plenty of willing girls to take her place. For many years there was an establishment at Temple House near the new St Paul's Church in Boxley Road where girls were trained for domestic service. It is understood to have been run by the gentry of Maidstone and neighbourhood. To there Lily and other ladies of the Big Houses would call to choose their maids. The steps and brass plate at Temple House seemed to passers-by to be perpetually scrubbed and polished in training sessions.

Edmund and Lily were generous hosts. Many a party was held, the Hall being big enough for dancing. Young guests ranged the house playing Hunt the Slipper and Sardines. Come the Summer and there were garden parties and tennis parties. Edmund was a very keen and knowledgeable gardener and could wax lyrical about the respective merits of horse manure and cow manure. The garden at Park House gained quite a reputation and the house was always full of flowers, which Edmund arranged. A beautiful stream meandered through the grounds and there were cascades of water into the lakes from a large rockery. They would both visit the Chelsea Flower Show and delight in buying new varieties. 1911 saw them hosting local Coronation Festivities for George V, with sports and games and a 'Meat Tea'. Wagons brought old people and children from outlying parts of the Parish and coronation mugs were presented to each child. The Maidstone Borough band played for 7 hours, presumably with a few rest periods.

The Home Farm was run for many years by Richard Luckhurst who lived at Old Harbourland. One of his sons, Bob Luckhurst, had the happiest of childhood memories. For the youngsters there was football, using a blown up pig's bladder, and cricket. Fast-running streams with trout to catch by dipping in your hand and tickling them. A countryside packed with orchards, hops, corn and livestock. For them no shortage of food. As Bob said, "We lived like fighting cocks".

The Great War interrupted life at Park House. We mention elsewhere that the Billiard Room became home for a while to wounded Belgian soldiers whom Lily helped to care for. Edmund was in his 50's and there was no questions of him joining the forces, especially with his poor eyesight. But they both contributed to the War effort in their own ways, and when the Vicar went to France as an Army chaplain, Edmund helped even more with Church services. When Peace came in 1918, life began to return to normal. Maybe some financial strains were felt, for in 1920 the Best-Dalisons sold off some of their properties in the village. These included Street Farm, The Hermitage, The Woodman Beerhouse and cottages in Forge Lane. Also Abbey Gate Farm and Harbourland Farm. At all events the slimmed-down Estate picked up on its pre-war heydays, and until another War came along there were great times at Park House. These we can enjoy through the memories of the Best-Shaw family.

The name Best-Shaw was not to be taken until the 1950's, but we will anticipate its use. Sir John Best-Shaw the elder was Lily's nephew, being the son of Lily's sister Elizabeth. In all Sir John had seven children. The elder of these would spend lazy vacations with Uncle Edmund and Aunt Lily in the late 1930's in company too with Tom Best-Dalison. They found the House and gardens a paradise. They had the run of the house, including the cellars, and one particular corridor was long enough for some indoor cricket. The balcony over the Hall was ideal for dropping pillows onto people below. There was no electricity, and only gas-lights downstairs, so that bed-time meant going up with a candle. Edmund seemed unhappy with the Cook, whose offerings he called "glacial". But the young Best-Shaws were much impressed to be offered a choice of three desserts. Edmund, however, described the choice as "dull, duller or dullest!"

In the Summer it was tea in the garden under the Cedar tree, brought out by a footman in his livery. Quince jam seemed a favourite. For amusement there were three grass tennis courts where Tom would organise tournaments. Park House had its own cricket pitch on the sportsfield, and young John Best-Shaw would get teams together. The girls would score, or in extremis make up a team. At other times they could just laze, watching fascinated as the gardeners left their billycans of milk in the stream to keep them cool – an idea which the Best-Shaw children copied with their own drinks.

Come Sunday it was time for Church. The family made their private way to services along the grass avenue which came out near Court Lodge Farm, the girls wearing hats and gloves and clutching their prayer books. Edmund invariably wore a frock-coat and top-hat to Church and, remembering that he was an ordained priest, there were also morning prayers at Park House. The scullery maid Winnie Weekes had remembered these around 1914, held before breakfast. Julia Best-Shaw remembers a red carpet being laid out in the Hall to kneel upon, and the sight of a row of servants' bottoms sticking up in the air.

And, of course, the servants were expected to attend Church with the family, although getting there by a different route. In Winnie Weekes' time all the servants had to wear their bonnets to Church.

The number and function of the servants changed over the years. For example, Mr Bodiam in 1899 was groom and gardener, and then became coachman, living with his wife and children above the Coach-house. His daughter Maud described their living conditions as being rather basic, and intimated that the horses fared rather better down below! Certainly the stables were beautifully decorated with attractive tiling. Mr Bodiam was less comfortable working with cars when these superseded horses. He became butler and Fred Vaughan joined the staff as chauffeur-cum-gardener. To Edmund and Lily the staff were known by their surnames, excepting someone there once called Nurse who was always Mr Nurse. Cries of 'Nurse' somehow seemed incongruous!

The bedrooms allocated to the servants were so chosen that their windows could not overlook the family in the gardens. They entered and left Park House by their own back doors. If members of the family passed by inside the house the servants would turn to face the other way. One ex-parishioner who was a boy in the 1940's tells of not only having to raise his cap if he met Edmund or Lily but that if he had no cap then he must take hold of his forelock and tug it. The same boy was once seen by Edmund throwing some orange peel into a hedge which provoked an outcry of disapproval. Here then was the respect and discipline of those times. Was it such a bad thing? The Boxley village up to the 1940's had clear figures of authority – landowners, Vicar, school-teachers, policeman. Even Parish Nurse Evelyn Trousdell cycling around in her uniform would command respect and obedience if she noticed any misdemeanours.

Running the Boxley scout group for many years was Tom Best-Dalison. Born in 1905, educated at Eton and Oxford, he never found any real vocation. He had a passion for motor cars and was to be seen roaring around in a Jaguar. Indeed, he once or twice took part in the Monte Carlo Rally. People recall his parents keeping both a Rolls and a Daimler, and Tom formed a close friendship with the chauffeur Fred Vaughan. In this he was clearly departing from the Master and Servant attitude of Edmund and Lily, and he had great plans for Park House at such time as he should come into his inheritance. A Garden Centre was one idea.

As previously mentioned, Tom was a great one for pranks and practical jokes, such as the small matter of hiding all the keys of Boxley House one day in conspiracy with the younger Styles. All in all a very jovial character and always game for a lark. He discovered that the lakes would more easily yield up their fish if he threw in bottles of carbide which then exploded and sent stunned fish floating to the surface. Much impressed, he thought that this could be adapted to catching rabbits and so he detonated a rabbit hole. The

BOXLEY PARISH

Two views of Park House, Boxley.

result was flying debris and permanent injury to one of his eyes. He would regale the scouts with this story as a warning against like adventures. Those same scouts he would drive down to Devon on camping holidays, the Jaguar laden with tent poles and canvas. The scouts themselves were asked for a small financial contribution, and no doubt Tom or his parents heavily subsidised the cost. Tom also gave his time to organising games of football for the boys from Boxley school on the Park House sportsfield.

And so we can begin to see the other side of the Best-Dalisons, away from the apparently stern employers. For example, countless villagers treasure memories of the Park House Christmas Parties. For many they were the highlights of their young lives. A large Christmas Tree stood in the Hall with a multitude of real candles which Edmund would help to light in a little ceremony. Bodiam the butler stood by with a wet sponge on a stick in case of accidents. Lily loved to dance, and Fred Vaughan and one or other of his children would struggle down the Ash path from their home in Park Cottage carrying a gramophone and records. At other times a pianist would be recruited. Lily would get everybody dancing, and Alan Vaughan remembers as a boy having to partner her at a cracking pace doing the "Dashing White Sergeant". This was in the 1940's when Lily was over 70, and she was obviously a sprightly old lady. Before receiving their presents the children sat on the shiny Hall stairs waiting for their names to be called. Tea was served in the dining room, sometimes with miniature Christmas cakes. Then the landings and Hall provided ample room for all the usual Best-Dalison party games.

The Best Dalisons on their way to church through the grounds of Park House.

Edmund and Lily sometimes played host to School prize-giving days. These were held in the Billiard Room, where the table was safely covered and the smaller children perched upon it. And the adults enjoyed their own jollities over the years. Lily, like Major Best's wife, kept a record. Worthy of mention is a Coming of Age Ball for Tom in 1926 attended by 200 guests. The lakes and cascade were lit up in the evening and at the conclusion Lily could not resist recording that as many as 26 chauffeurs were lined up to collect their masters and mistresses. The bellringers in the Boxley Tower paid their own compliment to Tom by ringing some Grandshire Doubles led by Wally Gosling.

But another War arrived. Despite his damaged eye and generally poor eyesight, Tom managed to join the Royal Navy Volunteer Reserve where he found perhaps the greatest fulfilment of his life. It was a time for evacuating children from London to the safer surroundings of the countryside, and Edmund and Lily now made the Billiard Room into a dormitory for several of the pupils of Alleyns School from Dulwich who had moved down to Maidstone. Lily, bless her, made what war-time economies she could think of. She took to wearing plimsolls at home to save shoe leather, drank beer instead of wine (but still out of a wine glass) and went into Maidstone by donkey and cart so as to save petrol.

By 1945 Edmund was 87 and Lily 78. Austerity gripped England in those early post-war years. The cost of running a Big House was increasingly difficult, and servants hard to find. The Dairy was now disused, the churns and butter pats lying around gathering dust. The cellars an idle strorehouse for a hundred years of family paraphernalia. Then in 1947 tragedy struck. Tom died at the early age of 42 and with him went his dreams for Park House under his own future stewardship. In many ways Park House died with him, and the old couple were broken-hearted and their Christian faith strained to the utmost. Tom had never married. Financially too it was a devastating blow, for the Estate had been made over to Tom and Death Duty hit the family hard.

In 1951 Lily died. For more than fifty years she had joined wholeheartedly in the life of the village and wider Parish. Her generosity knew no bounds, from outwardly visible gifts such as the Boxley Institute building (some way north of the King's Arms and long ago demolished) to quiet gestures. When one young lady was getting married Lily was most apologetic about the present they were giving because it was very old. The present turned out to be a couple of Chippendale chairs! They both gave liberally to the Church, which they loved so much. When the village blacksmith was nearing the end of his life Lily's concern was such that she offered to provide and pay for a night nurse. For another villager she paid for a specialist to treat his eyesight. Many literally worshipped her for these and other kindnesses. She ran the Mother's Union and the Boys' Bible Class. She had a great love for children. The sportsfield saw her on the touchline in all weathers cheering on the Bible Class footballers. On Easter Sundays she would go up to Park Cottage and hide eggs in the garden for the Vaughan children to find.

But still there was that Victorian order and discipline about her. Some recall that girls were expected to curtsey to her. She had her own way of grading people in conversation, so that her social equals were Dear Mrs White, those a little lower down the scale were Poor Mrs Grey, whilst Poor Little Miss Black was somewhat out of it. In Church she insisted upon absolutely no talking from going in until going out, and many a culprit received a frown or admonition. In conversation with a certain young parishioner one day she passed comment that she believed peasants were now being allowed into University. The young parishioner in question having just gained a place felt constrained to say that this was probably a good thing! Both she and Edmund became very hard of hearing. Jack and Rosemary Whitford came to live at Parsonage Farm in 1947, and Rosemary was invited by Edmund and Lily to have luncheon, so that they could begin to get to know her. Edmund sat at one end of a very long dining table, Lily at the other end, and Rosemary in between. Rosemary answered probing questions, and as each piece of information was gained, the answers were shouted from Edmund to Lily, such as, "SHE PLAYS THE PIANO!" Jack Whitford remembers calling to see them and finding that newspapers were never discarded, but rather left by the armchairs, one on top of the other, so that you had to thread your way through a maze of piles of 'The Times'.

In 1955 Edmund died well into his 90's. Into his last years he was fulfilling his duties as honorary curate, preaching from time to time. But his eyesight began to fail and he referred to his notes by a combination of torch and magnifying glass. Not surprisingly he lost his place occasionally and an un-Christian oath would escape his lips. Whilst seated in the family pew he began to miss parts of the sermon – prompting a loud question to Lily for all to hear, "Where's the feller gettin' to?" Tributes at his funeral rightly referred to him and Lily as two saintly souls.

The deaths of the three family members so close together resulted in heavy Death Duties. Park House was destined to share the fate of so many English Country Houses in the 1950's. Clearly uneconomical to run and in need of extensive repairs it was sold. In due course the house was demolished and parts of the grounds parcelled off as building plots. The Coach House was retained and converted to a dwelling, which took to itself the name of Park House. The plot owners were to inherit relics of the old park, such as the dog's graveyard, the splendid Apple Store, the Motor House and the lily pond.

Demolition was complete by 1957. The vast cellars lay open to the sky like empty eye sockets. With a sad symbolism there lay strewn within hundreds of broken champagne glasses, and hundreds again of Victorian dance cards with their little pencils attached. The party was over.

Park House, Sandling. Home of the Lushingtons.

CHAPTER 15
The Lushingtons

The home of the Lushington family was for over a hundred years, Park House, Maidstone. By adding the name of The County Town, it was thus distinguished from Park House, Boxley.

Originally a possession of the Diocese of Canterbury, the Park House Estate was purchased by Henry VIII from Archbishop Cranmer around 1540 whilst it was in the tenure of Sir Anthony Knivett. Having paid with his life for supporting his neighbour and friend, Sir Thomas Wyatt, Knivett's estate reverted to the Crown, and was leased to a William Smyth. Queen Elizabeth granted it to George Clark and thereafter it remained in private hands for almost four hundred years. Passing through the Brewer and Withins families, it was bought in 1690 by Sir Thomas Taylor, whose widow later re-married to Thomas Culpepper.

In 1701, concerned at the growing power of France and Spain, all the municipal leaders and justices of the County of Kent, signed a petition urging the House of Commons to have regard for the opinions of the people and to support those countries allied against the two super-powers. Five justices were chosen to take the petition to London, including Thomas Culpepper of Park House and Justinian Champneys of Vinters. Unfortunately, the Members of Parliament considered the petition to be impertinent and seditious, and the five were ordered to be imprisoned for the remainder of the Parliamentary session. Originally their penalty was not too harsh, as they were held in the Castle Tavern in Fleet Street. Fearing a possible attempt to release them by their disgruntled supporters, the Government had them moved to stricter incarceration. Alarmed at the strong feeling throughout the county that the imprisonment of the justices was illegal, it was considered expedient to discontinue the parliamentary session a month early, and the five were released. Feted as heroes, crowds cheered them all the way home. The citizens of Maidstone met them en masse at Blue Bell Hill, and celebrated that evening at Park House with a huge party, memorable for an immense bonfire and copious amounts of drink.

Lady Taylor's son, also Sir Thomas Taylor, sold it in 1735 to James Calder, who had previously been Deputy Governor of Gibraltar. The original house stood precisely astride the Maidstone/Boxley border. It is recorded that around 1790 the Maidstone parish officers were traversing the bounds of their parish, and determined to exercise their rights, demanded that they should be allowed to pass through the house. Sir Henry Calder, being confined to bed with gout, refused permission, but notwithstanding they insisted on their right, forced entry, and passed through. Incensed, Sir Henry had the house demolished and erected the present edifice some yards further north, and safely inside Boxley parish. Constructed from ragstone quarried from the lands on the other side of Chatham Road, the large square mansion with triple-bay bow windows was completed in 1792, but Sir Henry did not live to see it. The name of Park House, Maidstone was retained although it soon became referred to as Park House, Sandling.

Sir Henry's widow and his son, also Sir Henry, lived there for a while before renting it out, firstly to a Mr Osborne and then in 1828 to Edmund Henry Lushington, formerly a judge in Ceylon. After a number of years as tenants, the Lushingtons eventually bought the estate, and in 1859 increased its size by purchasing from Lord Romney the 24 acres of land on the opposite side of Chatham Road where later were built Moncktons Drive and Avenue and the southern half of the Ringlestone Estate. Many of the Lushingtons are commemorated by an array of tablets in Boxley Church, in what has come to be known as the Lushington corner. Quite a few of the family spent parts of their lives in the then Ceylon as tea planters or administrators. They were typical servants of the Empire. Amongst the tablets is one of particular interest, namely that of Edmund Law Lushington and his wife Cecilia, for she was a sister of Alfred Lord Tennyson. Edmund Law Lushington was a professor of Greek and later Lord Rector of Glasgow University. Until his retirement his work kept him absent from Park House for long periods. Indeed all three censuses between 1851 and 1871 record him as being away from home. A highly respected academic he was a member of 'The Society of Apostles', whose membership included his great friends Alfred, Lord Tennyson and Arthur Hallam. A marble bust commemorating Lushington is displayed in Maidstone Museum. After her husband died in 1893, Cecilia lived out her old age at Park House in company with her sister Matilda and daughter, also Cecilia, but known as Zilly. Tragically, Zilly was the only one of her four children whom Cecilia saw grow to any maturity. The two old ladies were eccentric characters who spent half their day in their private rooms and struck fear into various nephews and nieces who made duty calls. Latterly Cecilia scarcely left the house, and when she did pass through the hall she would pause to stroke and talk to the bust of a son who died in infancy. She would carry with her a black bag which she would fill with fancy cakes from the tea table and presumably consume in secret. When Matilda ventured forth it was in a Bath chair pulled by a donkey for a trot around the grounds. Upon Cecilia's death in 1909, Matilda and Zilly moved away and younger Lushingtons moved into Park House to bring back some life.

The marriage of his sister into the Lushington family brought Tennyson on many visits to Boxley. The local belief is that one of the Boxley streams was the inspiration for his poem "The Brook". People in his home county of Lincolnshire will claim that he had one of their own streams in mind, and the truth is probably that he drew upon an amalgam of images from many places. Having said that, the prologue to "The Princess" was definitely inspired by his visits to Boxley Abbey and Park House. The occasion of his sister's wedding in Boxley Church in 1842 (when he signed the register as one of the witnesses) probably prompted his passage from "In Memoriam" of "maidens of the place, that pelt us in the porch with flowers". At one time there stood a little thatched lodge in Lushington Park (for that is how it was known locally) where tradition has it that he would sit and write. During the early days of the Army's occupation it disappeared.

By the 1920's there were many Lushingtons living in the Maidstone area, and congregating at Park House from time to time. The Rev. Thomas Godfrey Law Lushington was Rural Dean of Sutton and occasionally preached at Boxley Church. His sister May was crippled and confined to a wheelchair, and always parked herself by the font for Church Services. When travelling by car it was necessary to use a hoist to get her on board. She was apparently a very sweet lady. Needless to say there was always the usual full array of servants. The 1851 census shows 9 live-in servants and neighbouring homes also contained gardeners, coachmen and women 'in service', who would have worked there.

Not all the estate was parkland. Close to Peel Street Hedges there was farmland, including orchards and cows and pigs. It seems that Thornhills Farm to the east of the Hedges also belonged to the family. The figure of Mr Richard Pantony would be seen between the farm and his dairy in Pantony's Lane, a yoke and buckets across his shoulders as he did his milking trips. Then with his horse and cart he would do the rounds in Boxley and the locality to deliver fresh milk twice daily from house to house.

Like all the Big Houses, the Lushingtons made their grounds available to local people for all manner of events such as Sunday school treats and Empire Day celebrations. One such was the fete held by The Maidstone Mechanics Institute who rented rooms in Chillington Manor, now the museum. Marquees were erected on the grassy slopes leading down to the river, and the lively scene was recorded for posterity by Tennyson in his prologue to 'The Princess'. One of the tablets in the Church records Henry Venables Lushington as the last owner of Park House and dying in 1936. As with Park House at Boxley, Death Duties hit hard. The house was bought by a builder, but in 1939 and the coming of war it passed into the hands of the Army. Mercifully it survives, having been incorporated into Invicta Barracks as the officers mess.

Since coming into the occupation of the military, the beauty of the parkland has become diminished and the public no longer has access. Residential housing has nibbled away its borders on three sides and the remaining portion lies wedged between Sandling Lane and Chatham Road. However a fine view of the house nestled in its parkland is obtainable from across the river at Buckland Fields near the Girls Grammar School.

CHAPTER 16

The Decline and Fall of Vinters

The glorious mansion built and improved by successive generations of Whatmans was not destined to survive the social and financial upheavals which began with the Great War. The last James Whatman died in 1887 leaving four daughters but no son. His widow Louisa Whatman lived on at Vinters, enjoying the income from the Estate and surrounded by servants. The Estate extended beyond the walls of Vinters park. It included Newnham Court, most of Weavering and Grove Green and pockets of land west of Sittingbourne Road and in the vicinity of Penenden Heath.

The ubiquitous Wally Gosling told a nice tale which gives the flavour of life at Vinters in the early 1900's. Boxley Church Choir used to go carol singing, concentrating on the big houses, and they would finish at Vinters. The butler "in all his glory" showed them in to where old Mrs Whatman sat as if on a throne, surrounded by family and friends. The Choir sang three of four carols, and then Mrs Whatman would offer her opinion about the performance. Next the choir were taken down to the Servants Hall which had great flagstones on the floor, wooden benches along each side, and a huge log fire. Laid out was an enormous supper to which Wally Gosling and his fellows "paid their respects". Finally a space was cleared for some dancing. The maids, footmen, grooms and gardeners would all appear together with a couple of fiddlers and a merry time was had by all, lasting late into the evening. There came the day when one strait-laced Church organist and choirmaster thought all this carousing undignified and he called a halt to it. The result was a revolt by the choir and a boycott of the next Sunday service!

Old Louisa died in 1905. Of her four daughters, Mary married to become Mrs Dugdale, but had no children. Ellen married William Trousdell who was an Army officer and who later farmed at Cobtree. They had at least eight children, and these Trousdells will be mentioned again in Chapter 17. Florence and young Louisa never married.

So far as James Whatman's Will can be understood, he left Vinters to be successively enjoyed by first his widow and then his daughters in seniority. So it was that Mary Dugdale first exercised control, and her husband was prime mover in pressing to "put Vinters in a state up to modern demands". He cited the need for bathrooms and electricity in particular. The Dugdales proposed funding these improvements by selling silver and furniture, which Florence and Louisa do not seem to have been very happy about. The situation was well illustrated when a Captain Pitt was negotiating to take a tenancy of Vinters and demanded numerous improvements. It seems he never got them, and he never proceeded. James Whatman had mortgaged Vinters and the entire estate a number of times, and at his death the massive sum of £68,400 plus interest was due. Despite his enormous holdings of property and land, his personal estate was insufficient to cover his debts. Although large portions of the estate were sold off, including the 11 acres of Heathfield House to R.J. Fremlin, the family laboured under the burden of repayments. A cross they were to bear right up until the estate was finally disposed of in 1954, when £4,200 still remained outstanding. Added to their problems were all the dilapidations to the old house that had accrued over the years.

Louisa Whatman to the right, in a family snapshot. Jeanette Balston seated and Kate Balston (née Trousdell) to the left.

Mrs Dugdale herself seems to have lived at Vinters for a while following her mother's death. Florence and Louisa had found the mansion too vast a home, and around 1912 they moved into Newnham Court which had been built for them. This is the "true" Newnham Court, which name is being assumed by the Shopping Village which occupies the site of Newnham Court Farm.

So it was that from about 1912 the Whatman family ceased to live at Vinters. It was let to Sir Reginald McLeod who maintained a full staff and made the grounds available for local events. There was an annual treat for the children of the parish, augmented by orphans from a Home in Boxley Road. The children played games, took boats on the lake, and finished with a strawberry tea in the Servants Hall and then presents to go away with.

Florence died in 1923, rather dramatically on a train between Ashford and Maidstone East. But Louisa went on and strode Boxley's stage until the 1950's.

She literally strode, because it was her habit to walk to her destinations if she possibly could. In this she showed a determined disregard for any traffic on the road. Thus if walking down the Sittingbourne Road into Maidstone, and the sun was shining where there was no footpath, then that was where she chose to be. She was a regular churchgoer at both Boxley and Grove Green. Boxley was a fair step from Newnham Court, but she went cross-country north of the Chiltern Hundreds along a footpath known as The Hockers and out to Boxley Street. At this point her course was firmly set in the middle of the road. She did not believe in motor-cars, but did have a carriage available to her which she would use occasionally, driven by Mr Voules her coachman. But not on Sundays, for she explained that her father never called out his coachman and horses on the Sabbath and neither would she. It is believed that the coach had rubber wheels and the horses rubber hooves. She wore elaborate hats to Church . At the age of 80 the long walk left her shaking with weariness and the feathers on her imposing hat shook in sympathy in the pew.

Louisa was a very distinctive figure for besides her hats she always wore a long black dress, save that in Lent she wore mauve. She would also often have Pekingese dogs trotting about her. Many people, children especially, went in some fear of her. When she entered Grove Green Church, everybody stood and some men even tugged their forelocks. She owned many houses in Weavering Street and would carry out regular tours of inspection of both tenants and buildings. Even the length of a girl's hem could invite her disapproval. But then again, knowledge of a sick tenant would bring a kind visit. During the second war she took in one of the Alleyn's schoolboys who had been evacuated to the parish, a rather shy boy. Louisa and John would sup Earl Grey tea together when he returned from school, which evokes a charming picture.

Louisa's walks also took her visiting relatives such as the Balstons and Trousdells. Jeanette Balston tells of one such visit. Now towards the end of her life Louisa's eyesight began to fail. In her circles no lady would ever answer her own front door because that was the maid's job. Jeanette opened the door herself to poorly-sighted Louisa and was asked whether Mrs Balston was at home. Jeanette said that she would go and enquire, disappeared for a moment, and re-presented herself as Mrs Balston! Down in Vinters Road lived Enid and Evelyn Trousdell who did employ a maid to open the door to Louisa. The maid was then berated with the banging of a walking stick and a demand to know where the nieces were and what they were up to.

And what of Vinters itself? By the 1930's the mansion had no tenants, for who could afford its upkeep? A small band of servants did their best to keep it ticking over and almost every day Louisa would walk over from Newnham Court for an inspection. Inevitably the walled garden, the many glasshouses, and the grounds in general began to deteriorate. Fruit trees were now more for the benefit of scrumpers. Mulberries, quinces and medlars mixed with varieties of apples and pears. Most of the old parkland remained as grassland

Vinters

Newnham Court, built circa 1912 for Florence and Louisa Whatman.

to be grazed by sheep and cattle. But there was one corner which was lively enough. At the top of Huntsman's Lane was an old ragstone quarry let out to the local builder Mr J.W. Bridge. As well as taking out the stone he used part as a shooting club and part for the Quarry Tennis Club, with four courts and a wooden club house. Here was much sport and laughter. Energetic man that he was, Mr Bridge also ran a Scout Troop who camped and exercised hereabouts.

Then in 1939 war came again, and like so many Big Houses, Vinters was used by the military. Probably because it was in the gentle hands of the Women's Royal Army Corps the house survived fairly well. In the park were built Nissen huts for extra accommodation, later to be used for prisoners of war and finally by squatters during the post-war housing shortage. From war-time and beyond, the precious furniture and effects were crammed for storage into two rooms which Mr Bridge padlocked and sealed with wax, impressed with his signet ring. He would then carry out periodic checks on the rooms, and with him one day was his grandson John Dadd. As a door opened, the sudden movement of air set a large Victorian clockwork doll walking across the room, much to their fright. To the young John Dadd these rooms were an Aladdin's cave of strange and wonderful things, such as archery targets and arrows and ladies bustles which were made of pigs bladders to be inflated.

We are now into the post-war years. Louisa had a few repairs done to the house and it seems that she even began to harbour dreams of returning to live there, however unrealistic. But in 1948 there was a large auction sale of the contents. In 1950 she died aged 92, and soon after the mansion and Estate were sold, piece-meal in 64 lots. Included in the sales was Old Newnham Court and its farm. Tenants in Weavering in particular jumped at the chance to buy their freeholds. The major purchaser of the mansion and parkland was a local builder. A while before, the Army had tried to buy a substantial area for military use, but the local council blocked that idea.

In time housing development has taken place on the rich agricultural land that lay towards Sittingbourne Road. The Crematorium was built, its entrance coinciding with a drive that led to the mansion from the Bearsted Road. The long dip to the east of the Crematorium known locally as Happy Valley does at least remain in something of its old beauty. A Television Studio to the east of the park and schools and playing fields to the south have all encroached. The mansion itself fell steadily into disrepair as uses for it failed to be found. One suggestion was a Golf course with the mansion as Club House. In the end it was to be destroyed by a fire and by the 1960's what ruins remained were levelled to the ground. A dedicated band of people ensure that at least some of the old parkland remains for public enjoyment and as a haven for wildlife. The Vinters Valley Trust have battled successfully to achieve this. There are magnificent specimens of ornamental trees, from obscure species of oak to Giant Redwoods, and even palms. Orchids and other wild flowers thrive. One can sit on the Ha-ha and gaze out across a buttercup filled meadow at a rural scene that successive James Whatmans would have known. The lake survives, and the paths that worked their way down to it can still be traversed, as the walker reflects upon those long-gone glorious days which are now a fast-fading memory.

Vinters with the lake in the foreground.

CHAPTER 17

The Second World War

The twenty-one peaceful years since 1918 were now to be followed by six long years of war. The Vicar of Boxley during the early war years was Rev. John Watt, and his wife Helen recorded some memories upon which parts of this chapter draw.

On a Sunday in September 1939 the Vicar was conducting a service when the wail of that famous first siren floated into the Church. Very calmly John Watt spoke: "I think we should all disperse quietly to our homes". And so the congregation filed out to the Green and in sight of the lovely wooded hills and orchards. It all looked so peaceful, but there was a sense of foreboding in the air. That siren had been a false alarm, but there were many more to come in deadly earnest.

The experiences of the civilian population during the recent Spanish Civil War had prepared Britain for a war fought from the air. The digging of air-raid shelters, the fitting of gas masks and the stand-bys of buckets of sand and stirrup pumps to deal with incendiary bombs were now the order of the day. So too the fitting of black-out curtains. London schools were evacuated to the presumed safety of the countryside, and Boxley received the boy pupils of Alleyn's school from Dulwich. The boys attended school in Maidstone and they and the masters were accommodated with families all around the Parish. In their short time here the masters and pupils made quite an impact, sharing their music and drama in which some of the village girls joined. Indeed, more than one romance began and lasted from those years.

1940 was the year of Dunkirk, and some weary soldiers who had been rescued from the beaches found transitory rest on the floor of the Vicarage nursery. And now the dreaded war from the air was unleashed with the Battle of Britain. At the time a 15 year old attending Maidstone Grammar School, Derek Sayer was living near Penenden Heath, and we can share his memories too. Boxley and the Heath were on a flight path to London, and wave after wave of German bombers passed overhead, with British fighters swooping down upon them. The sky was full of vapour trails and now and again parachutes and crashing planes. When the local lads saw a plane coming down they would cycle furiously to try and get there before the Home Guard or Police or Regular soldiers. The sky was also full of the noise of cannon fire and of anti-aircraft guns. The exploding shells filled the air with metal fragments of shrapnel, which came down with a strange whooshing sound. The recovery of shrapnel was another exciting pastime for the boys.

On their way in the German bombers had fighter escorts, but because the fighters carried less fuel they had to turn back early. The bombers themselves had to get back as best they could, and would fly very low over the Heath, hoping to gain some protection that way. But German fighters and bombers met their fate around Boxley Parish.

P.C. Ted Kirby should really have retired by 1939 after 20 years in the Parish, added to his soldiering in the Great War, but he stayed on. There was an occasion when a Junkers bomber crashed near Boarley Farm and the pilot surrendered to the Farmer there, who rang Ted to come and collect the prisoner. Making his way to the scene, Ted heard a noise behind a hedge and discovered another of the bomber's crew who also surrendered. Being an old soldier himself, Ted was a little affronted when he got to Boarley Farm and found the first German being entertained with a cup of friendly tea. And Ted it was again who was called over to neighbouring Aylesford where another couple of German aircrew had come down. One of Ted's sons joined him and the two of them hurried over and arrived just in time to rescue the Germans from the good women of Aylesford who had cornered them and were about to inflict some awful punishment.

Over the hill at Grange Farm, Bob Style's men were harvesting when a German baled out and arrived amongst them. He soon surrendered when an array of pitch forks were thrust towards him. One bloodthirsty harvester was all for getting an axe, with cries of "Let's cut 'is 'ead 'orf!" His companions persuaded him that this was no way for an Englishman to behave, and transport was found for them to take a bemused German to Chatham Police Station. There was a very real fear of invasion in 1940, and the flat land around Grange Farm was considered a likely place for German gliders to land and disgorge troops. To foil them there were strung out thick wires, which also foiled the harvesters and caused them annoyance. Near Boxley Grange two 4.5 inch guns were emplaced. At Boxley House the Styles were playing tennis, and in the spirit of Drake they determined to finish their game despite the air battles above them. Mrs Style was watching the tennis from her deckchair and wearing a Panama hat. When they eventually adjourned to the house and she took her hat off there was a rattle on the hall floor as pieces of shrapnel fell out. Winston Churchill was exhorting the nation to fight any invaders on the beaches and in the hedgerows and that "we will never surrender". It is a romantic thought to wonder whether Bob Style and his two crackshot daughters would have exchanged pheasants for German paratroopers and taken pot-shots had the occasion arisen. Ursula Style was now married to a Naval Officer Richard White, and he gained national attention by commanding a ship which achieved the remarkable feat of sinking two German U-boats within a very short space of time. Back in Boxley and drinking in the

King's Arms, he tried to persuade a young local naval rating to join his ship. The offer was declined, as the rating felt it best to avoid U-boats rather than go looking for them.

Meanwhile at the Vicarage yet another German had dropped in and got tangled up in the Fig tree. The Vicar and Fuller the gardener persuaded him first to throw away his pistol and then climb down. Despite the calls for assistance, nobody came to collect the German for 24 hours, during which time he sat making eyes at Ivy the maid. When eventually the authorities came it was in the shape of two armoured troop carriers. As the whole area seemed littered with the enemy one supposes that they were on a house to house collection.

It is not clear what the Home Guard were doing at this time. Boxley had the Sandling Platoon, a body of men based first at Boarley Oasts and then at the Yew Tree pub. Their duties included guarding the Boarley Water Reservoir and patrolling the Parish. Hot soup and hot chocolate was brought out to them by a grateful and admiring public. On some weekends they would be off to the coast on guard duty. One day the Boxley lads were having live grenade practice in the Detling chalk hole. Their officer offered to demonstrate, but only succeeded in projecting his missile a few yards. Panic ensued. At Harvest time those who were farm-workers were on night patrol and then in the fields until 7 p.m. and were prone to fall asleep standing up. Food production became increasingly vital as the U-boats strangled the shipping supplies. The harvesters were encouraged with extra food to sustain them, in the form of harvest rations. Some of the older children were also encouraged by these goodies to lend a hand on the land.

In August 1940 the Parish was sucked indirectly into one of the most tragic events of the War in the Maidstone area. Rev. John Watt was visiting chaplain to the R.A.F. station in Detling. He had just enjoyed lunch with some officers when about 50 German planes appeared from nowhere and strafed the airfield. Something must have gone wrong with the warning systems for no siren had sounded. The Vicar has left a graphic account of what ensued, but this belongs properly with the history of Detling. Suffice to say that 37 men and 4 officers (including 2 that he had just lunched with) were killed and countless wounded. Rev. Watt was very badly shaken and suffered two black eyes and other bruises. He had a lucky escape. After this experience he had a few sleepless nights, after which Ruth Saveall (who was working at the Vicarage as a maid) would take him a breakfast tray in bed at 8 a.m. One such day at 7.45 a.m. the siren went and soon a colossal battle was in progress overhead with pieces of shrapnel singing down into the garden. Eventually at 8.25 Ruth appeared with the nicely understated excuse that, "I'm sorry I'm late with your tray Mr Watt, but there was a good deal of shrapnel flying around". Years later (and Ruth lived to see her 100th birthday) she recalled probably that self same day when a German bullet or piece of shrapnel came through the kitchen window at the

Vicarage and just missed her. Likewise she recalled the Vicar's homecoming all black and blue and dusty after that awful day at Detling.

It must sometimes have seemed that the Vicarage (or was it the Vicar?) was being singled out. On yet another occasion John Watt was shaving when a piece of shrapnel embedded itself beside the mirror. Shaken, he moved elsewhere to sit down with his breakfast coffee and a second piece came through the window. Retiring next to the nursery to read his paper yet another piece came through that window and so scared the budgerigar that it lay down with its feet in the air, gave a squawk, and died.

Bombs as well as shrapnel fell upon Boxley. On one occasion a stick of bombs fell straddling Park House, the Vicarage and Boxley Abbey. Let Helen Watt take up the story.

"It was hot weather and, as John insisted on sleeping with his bedroom window shut and the blackout curtains drawn across, I regretfully retired to a room on the other side of the passage where I could open my window. We still had one domestic, a little girl called Ivy who slept on the other side of the staircase from my temporary room. On this night I heard the first bomb fall, and then the next a little nearer, and realised that they were coming our way. Knowing that it would be safe to put on the light in John's room, and being unwilling to die alone, I dashed over the passage and opened his door. I put on his light and saw him lying on his side blissfully asleep, and sticking out from under his bed a round pink flannel behind. "What on earth are you doing Ivy?" I called. She crept out and said, "Me Mum says it is safer under the bed, and I thought I'd like to die under the Vicar!" I shook John and yelled "Bombs John, wake up!" He stirred sleepily and muttered, "Well, go and make some tea". What a comforting man".

Helen Watt related what happened down at Park House. Mr and Mrs Best-Dalison were now sleeping alone in their vast mansion, with servants coming in by day. They slept in separate rooms and were both quite deaf. The following morning Mrs Best-Dalison went into her husband's room and said, "Edmund, something seems to have come through the roof of the hall in the night". An examination showed that it was the first of the stick of bombs which mercifully had not exploded. The two old dears had slept peacefully through it all.

Also deaf was Mrs Mills, widow of the village blacksmith who had not long before died. She lived in Forge Lane and the corner of her house was struck by one of our own anti-aircraft shells. Neighbours rushing to the scene found her too sleeping through it all.

Farm workers on the Boxley House Estate over the hill experienced bombs as well. Amos Golding recalls a companion having trimmed a hedge and burnt the cuttings, and then damping down the flames for the night. Or so he thought, because the fire started up again and the flare caught the attention of a German Bomber which unloaded a bomb or two on it. At harvest time they had built several hay stacks and these again attracted bombs. It must be remembered that the North Downs really were a landmark corridor for the Luftwaffe, and if they were returning home with bombs on board, then they would unload them where they could. Amos Golding's worst experience was the day of the Detling Air-raid, when he and some others were working close by at Pollyfields Farm. He recalls the Bombers sweeping in from the direction of Sheerness (having outflanked the radar perhaps) and blitzing the Airfield. The farm workers turned the frightened work horses loose to fend for themselves, and the farm workers sought shelter by a shed which shook as the explosions occurred. Worse of all were the screams of the wounded and injured.

By the end of September 1940 the Battle of Britain had been won and the immediate threat of invasion removed. The Germans now turned their attention to night-time bombing. The Blitz on London had begun, and we can rejoin the memories of our schoolboy Derek Sayer close by Penenden Heath.

The warning sirens would start wailing at about 10 p.m. and the "All Clear" would not be sounded until the early hours. Far to the west the sky was aglow as London's Dockland was burning. The ARP (Air Raid Patrol) had a hut on the Heath and Derek made himself useful running messages. An old First War Tank used to stand on the corner of the Heath and this and the railings which surrounded the Heath were removed to be melted down for the war effort. In the night sky the beams of searchlights swept to and fro, trying to pick out the enemy bombers. The Anti-aircraft guns fired away, more in hope than expectation of hitting anything. There was a gun site just north of the putting green.

Into 1941 the Alleyns boys moved away from the Parish. So much for a safe refuge! They were replaced by a Young Soldiers battalion of the Royal West Kents who were billeted in tents in the Best-Dalisons' fields. Some of the officers were afforded baths at the Vicarage. The soldiers themselves inevitably found time to cavort with some of the village maidens. Throughout the War the Army camped around the Parish, taking over Vinters, Sandling Place, Park House Maidstone and sometimes pitching tents on the Heath. Close by Stone House there were huts to store ammunition.

Wally Gosling had done his soldiering in the "first lot" and was now a special constable. There was an ARP or Fire Watching Team of four based at Boxley school. Hindsight considers their presence worse than useless because they were so shut away that they knew nothing of what was going on outside. Wally used to finish his long evening beat by calling in there at about 9 p.m. to make sure all was well. A pack of cards would come out, they would all have a drink or three, and Wally confessed to sometimes not getting home until 2 or 3 in the morning. His splendid wife would sympathise that his police duties should keep him out so very late. Another place where the lights burnt late was the Kings Arms. Boxley seemed to have its own licensing hours, and even Rev. Watt was allegedly in there turned midnight, scoring at darts and drinking with the worst of them. The Landlord saved some special beer to be maturing until peace came, and when it did there were some very happy customers.

Gradually the tide of War began to turn, and the fight was carried to the enemy. Now allied bombers were flying in the opposite direction, American Flying Fortresses by day and the British by night. One cannot help wondering whether emigrated Wyatt blood flowed through the veins of those American air crew, setting off over the lands of their ancestors to do battle. But come 1944 and Hitler unleashed a final terror into our skies. One day Derek Sayer saw what he thought was a plane in trouble with flames spurting from its rear. He was soon to learn that this was one of the first Flying Bombs, or VI Rockets. Again he was to have a grandstand view as the British fighters intercepted the VI's, sometimes flying alongside to tip their wings and send them crashing into the empty countryside around Boxley. It was out towards Detling that one of the first was brought down, and there was much secrecy as the authorities investigated the wreckage. The flights of these rockets was certainly something to remember. One onlooker recalls some at different times which almost appeared to be following the Pilgrim's Way on their path towards London. One was caught by a British fighter and shot down near the London Road outside Maidstone. The explosion sent such a blast and shock-wave that corn in the fields by the Pilgrim's Way was laid over.

Next came the improved V2 Rockets, which flew so fast that the RAF could not catch them. It was only when their launch sites were over-run following D-Day that the skies over Boxley finally fell quiet. But beforehand damage was caused, including the east window of the Church being blown out. By the entrance to Cobtree stood a cottage where lived Ernie Gates and his wife. Mr Gates worked at Sir Garrard Tyrrwhit-Drake's Zoo. A Flying Bomb cut out overhead and plummeted down, and onlookers swore that the cottage was lifted off its foundations by the explosion before settling down again. Rescuers found Mrs Gates inside desperately trying to hold the ceiling up with her raised arms. The blast sent a neighbour a little distance away flying across his bedroom. One unusual arrival from the sky was a landmine, dropped by parachute and which was probably intended for Detling Airfield. Indeed, the western edge of the Parish towards Detling almost seemed to attract explosions from the sky. Apart from the odd cow being killed no great damage resulted.

In the months leading up to D-Day, Boxley was part of the armed camp which Southern England had become. There were troops camped out towards Bredhurst and down in Vinters Park. There were Bren-gun carriers at Park House and ammunition dumps by Stone House. There were tanks parked close by Penenden Heath, indeed the state of Woodland Way is put down to the weight of tanks upon it. Military check-points were set up near the Running Horse and at the top of Boxley Hill. Around Grange Farm, mock installations were set up as part of the deception to confuse the Germans as to where the invasion was to take place.

In Vinters Park there were French-Canadian soldiers camped, and one evening they threw a large white covering over a lorry parked up on the heights opposite the lake. They then used it as a screen and started a film-show. They so lit up the night sky that enraged Military Police (who had their own camp down by the Ashford Road) rushed up to put a stop to it.

So Boxley did not have a particularly quiet time. Away from the Home Front, many people were away in the services and many were to sacrifice their lives by land, sea and air. And just as after the Great War life was never to be the same again, so too in 1945 moods had changed and attitudes had hardened.

BOXLEY PARISH

The wedding of Frank Balston and Kate Trousdell in 1909. One of the pageboys is a very young Tom Best-Dalison.

CHAPTER 18
The Balstons and the Trousdells

In 1774 James Whatman was looking for an apprentice. Christ's Hospital School had a reputation for producing well-educated boys who were suitable for training in business and commerce, and it was from there that James Whatman recruited fifteen years old William Balston. From the hurly burly of London, William was transported to the rural delights of Turkey Mill where he became a member of the Whatman household. In 1787/88 the family moved to Vinters and, when they finally left several generations later, they still referred to "Mr Balston's room".

In 1793 Whatman's health began to fail and he decided to sell his business. He had trained William well and had already given him a share in the business, but doubted William's ability to run a business on his own. William, however, found some partners, and a new papermaking firm of Hollingworth & Balston took over at Turkey Mill, with William continuing to live at Vinters. Indeed, Whatman lent him £5000 to help buy into the partnership. Business prospered at first, then the Napoleonic wars and some industrial unrest over wages caused set-backs and the partnership split up. From 1805 William fulfilled an ambition and built a new mill for himself at Springfield, taking the valuable Whatman watermark with him. This was the very first mill to be driven by a steam engine. In 1806 he married, the new mill proved a success, and seven sons and three daughters were born. William retained the valued friendship of the Whatman family right up until his death in 1849. Connections with Boxley continued through the generations, particularly when William's grandson Richard Balston lived for some years at Boxley Abbey where several of his many children were born. In 1909 one of Richard's six sons, Frank, married Ellen (known as Kate) Trousdell, who was a granddaughter of the last James Whatman. So it was that after many years descendants of the second James Whatman and his apprentice William Balston were united in matrimony.

The wedding was reported in great detail by the South Eastern Gazette:-
"The families of both parties are held in the highest respect in the town of Maidstone, with which they have so long been associated, and it was, therefore, not surprising to find the ancient Parish Church of Boxley filled with the elite of the neighbourhood on such a happy occasion. Long before the ceremony was timed to commence, it was evident that the accommodation afforded by

the edifice would be taxed to the utmost extent, and this, in spite of the fact that admission could only be obtained by special permit. The porch was filled with persons unable to obtain seats, whilst large crowds of well-wishers collected on the village green awaiting the arrival of the bridal party. Inside the Church the scene was one which will live long in the recollection of many, the effect of the lavish floral decorations, combined with the elegant costumes of many of the ladies present, being extremely picturesque. The village, too, was prettily decorated for the occasion, and at the entrance gates to Park House, where the reception was subsequently held, an arch of evergreens had been erected, on which, in silver letters on a red background, were the words 'God bless them' and on the other side 'Bon Voyage' with the monograms of the bride and bridegroom."

Here was Edwardian Boxley in all its pomp and glory. A guard of honour was formed by some thirty employees of Springfield Mill who belonged to the Territorial Army. One of the pages was a young cousin Tom Best-Dalison in a white satin suit and a white felt hat with feathers. The guests were a roll-call of names associated with Boxley - Whatman, Marsham, Shaw, Mercer, Style, Lushington, Sir Reginald MacLeod as well as the Balston and Trousdell families themselves.

The Trousdell connection with the Whatmans began with the marriage in 1875 of an Irish Army officer William Trousdell with Ellen, second daughter of the last James Whatman. William had been an Army officer and he went on to farm as a tenant at Cobtree for some years. He and Ellen were to produce a large family. Of his sons, William (known as Hugh) was lost at sea in 1915, whilst the Great War also claimed the life of Maurice killed in action after winning the Military Cross. Two other sons, Charles (known as Carlo) and Alick also won the same gallantry medal. Carlo was a particularly adventurous man and spent many years abroad, which included gold mining and tin mining, and whose death was probably hastened by being beaten up as an elderly man by natives in Africa. He never married, his fiancee having tragically died. Alick lived on until 1965 and left children. He also left to Boxley Church in his Will the ownership of the outer porch which had vested in the Whatman family for so many years. The porch bears a memorial tablet to his two brothers lost between 1914 and 1918.

The influenza epidemic of 1918 (which for some strange reason seemed to strike down young healthy adults rather than the very young or the elderly) claimed the life of the Boxley curate Cecil Hilton who is believed to have been engaged to one of the daughters, Evelyn Trousdell. She was never to marry, but gave devoted years to Boxley as Parish nurse. Her uniformed figure riding around on her bicycle with a black bag was a comforting feature of the locality. She was much loved and delivered countless Boxley babies, whom she forever afterwards referred to as "my babies". The Trousdell family, and latterly Evelyn and another unmarried sister Edith, lived at a lovely old house "Maryland" on the edge of the parish in Vinters Road, now demolished. And Evelyn's and Edith's sister Kate it was who married Frank Balston in that grand wedding in 1909 before mentioned.

After Louisa Whatman's death in 1950 there was a nice family symmetry when Frank Balston's son Hugh went to live at her home at Newnham Court in 1954 and carried the family's Boxley connections into another generation. Hugh and his elder brother Peter were the first paper-maker descendants of both the Whatmans and the Balstons. Peter Balston lost his life in the Second War whilst serving with the RAF.

Newnham Court had for many years been the quiet and secluded residence of an elderly Louisa. Most of the rooms were unused, with dust covers thrown over the furniture. Brown paint work added to the atmosphere of austerity. Hugh and Jeanette Balston soon transformed the house, and their five children brought noisy activity to every corner. Why, even electricity and a telephone were introduced!

Court Lodge Farmhouse with glimpses of the Malthouse and Hermitage at the top.

CHAPTER 19

Boxley Village

Boxley Village straggles the length of the road from Harbourland, due north to the foot of the Downs, with short diversions west into Grange Lane and east along the Pilgrim's Way to Warren Farm. Boxley Parish was originally divided into four quarters, Sandling, Weavering, The Hill and Boxley Street, with the village comprising almost all of the latter section.

The area as George Wallis described it in our chapter on Victorian Times had until then probably changed little from Norman times. The Saxons almost certainly had a church on the present site, and one envisages peasant hovels and farming activity. From 1066, The Conqueror's Norman followers having been granted land were quite likely setting up their homes hereabouts, and lording it over the defeated populace. The foundation of the Norman Abbey in 1146 would have been the catalyst for the village that was to swell to its heydays of the Big Houses up to the 1940's.

The very name of Park House suggests parkland, and until quite recent times the immediate surrounds of Boxley House were known as Boxley Park. The whole of the eastern side of the village street, apart from the area immediately around the church, was originally enclosed by Sir Thomas Wyatt and formed 'The Ley Park of Boxley' and ascribed to his own occupation in the 1554 attainder record. A 1667 marriage settlement between Thomas Oliver and Sara, daughter of Sara Higford of Boxley, refers to the latter's 'Mansion House and capital messuage, barn, stables, outhouses, yard, garden and orchard plus a piece of meadow or pasture commonly called The Park, alias Lea Park, containing approximately 50 acres in Boxley'. Wyatt's 'Ley Park' was probably a collection of the old open-field strips, converted from arable land to pasture to provide food for livestock, whose droppings would enrich the land for future crop-growing. Often such 'leys' would become permanent pasture, probably as a deer park or for cattle. Intriguingly, this particular park was bisected by a 'ley line' (a prehistoric track joining two prominent points in the landscape along which is detected a strong magnetic pull) which could provide another explanation for the name.

Strolling through the village today, the houses and farm buildings appear to be almost entirely of Victorian construction, or are older timber-framed buildings with a later facade of brick and hung-tiles. This mellow uniformity is hardly surprising, given that almost the entire village was owned by just three families by the time of the ascension of Queen Victoria. Virtually the entire western side of the road was owned by the Fowle family whilst the eastern side was divided between the Park House and Boxley House estates. Lord Romney and Maudistly Best were responsible for much of the construction and face-lifting, and the proximity of the local tile and brick kilns provided an economical source of materials.

In times past there was no Motorway to disturb the peace at Harbourland. Before 1940 the same farmhouse building stood on the corner of what is now Harbourland Close. Here Cyril Hassam lived, and behind was his slaughterhouse. His home-made sausages gained some fame. The local children would peep through gaps in the fence to watch the gory sight of animals being killed by a blow with a pole axe. During the Second War the favoured few could augment their meat rations with some tasty liver or similar offal. Before Cyril Hassam, it was the Bricknell family who farmed here, and down the track which is now the Close were some cottages. The stretch of road through Harbourland was and is known as Dove Hill, and on its eastern side Cyril Hassam ran a piggery. Standing high behind the Bull Public House are Bull Cottages, built by George Wallis in 1877 for Major Best's Park House Estate Workers. A single storey outbuilding was included, half of which was a bakehouse with a large oven, and the rest comprised of two wood sheds and two earth closets. They were built on the site of a very old cottage bought by Major Best in 1874 when Daniel Scratton's estate was sold. The steps that led from the road up to the original cottage are still there. The gate of Number 1 continues to bear the legend, 'air raid warden', a legacy of the last war.

Just north of Harbourland Close stands the imposing white Harbourland House. Here lived Mr C.E. Roper and his sister. He a Maidstone solicitor who turned out for the village cricket team prior to The Great War and enjoyed the local shooting parties, and Miss Roper the organiser of The Girls Friendly Society. Over the years she would hold popular reunions for her 'old girls'. The house was built at the end of William IV's reign where previously had stood a cottage occupied by John Huggett. In 1750 Jeremiah Parker, landlord of The Bull Inn, had purchased from Richard Ironmonger a cottage called Harbourland Hill with an acre of land, in occupation of John Froud. In 1784 William Carter purchased it from Parker's heirs, it being occupied for a number of years by Burgess Masters. It was then conveyed to Pierce Edgcumbe who leased it to Huggett. In 1838 Richard Dark Edgcumbe leased to Edward Munk, grocer of Maidstone, his newly erected house with a garden, stable and a small chaisehouse. Before the Ropers, who occupied it from 1899 through to the 1950's, there were a succession of wealthy tenants including vicars, bankers, and in the 1890's, George Drayson of Smythe & Drayson, slate and timber merchants.

Beyond the grounds, where a row of modern cottages lie at right angles to the road, previously stood three cottages built in 1784 by John Parks, bricklayer of Boxley. In 1798 he offered them for sale by auction at The Bull, but evidently they failed to find a buyer as they formed part of his will in 1807. In 1832 a Miss Elizabeth Parry purchased them, occupying one cottage, with Henry Parks and Edward Lane in the others. Her heir sold them to James Best in 1848 and they became estate cottages, before being demolished to make way for today's dwellings.

Next door was a plot of land which in 1767 was described as having a messuage or tenement now converted into two tenements, with an oasthouse, in the tenures of Richard Sutherland and William Lucas, yeoman. It was owned by the Athawes family for about 150 years, until Major Best purchased it in 1888. The tithe map of 1844 shows it as being in the tenure of Robert Lucas. Sadly, these buildings are now also gone, but directly opposite stands the lovely cottage known as Old Harbourland, now the home of Dr. Bob Spain. Dr. Spain has recently discovered and obtained a copy of a delightful water colour showing Old Harbourland and the cottage attached to the oasthouse which stood opposite. A listed building, the house is timber-framed and said to date from the 16th Century, being partly built in the 18th Century, which is probably when it was re-roofed. Dr. Spain informs us that there are earlier roof timbers inside the present roof, bearing evidence of smoke blackening, indicating an original open hearth.

Further additions were made in the 19th Century which is when the hung tiles would have been added. It is probably the 'farm of $12^{1}/_{2}$ acres at Harbourland', tenanted by Robert Warren in 1554. In 1806 William Coleman leased to Passwater Usher the dwelling house, oasthouse, buildings, yard, garden and cottage with 14 acres called Harbourland Farm. Thomas Best absorbed it into the Park Farm Estate in 1814. By the mid 1840's, William Benge had the tenancy and ran a beerhouse from the premises as did his successors, William and Thomas Miles, up to the 1860's. The barn had been converted into accommodation by 1849 (and may indeed be the cottage referred to in 1806) and Miles farmed only $13^{1}/_{2}$ acres. It would appear that the farmland then became divorced from the house, because from at least 1878-1881 George Orford, a bricklayer, ran Old Harbourland purely as a beerhouse, paying rent to the then tenant of Harbourland Farm Thomas Betts. Between the wars, Richard Luckhurst who ran the Home Farm at Park House for the Best-Dalisons resided here.

Standing alongside is Barn Cottage, converted from the barn of Harbourland Farm. Four of its bays are late 16th Century, with a fifth being added in the mid to late 18th Century, together with a pair of oasts. At the end of that century, the two northernmost bays were converted into a cottage at which time the stables were added. The right side oast displays a rare example of part of the stud and plaster partition between the plenum chamber and the unheated section of the oast. In 1849 it was the home of Sanders Parks, whose brother Joseph lived in the row of cottages just back down the road. Like John

Parks, they also worked as builders and then became wheelwrights and later motor-body builders in Sandling. Today, all but the stables have been converted into a house. The farm buildings remain on the other side of the road.

Just beyond Barn Cottage, a roadway known as Back Lane or Sandy Lane hairpins back and leads under the motorway to Penenden Heath. Originally, this was the main way from Boxley to Maidstone, bisecting the much larger Heath, across where now is Faraday Road, and continuing from Heathfield Road along what today is the footpath known as The Hedges. Down the lane, sitting back from the road behind its pond, is Stone House which bears a date stone of 1758. Doubtless this records the date when improvements were carried out, because it is certainly older, believed by some to have originally been built earlier in the century as a pair of labourer's cottages. However, Park House Estate Maps of 1697 and 1768 both show it as Tile Kiln Farmhouse, with yards and orchards, of almost 21 acres, and tenanted by Samuel Athawes. Alongside was Workhouse Yard and Kiln. This was probably the tile kiln run by Robert Hartridge who farmed 12 acres at Harbourland and who in 1670 supplied 20,000 bricks and 2,000 tiles to the stores at Chatham Dockyard. At the right end of Stonehouse a rear wing was constructed in the 19th Century, as the laundry house to Park House. In 1841 it was known as Stone Cottage and occupied by Thomas Jarrett and 10 years later its occupants were Edward Shephard, a pauper and his wife Abigail, the laundress. One of the Park House chauffeur's sons Colin Vaughan has an embarrassing memory of collecting all the clean laundry in a cart from the then occupant, the well-remembered Nellie Pearce. Somehow, on the journey back, he managed to tip it out, which incident made him none too popular. The wooden outhouse was the workshop for the estate carpenter and bricklayer.

Wallenberg, in The Place Names of Kent, says that the first known reference to Harbourland was in 1313 when it is written as Hereburgland. He defines it as being the land of Hereburh- a female name. In our first chapter we suggest it may have been a 'Cold Harbour' for travellers. Its name has been recorded in diverse forms down the centuries from Harbyland and Harveyland to Harberland and Barberland, and even Abbeyland. The lands of Harbourland appear to have been split from early times into three different farms whose convoluted ownership is difficult to follow. The powerful Brewer family held a messuage and 5 pieces of land here in 1616, which Isaac Caillovel later sold to John Marten, when it had 25 acres. In 1787 Arthur Holdsworth descendant of John Lane, sold it to William Carter together with the right of common pasture on Penenden Heath.

Moving on towards the village, the road to the left leading to Boarley and Sandling, is Grange Lane. Down here is the sheepwash, where one of the Boxley streams flows under the road and makes its way first into Cuckoo Woods and eventually on to the Medway opposite Allington castle grounds. The steep slope of the meadowland has attracted tobogganing by the local children. Here too, Gypsies used to camp with their colourful caravans, and were often out and about selling wooden clothes pegs. The children from Sandling, who came this way to school, used to keep together in a close group, for gypsies inspired a little apprehension. Some of these fields belonged to Harbourland Farm and on the rest stood the tenement, with a barn, stable, garden and orchard known as Lestens or Listons Tenement, occupied by Robert Warren back in 1554. This land later formed part of another of the Harbourland farms which John Astley passed to Norton Knatchbull, who in turn sold it to the Charltons. For many years it was tenanted by the Gouldsmith family, during which time part of its 50 acres was the $3\frac{1}{2}$ acre field known as Capon Panne which the Wyatts record included as part of its rent, 3 capons at Christmas. This name became twisted in local people's memories and it became known as 'Pot and Pan'.

For many years there was a brick and tile kiln in Grange Lane, east of the Abbey, where Cookes Cottage stands. The cottage was originally known as Brickkiln or Brickill Cottage and its current name is taken from that of John Cooke, a navy pensioner who lived there in 1881. It is from here that many of the bricks and the hung tiles came in Victorian times to construct cottages and farmbuildings. The kiln appears to have been constructed by William Fowle in the early years of the 19th Century on land known as Upper Thistly Field. In 1832 it was being run by Saunders and Hook, and had two cottages. Later the cottage had an integral coach and wagon house, and a stable as befitted a man of substance such as Henry Towsley, brick, tile and drainpipe manufacturer who lived there in the 1860's. Behind it is a large pond which could tell some stories. It seems that this was originally a pit where clay or brick earth, was excavated for brick-making. At the end of one day the workmen left their tools in there, and went home. When they returned in the morning the pit had completely filled with water and tools and machinery were lost. Tales are told of the Army ditching ammunition in the pond after the Second War. Local boys would try and fish, and usually just succeeded in pulling up tiles. P.C. Ted Kirby, next mentioned, broke the ice one winter's day and plumbed its depth to some 80 feet at its deepest point.

Cooke's Cottage was the home for many years of the village policeman Ted Kirby, who raised four sons there. After soldiering in the Great War he came to Boxley in 1919 and stayed to maintain law and order right up until 1944. Such long service in one locality was very rare, because Police policy was to move the men around before they got too well known and connected. But, shall we say, popular demand resulted in his long tenure. He was a man highly respected by all and sundry. His area was the whole of Boxley Parish, from the River to Weavering Street, and from the Downs to Penenden Heath. He must have cycled a fair number of miles. When not on duty he loved nothing better than shooting game. Boxley in those days must have reverberated to the sound of guns, for rabbits and hares and blackbirds, as well as partridge and pheasant were regularly and seasonally shot in all corners.

Life for the Kirbys at Cooke's cottage would seem very hard to modern sensibilities. There was a very deep well, but this had become disused. Water was collected off the roof, or in dry spells was brought by container by Jim Clifford at Abbey Farm. There was neither gas nor electricity. Cooking was on a coal-fired range, and lighting by candles or oil lamps. The toilet was an outside earth closet. But any of the Kirby boys would tell you that it was a happy life.

South of Grange Lane, and now cut-off by the motorway, was Lower Grange Farm, originally known as Nether Grange or Nether Graving. Run by Maud Foster at the start of this century, as farm steward to Mrs Best-Dalison. As its name suggests, this farm would have helped supply and store for the needs of the Abbey in its early years. Today only a small farm, it was in Sir Thomas Wyatt's time one of the five largest farms in the parish, when its 134^1/$_2$ acres were let to John Stile. Granted by Queen Mary to George Clarke, the estate came into the possession of Robert Bruer (Brewer) in 1579 following his marriage to Mariam Clarke, by when it had swelled to 340 acres and incorporated much of Sandling. John Mason, the timber-merchant leased it from the Brewers in 1679, it then being sold to Sir Francis Withins who conveyed it to Sir Thomas Taylor. From then it became subsumed into the Park House (Sandling) Estate until finally being sold by The Lushingtons in 1821. No longer an important property, much of its land was sold off, large sections coming into the possession of The Fowle family. By 1774, the tenant farmer Dawbarn Wattel had only 75 acres. The old house originally stood to the east of the modern building with a pond in between. The Athawes family held it through the 18th Century, and then the Roots family farmed its 40 acres throughout the first two thirds of the 19th, until the Bests bought it and leased it to Louis Jarrett for the next thirty-odd years.

Returning to the main road leading to Boxley village, one of the village pounds, where straying cattle etc. were impounded, stood opposite Grange Lane. There is now a long stretch of open country without habitation, but this was not always so, because around 1884 Major Best had re-routed the road, moving it westwards away from his new Park House. In the process an attractive house, known as Boxley Cottage found itself on the opposite side of the road, and about the turn of the century was demolished. In 1709, John Alexander leased to Edward Johnson – 'his tenement, lately built, with an orchard of 3 roods'. By 1770 it had been converted into two dwellings and remained so when in 1788 William Brooke sold it to Thomas Best. It became known as Herdsmans Cottage, and later Lambs Cottage, after Samuel Lamb the tenant who lived there and farmed 120 acres of the Park Farm Estate. In 1881 it housed William Austen, the Park House coachman and Joseph Sedgwick, curate of Boxley, his wife, two children, three servants and three

BOXLEY VILLAGE

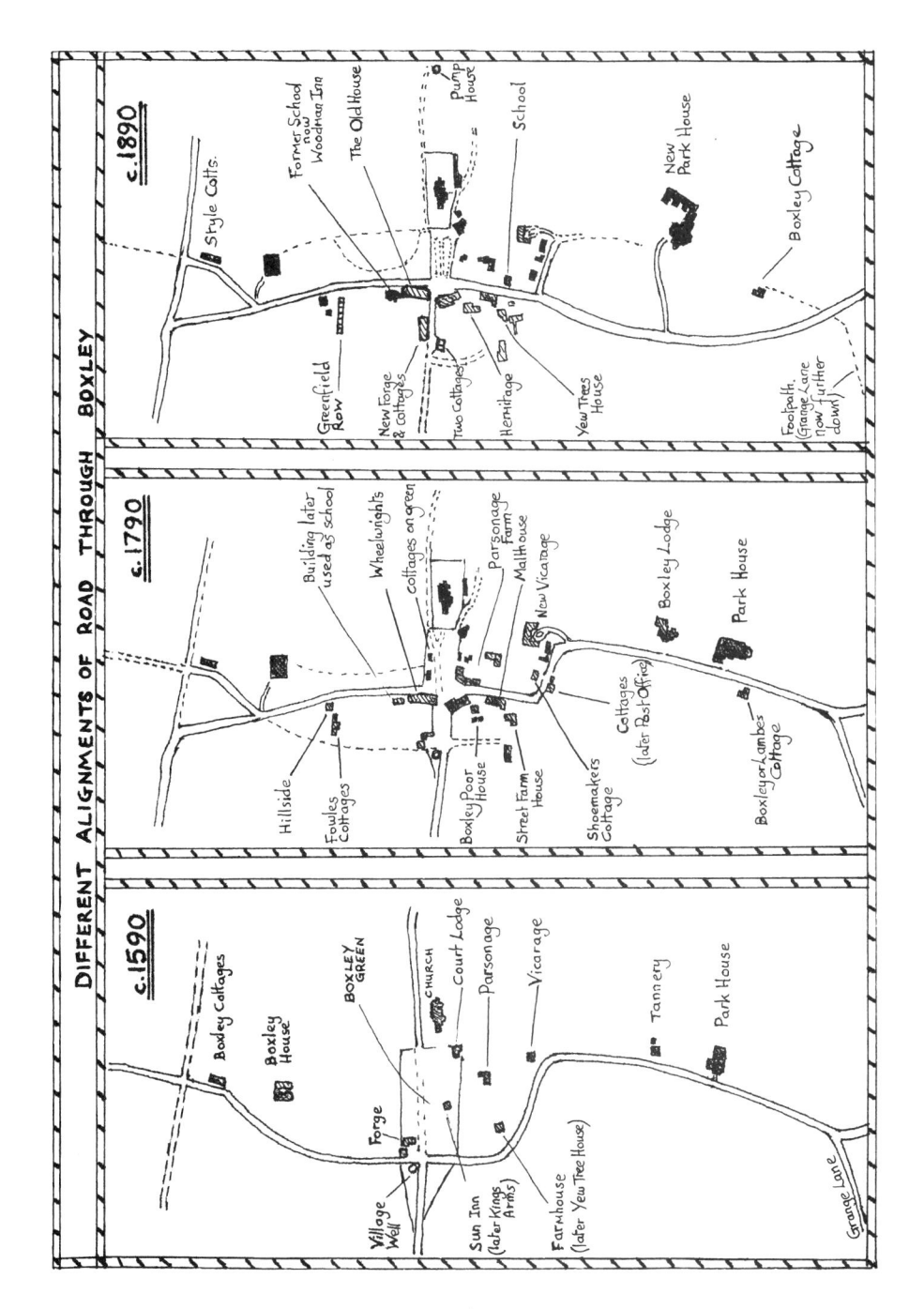

'pupils' aged 13. One presumes that his wife was running a private school. With the removal of the house, the road lapsed into rural tranquillity, at least until the onslaught of the motorcar. Up to the 1930's at least, there were orchards alongside the road, proudly showing their colours at blossom-time.

The first dwelling in the village on the Harbourland approach is Park Cottage, originally a pair of cottages owned by the Park House Estate. In one of the cottages lived for many years William Prince, the butler and his family. Of his children Percy was killed in The Great War, and his daughter was Miss Eleanor Prince who taught for many years at the village school. In the other cottage there later lived Fred Vaughan the chauffeur and his large family. Two old cottages used to stand on this spot. Once the property of the Fowle family they were purchased by Major Best who demolished them to make way for the re-aligned road. For decades one of them had been the home of the Davis family. John was a shoemaker and his wife, Harriet was running the village post office from there in 1852, which job was carried on in the 1860's by her daughter Sophia. On the opposite side of what is now the entrance road to the Vicarage, (and which originally also served Park House and Boxley Lodge) once stood a cottage. Together with another further along the driveway, they were owned by Abel Roots. This first cottage was known as Shoemakers Cottage, after the profession of Thomas May, who lived and kept a shop there.

To the left of the road was a large sheep-dip pond, and then, as now, the buildings of Street Farm. From oblique references in documents, and descriptions and sketch maps in title deeds we have concluded that up to the 17th Century, the main road through Boxley took a distinctly different route than it does today. We have already stated that coming south it ran along the lane which leads to the Vicarage and down past Boxley Lodge and Park House to Harbourland. From the present junction of the lane to the Vicarage with the main road it originally went straight across, curving round through the buildings of Street Farm, and running through where now stands Anvil Cottage at the top of Forge Lane. Crossing Forge Lane, it ran up past the far end of Greenfield Cottages, then alongside what is now the waterworks, with part of its course preserved past Styles and Hatchetts Cottages. From there it passed across the Pilgrim's Way, up the bridleway that climbs the escarpment, where it divided, with one lane passing to the west of Harp Farm and the other bearing right to Lidsing. This left the then much larger village green and the cluster of ecclesiastical properties, in peaceful isolation.

In the 16th and 17th Centuries the lands that became Street Farm belonged firstly to The Wyatts, and then to the Brewer family. The farm was originally a smallholding of 18 acres, composed of a farmhouse, barn 2, stables, outhouses, and four fields. The internal boundaries were later altered to make 6 small fields which stretched south along the westside of Boxley Street. They included an apple orchard, 4 acres of cherries, 4 acres of hops and the 2 acre Priests Mead. From at least the start of the 18th Century it was known as Southgates

Farm after the family who owned it. In 1698, Robert Leche of Vintners in Boxley had sold Chillington Manor House, which today houses The Maidstone Museum, to Robert Southgate, a fruiterer by trade. Southgate was the occupier at the time, the previous tenant having been Edwin Wiat of Boxley, serjeant-at-law. It is quite likely that the Southgates were already the owners, and perhaps had been occupiers of the Boxley farm for some years prior to this. However their name does not appear on the Hearth Tax of 1664. Robert Southgate's son, also named Robert, inherited. Unfortunately he became bankrupt in 1743 when he was described as a fruiterer and cider-maker. Although in reduced circumstances, the Southgates continued ownership of the farm until Robert's death. In 1764 Edward Fowle and Mary Driver (widow of Richard Driver the builder of the Running Horse Inn) purchased the farm from William Southgate the heir of Robert Southgate. The farm was then in the tenancy of John Nichols. Prior to him its occupants had been William Alexander and Charles Alexander, who had replaced William Godden in 1720.

The Fowles had been tenants of Parsonage Farm since 1753 and probably lived there from about 1758. Edward continued to increase the family's holdings, including purchasing a half share of Boxley Abbey. By 1774 he owned most of the land lying west of The Street, stretching back to the Abbey and south to the Marley Stream, all of which 144 acres was known as 'The Great Farm'. The Fowle family owned vast tracts of the parish, encompassing Cobtree, most of the Nether Grange Estate, the Abbey lands, property in Grove Green and in Weavering and in neighbouring Aylesford. They also rented various lands such as those of The Parsonage which lay 'over-the-hill'. When Edward died in 1789 his lands were divided amongst his sons, Edward, George and William. Two years prior to his death, he made a new will in which his other sons were required to relinquish all their rights in the farm centred on Boxley village in favour of William, who by this time had made his home at The Yews. William's inheritance was dependant on allowing his father's second-wife and widow Jane to reside at The Parsonage together with her servants and family, or if she chose to move to The Yews. Jane chose The Parsonage and thereafter what we now know as Street Farm began to fully evolve.

Outliving his brothers, William, whose 'strangeness' was later to be immortalised following his interment beneath his mill, inherited virtually all of the lands. Very much 'his own man', it was he who removed the original White Horse Stone and destroyed other megaliths. His bastard son William Pattenden took the Fowle name on his inheritance in 1815. He became a pillar of the community, frequently a church warden, and surveyor of the highways for Boxley Street Quarter, with a seat on the vestry committee. His work for the parish ceased abruptly in 1836 following a row with the vicar Reverend Griffith over William's refusal to make available any land in the village centre for the construction of a new school. At his death three years later, he too insisted on being buried under the mill. His will contained a full inventory of all his possessions, both in the house and the farm. The house contents included items in the dairy and a large quantity of beer and brewing equipment in the cellar. It is possible that this equipment was transferred to the Great Barn, becoming Boxley Abbey Brewery. In the outbuildings were 2 wagons, 7 dung carts, a millers cart, a light spring cart, a gig, a hutch (cart for carrying ore), 2 bavin tugs, 4 ploughs and 5 harrows. Livestock included 111 ewes in lamb, 24 fat sheep, 101 tegs (two year old sheep), and 2 rams. He left all his property to his brother-in-law, William Sharp Avery, in trust until his 4 children attained their majority. At the death of his eldest son William Fowle in 1865, the Fowle dynasty in Boxley came to an end when Robert Fowle sold the majority of the estate to Major Best.

The Farmhouse to Street Farm is today known as Yew Trees House and is a separate residence. Previously it has borne the names Yew Trees Hall and The Yews, whilst the Fowles dubbed the farm and house, The Homestead. The oldest part of the house is the rear, north-west section which was possibly built as early as the 15th Century, abutting the old road which ran west of it. Originally a half-timbered yeoman's cottage, it was converted into a substantial residence by the construction of a new wing in the Tudor or Stuart period. Unusually, much of the original building material is still evident, such as 15 inch wide floorboards bearing adze marks, and a 'wattle and daub' internal lining. Around the beginning of Queen Anne's reign the open sides of the 'L' shape were closed in, and a new facade added. The new portion included a kitchen with a huge inglenook, and an attached dairy with an internal wall. Probably at the same time, the exceptionally large sash windows with their narrow glazing bars and shutter surrounds, were added. They are considered prime Items of Architectural Interest. Moulded glass medicine bottles have been found placed beneath the threshold of an original outer doorway in the earliest building. They are known as 'witches bottles', put there to prevent the entry of the unholy. However, it is in the garden that one finds one of its main delights, a pair of late 17th Century 'bee boles'. These are recesses in the garden wall, in this case with rounded arches, in which bee skeps were set. Unusually, these were tiled at the top with peg-tiles in order to keep the straw skeps dry. A possibly 18th Century octagonal framed summerhouse with thatched roof also stands in the 2/3 acre walled garden.

Once in the possession of the Bests, both Street Farm and Yew Trees House were occupied by tenant farmers. Firstly James and then Robert Fauchon, farmed the 250 acres, after which the house became divorced from the farm. Hubert Foster, then others of his family resided at the house whilst James Clifford ran Street Farm through his resident bailiffs, Alf Costen and then Fred Sage. Clifford had been the Best's tenant at Abbey Gate Farm since 1891, and he combined the two farms, eventually purchasing the now 313 acre farm in 1920.

Mr Ronald Howard, who bought Yew Trees House in 1970, has provided a wealth of information on the interior of the house, and relates that his predecessor, on purchasing the house in 1957, altered the name from The Yews. At the time it was popular amongst the 'In Crowd' of Society, to divide the population into 'The U's', and 'Non-U's, dependant on social acceptability. 'U' – being Upper Class. The house name thus acquired a derogatory connotation, which necessitated the change.

Next to Yew Trees House stands The Malt House. Built in the mid 18th Century, for many years it served as such but had at times also been called The Granary. It was owned and probably built by the Fowles, who ran the business themselves until about 1830 when it was let to Thomas Filmer whose daughter was destined to marry the young William Fowle at the tender age of 16. Mark Atkins took over in 1844 and the Atkins family continued to run it in to this century. The furthest kiln from the road was converted into a cottage at the end of the 19th Century, whilst the rest of the building was put to a variety of uses, not least of which was a rifle range. Malthouse Cottage housed the post office for a number of years. When the beerhouse further up The Street changed hands in 1910, the new landlord decided to concentrate on his customers' alcoholic requirements, and once again new premises were required for the post office, and also a new proprietor. Mrs Ann Mannering, the wife of the recently retired school headmaster Albert, took on the role of postmistress, setting up shop in the conveniently sited little cottage. Around 1920, when Ann would have been 76, Mrs Mary Goldsmith took over, running it as a post office and stationers up to 1934. It was very small, with room for only 2 people at a time, and the proprietors would come through from the back when the bell rang.

Alongside The Malthouse is The Hermitage whose age has been the subject of some local debate. What is certain is that this is the site of The Boxley Poorhouse. In 1748, Sam Hollister, a Brewer who owned The Kings Arms, leased part of the 1 acre cherry orchard that formed most of the Inn's grounds, to the churchwardens, overseers of the poor and local luminaries. The purpose was to enable them to 'erect a house for lodging, keeping, and maintaining and employing the poor'. It is worth recording the names of the lessees as they form a roll call of the prominent people of the parish. William Alexander, wheelwright by Boxley Green, Thomas Hatch the younger, farmer of Warren Farm, Richard Clifford, blacksmith by Boxley Green and Joseph Cordwell, papermaker at Poll Mill were the overseers. The sixteen others were the local gentry:– James Best of Park House, William Champneys of Vinters and Samuel Athawes the elder of Boxley Lodge and The Parsonage. Farmers:- Samuel Athawes the younger of Newnham Court, Thomas Hatch the elder of Boarley and Tyland Farms, Edward Whitaker late of Abbey Gate Farm, Richard Bridgland of Weavering, Charles Alexander of Street Farm, John Williamson and Edward Kennard. Prominent tradesmen:– James Whatman, papermaker of Turkey Mill, Thomas Dean papermaker at Sandling Paper Mill, Nathaniel Turner tanner at Sandling, Richard Driver, saddler and landlord of The Running Horse, Edward Russell papermaker at Forstall Mill and John Crispe, butcher. The Poor House functioned from 1748-1836 and its work is dealt with in another Chapter 7. In 1836 it was put up for sale, described as 'a substantial brick building with a large garden, walled in on three sides'. It was purchased by James Roots of The Lower Grange and as a condition of sale he agreed neither to convert the present building into cottages nor erect new ones on any portion of the ground. His son Abel Roots owned the property in 1849 when it was a house and shop. Abel had trained as a shoemaker, but by this time was also the miller at Aylesford Corn Mill, and had inherited much property. In 1890, Major Best bought 'The Hermitage with a cottage, near the workhouse buildings, nearly all pulled down'. Considering the 'condition of sale', it is not likely that any major reconstruction was entered into soon after purchase. The ordnance survey map of 1865 appears to show a slightly different shaped building than that of today, but this could indicate that the bay windows were added at a later date. It was probably built after 1850 but just possibly could incorporate part of the original structure of a century earlier. It is a beautifully proportioned building, with a fascinating cellar and interesting attic rooms. Outside are the remains of the old earth closet, apparently a two-seater, and the large garden is indeed "walled in on three sides". Of particular interest is the detached cottage in the grounds, originally a coach-house with a stable at the rear and a hay-loft and groom's quarters above. The stable is wonderfully intact, with two stalls.

Major Best set something of a precedent in having curates or other clerics as his tenants at 'The Hermitage'. Lily Best-Dalison inherited it, and around 1907 she was anxious to both provide accommodation for a new bachelor curate, Cecil Hilton, and someone to care for him. A certain Captain Saveall and his family were looking for a new home. The two needs met, and the Savealls came to 'The Hermitage' on condition that they shared with and cared for the curate. There were two sons, Hugh who worked on the Style's farms before emigrating to Canada, and Bob who was killed in the Great War. Of the two daughters, Ruth lived to see her hundredth birthday and to pass on her memories going back before 1914. She spoke of "a lovely little village, everybody so friendly".

Next door is the 'Kings Arms' public house, of which more in a separate chapter. The southern end was for some years a shop and for a while the village post office. Post offices were very important and well used in those earlier years, and locations varied around the parish. For example, on the Sandling side of the parish there was once one at the old St Andrew's Chapel near the Abbey, and for much longer one was at the timber frame building near Gibraltar Lane. During his long incumbency the Rev. Hale was a frequent and popular customer in the pub. Perhaps the best known resident was the

BOXLEY VILLAGE

Guests gathering on Boxley Green for a wedding, circa 1910.

Boxley Vicarage pre 1914. The attic windows and the wing to the left have since gone.

formidable Mote cricketer Ned Hickmott whose mother was licensee for many years. He was groundsman as well as player, and in 1884 was playing with Rev. Henry Trower who was senior curate at Boxley for 14 years, and who scored a packet of runs. Tom Osborn in his History of the Mote Club refers to Ned as a polished oarsman and one of the best swimmers in the South of England, and being very fond of riding to hounds. He died in 1934 and was clearly a great character.

'The King's Arms' stands on the corner of Forge Lane, which has borne that name for little more than a century. Prior to this it was always known as Boxley Green, because originally The Green stretched right across from the church up to where the original road passed, where now is Anvil Cottage. The Green was also much wider, taking in part of The Parsonage grounds and those of Boxley House. A map of 1743 shows that there were two cottages on the Boxley House side of the Green, but these did not outlast the century.

George Wallis recounted the small boys' school which was in Forge Lane. Was it since demolished, or might all or part of it be the end building on the left, now known as Anvil Cottage, which in 1849 was a pair of cottages? Opposite this cottage was the village pump, protected from the weather within a building called The Roundhouse. Water was drawn up from below by use of a large wheel. A similar well still stands at Well Cottage at Grove Green. Intriguingly, there stands today in the garden of the Kings Arms a circular structure used as a raised flower bed. On opposite sides of the rim are shaped projections that could have enclosed the supports for the wheel spindle. Was the well surround moved to The Kings Arms garden when it was no longer required? Until the water pumping station was built in 1939, the village relied entirely upon its abundance of natural springs and streams for its supply. Many houses had their own wells.

Near the well in Forge Lane stood a limekiln and limekilnhouse, which were demolished about 1870, and next to it was the forge which later gave its name to the lane. There had been a forge there since at least the 16th Century. In 1680 John Charlton leased two tenements and a smith's forge in occupation of William Miles who remained there for at least a further 25 years, before being replaced by John Goldsmith. By 1719, Richard Clifford was the blacksmith and the forge house stayed in the family until Thomas Clifford's three daughters sold it in 1847 to Lord Romney. Originally, the house stood further back on the edge of the green with the 'L' shaped forge projecting onto the green. It appears that the house was demolished in the 1830's leaving only the stable at the rear, and new cottages were built around the forge, which by 1841 was being run by George Barrow, succeeded by his son James. Thomas and Charles Taylor took over in the mid 1880's and for a time ran the post office from their cottage.

Mr Henry Mills was the Blacksmith best remembered, arriving in the village in 1916 as successor to Mr Shilling. Not long afterwards he was joined by

BOXLEY VILLAGE

The Woodman Pub. The sign above the car refers to Tea Gardens.

Shilling & Cripps Wheelwrights premises, sited below the Woodman. The sign reads 'Wheelwrights, Carpenters and Decorators'.

Mr Young, who was the Shoeing Smith. Mr Mills and his wife and daughter lived on the premises, and Mr Young and his family lived next door. The Forge had double doors which opened to reveal two sets of fires with bellows. An old set of bellows stands outside today. Mr Mills dealt with general ironwork, particularly the repair of agricultural implements, and Harvest-time was when he was at his busiest. He used to travel out to many of his customers, carrying his gear in a cart. Pulling the cart was his donkey Jenny, which he had obtained from some gypsies. The poor creature was thin and flea-infested when he first had her, but he nursed her to health. Jenny used to be tethered to a post on The Green, and very artfully the post was moved up and down so that Jenny had fresh pasture, and the grass was kept close cropped! In the winter Jenny was stabled at The Vicarage.

By 1938 Mr Mills was ailing and had to retire. He was desperate to avoid Jenny going to a slaughterhouse, and a home was found for her on a local farm. But Jenny pined for her master and died, so the vet said of a broken heart. The Vicar's wife broke the news to Mr Mills who sighed and said, "I reckon she missed her routine". When Helen Watt enquired what that might be, he said "Well, every night she had some carrots and then I gave her one or two draws on my pipe". Mr Mills died himself soon afterwards.

The cottages in Forge Lane, which following their purchase from the Fowle family formed part of the Park House Estate, were sold off by the Best-Dalisons soon after The Great War.

'The Old House' a listed building, which stands on the corner of Forge Lane and Boxley Street, was once three smaller cottages. They had evolved out of a house and wheelwright's shop which formed the northern-most section and stood originally on the Green's edge. In 1750 it was run by William Alexander, who was succeeded by John Nicholls, Robert Spencer and John Parks. Parks then leased it to John Hassell throughout the 1790's until replaced by William Merrall about 1799. Father and son of the same name plied their trade there, with Merrall the younger running a beer house there as well in 1832. In 1859 Thomas Ongley who also had the wheelwright's shop at Sandling, took over. With Thomas Oxley, master carpenter and wheelwright there towards the end of the century. At the start of this century, wagons could be seen standing outside the two enormous doors, awaiting repair at the capable hands of Isaac Cripps. Mrs Cripps was Nanny to the Styles children over at Boxley House. As properties began to encroach upon the Green, the wheelwright's house was extended, becoming a row of three cottages. Close scrutiny of the 18th Century facade reveals the original doorways, and it bears a Sun Fire Insurance Mark. Insurance companies had set up their own fire brigades, the Sun Fire Office being one of the first, in 1710. The metal badge, bearing the company's trade mark served both as an advertisement and as identification for the primitive fire engines. Many stories are recounted of fire brigades fighting the fire in a building whose owner had paid the premium, and then standing watching whilst neighbouring properties burned to the ground! It is believed that the cottage on the corner was being run as a shop by Richard Clifford junior in 1835, and it bore the name of Clifford's Cottage for many years. After the Great War, this cottage was known as The Nurses Cottage, and indeed Parish Nurse Evelyn Trousdell lived there for a while, as presumably had her predecessors. From the late 1930's Wally Gosling and his family made it their home.

Close by to the north was the tin building known as Boxley Institute. Provided by the Best-Dalisons, it served many village uses for both young and old, from The Mothers Union to The Girl Guides. Old maps also refer to it as The Reading Room, and latterly it became a lending library, before being demolished some time ago. It stood on the site of another village pound.

Still standing, and today named 'Woodmans' is the building which functioned for some years as The Woodman public house. It is uncertain quite when it was built, but its somewhat austere red-brick facade is constructed in the style known as Flemish Bond which became most popular in the 18th Century. The first reference to it we have found, is on the Fowle's Estate Map of 1837, where it is shown as 'The National School'. The 1841 census has it occupied by Mary Stedman, schoolmistress and the 1844 tithe map clearly depicts it as a school and playground. We believe that after 1834, when Lord Romney withdrew from discussions concerning the construction of a new school, funds were obtained from 'The National Society' and this building was rented from William Fowle and served as the school until 1846. It was already old at that time, as a letter of 1845 speaks of the fact that it was in bad need of internal repair. By 1850 it was in the hands of George Baker, who lived up to his name and was indeed a baker. However, the merry cries of children were replaced by those of their merry elders, because George also turned the premises into a beerhouse called Woodman's House. The parish records show that a William Hickmott was running a beerhouse in the village between late 1846 and 1848. It is quite likely that he was related to the John Hickmott who took over The King's Arms in 1854, and William may well have taken over the old school premises when they became vacant . George Baker continued to run the premises as a beerhouse and shop into the 1870's, but by 1879 he had been replaced by James May. James and his sister Harriet continued the beerhouse but turned the shop into a grocers and by the 1890's it had also become the village post office. Between 1903 and 1908, the building continued to perform all 3 functions under the occupancy of Mrs Maria Giles, and thereafter Thomas Pearce into the 1920's.

At the beginning of the 1930's The Woodman finally came of age as a fully fledged public house with the arrival of its best remembered proprietor. William Day was believed to have a show-business background, reminding some people of Danny Kaye. He would hit out tunes on the piano and provided a lot of fun and laughter. Rumour has it that the licensing hours were something of a moveable feast, and those in the know would creep in by the backdoor via Wally Gosling's back garden. From the beginning of the century up to the start of the Second World War, residents of Maidstone enjoyed a walk to Boxley, and there was welcome refreshment provided at the Kings Arms and the Woodman. Each also offered teas in their gardens, and Woodman sausage suppers were popular. Parties of cyclists would descend, and a relative of Mr Day's recalls the daunting sight of dirty plates piled up high awaiting washing-up. Other visitors might enjoy a picnic in the parkland around Boxley House, perhaps watching the local cricket team. The increase in mechanised transport prompted by the war, coupled with the Woodman's lack of parking facilities and the onset of other popular entertainment, led to a slow decline in custom. In the late 1940's Percival Sadler took over for a few years, before the pub finally closed and was converted to a private residence.

In 1865 Major Best decided to buy the Fowle Estate from Robert Fowle. Lord Romney requested that he be allowed to purchase all the land and property northwards of Forge Lane, in order to prevent further housebuilding, and thus safeguard the peace and privacy of Boxley House. Major Best wanted part of the land to provide gardens for the beerhouse and the cottages on Forge Lane, but agreed that Romney could purchase the land north of the beerhouse with the ten cottages that stood thereon. Today there is a growing number of post-war houses above Woodmans, but in 1750 there were just 3 cottages owned by John Shornden, who sold them to Joseph Cordwell, the papermaker at Poll Mill. When his daughter Frances Bennett sold them to George Fowle in 1791, their number had grown to five. A deed of 1832 states that only two of these then remained, in the occupation of a Mrs Pilvin and John Wallis. He was the cordwainer (shoemaker and leather worker), father of George Ephraim Wallis and veteran of The Peninsular War in Spain where he fought against the might of Napoleon's armies at the battles of Vittoria and The Pyrenees. It is probable that Wallis's cottage was the 'Hillside Cottage' that stands there today. The deed also mentions that 5 cottages had been erected opposite these earlier cottages on part of the same plot, which itself formed a part of Green Field. By 1865 this row had become 8 cottages, which ran at right angles to the present main street, joining it to the site of the old road which lead over the hill. By 1880 these had become known as 'Boxley Barracks' or 'Barracks Row', perhaps from their barrack-like appearance. Certainly, census records appear to show that their occupants have always been employees of The Boxley House Estate, with the only uniformed residents being various village policemen. Over the years, adjoining walls were knocked down to increase the size of dwellings until the 8 cottages became the 4 they are today, named 'Greenfield Cottages' after the field in which they stood.

In 1932, Robert Styles sold the triangular plot between the old and present roads and The Pilgrim's Way to the Maidstone Waterworks Company. They bored a shaft 245 feet deep, sunk through the middle and lower chalk into the

Gault Clay, to tap the natural reservoirs, and built the pumping station in 1939. By 1943 it was reported that some 3828 feet of adits of approximately 6 feet in width, had been driven into the base of the lower chalk, and water was being extracted at a rate of up to 66000 gallons an hour. The company also bought land for what were called 'The Enginemen's Cottages'. close by to the north. It was part of the contract that a free supply of water was to be supplied to Boxley House and the estate cottages, and also to Harp Farm and Upper Grange Farm, over the hill. This was a fair deal, as time was to tell that The Company's water extraction was to severely diminish the flow of natural water to village wells, and that of the springs which fed the Boxley streams. When the building work was finished, Wally Gosling gladly seized the chance of earning a bob-or-two, through grassing the surrounds.

Along the preserved section of the old road, that borders the waterworks to the east, are the pretty Styles and Hatchets Cottages, once known as Boxley House Cottages. It would appear that these ancient dwellings were contemporary with the original Boxley House, having been built in the late 16th Century, although the addition to the north is 20th Century. They are timber-framed, refaced with red brick at ground level, and tile above, retaining the overhang of the first floor on a bressumer beam. Built specifically as the homes of Estate retainers, they served that purpose down the centuries until the estate was sold in 1890. However, John Parks, the builder, who was also The Parish Clerk, lived there in the 1850's. Like so many terraced cottages, the three have been knocked through to improve the accommodation.

Venturing east along the Pilgrim's Way are just two dwellings within the compass of the village. Perched up high on the north side is The Summerhouse which has a fascinating history. Its origins might go back to the 1100's as a Hunter's Lodge, but more certainly most of what you see today was built in Georgian times by the second Lord Romney (then owner of the Boxley House Estate) as a summerhouse. Under the ownership of Robert Style it became a Gamekeeper's Lodge, and home to his keeper Jesse Hodge, who had three daughters. Two of these, Elsie and Rose, went into service at Boxley House. Jesse was succeeded by Tom Hill. In recent times the Summerhouse has become a private dwelling and been extended and improved. Its views are spectacular.

A little further along on the right is the huddle of buildings that is Warren Farm. Originally part of the Wyatt estates, it was probably the '48 acre farm held through indenture by Nicholas Coveney', in 1554, and has formed part of the Boxley House Estate for centuries. Occupied by a long succession of tenant farmers, estate workers (such as Lord Romney's coachman in the 1800's), and latterly farm bailiffs. In the mid 18th Century it was one of a group of farms run by Thomas Hatch and his family. When he emigrated in 1852, Robert Lucas relinquished the tenancy to William Bridgland who was to stay for some 30 years. When Albert Style bought it from Lord Aylesford in 1884, it was occupied by Thomas Barney, erstwhile landlord of the Bull Inn, and had 91 acres, nestling beneath the Downs. They stretched on both sides of the lane from today's Boxley Hill almost to Detling. At that time its farmhouse, which dates from the 16th Century, was surrounded by a stable, cow lodge, well house, cart lodge, chicken house and pig sty. It obviously takes its name from the old rabbit warren close by, and at one time the tenants were obliged to supply the church with a number of rabbits annually.

Returning now to the top of the village street, next to Styles cottage is the 4th Boxley House Cottage, known as Gardeners Cottage and then Boxley House itself, the subject of a separate chapter. The comings and goings and doings of the family and all the servants and Estate workers added to the colour and vibrancy of the village for many years. Thanks to the Styles family, the village cricket team could play in the grounds for forty years or more. Wally Gosling tended the pitch as lovingly as he tended the graveyard. The church has a chapter of its own to tell its story.

Close by the church is Court Lodge Farm, run from around the mid 1850's by several generations of the Foster family. Between the Wars it was Harry Foster and then his son Dick Foster who ran a real mixed farm of fruit, cereals and livestock. A number of men were employed, and it was horses then not tractors. Uncle Hugh Foster lived at The Yews, Maud Foster farmed at Lower Grange Farm. Then there was Dick's sister Biddy, who helped run the Sunday School. Dick Foster was churchwarden for many years, and as well as farming he carried on the profession of an Auctioneer, especially at livestock sales. Opinion was that he could sell sand to the Arabs. He was also an extremely fine club cricketer for the Mote, inspired perhaps in his youth by Ned Hickmott from the Kings Arms? Several shrewd judges thought Dick a good enough bowler for the Kent side. Doubtless from his Church-Warden's pew in church, he would consider the length of the aisle and wonder if it might take spin! Dick's son Mike Foster has also been a stalwart cricketer for The Mote.

Court Lodge Farmhouse is a fascinating building. Its hung tiles give it a Victorian appearance, but these are a later addition. The oldest part, that is parallel to the Street, dates from the mid 1500's, whilst the recessed range to the right is late 1500's. Additions were made in the 1600's and again in the 1800's, when its timberframe was also disguised with cladding. Its inglenook fireplaces testify to its age, and there is a particularly grand fireplace that adds to its claims to be the house of Henry VIII's surgeon, Thomas Vicary. See Chapter 27.

Although there may be doubt as to whether the premises of Court Lodge were Vicary's house, the lands which formed its farm were assuredly all part of Vicary's lands, some fields still carrying the same names today which they have done for at least 450 years. A map of 1743, bears the earliest denomination of it as Court Lodge Farm that we have found, at which time its 177½ acres belonged to Leonard Bartholomew. His ancestor Philip Bartholomew had inherited the property in 1672 from the Clarke family, who had been granted it following Wyatt's attainder. On Leonard's death in 1757 it passed to his brother-in-law Captain Francis Geary. In 1832 James Best bought it from William Geary, when it was in the tenancy of George Hills. The Bests were able to prove that originally Court Lodge Farm belonged to Boxley Abbey, and thus they were exempt from paying tithes. A deed of 1669 provides the name of its earliest known occupant, Robert Payne. It states that John Clarke had mortgaged the premises with 140 acres, where Robert Payne had dwelt, now in the tenure of Walter Viney. By 1750 the tenant was James Goldsmith, and by 1791 Anthony Whitting. In 1786, Anthony's son Thomas was apprenticed to Robert Harris, who together with William Charles ran the 'felt factory' at Sandling Mill. The 1844 tithe map shows it in occupation of George Ware, who was still there in 1851. Then came the Foster dynasty, starting with Charles in about 1853, who was to farm there as Major Best's bailiff into this century, before handing over to Harry Foster.

Adjoining Court Lodge is an even older property, also vying for the right to be known as Vicary's House, perhaps with the more credence. Parsonage Farm lies secluded behind the high walls on the east side of The Street, which screen it from the constant flow of traffic. It is the third oldest building in all of Boxley, surpassed in venerability only by the church, and perhaps St Andrew's Chapel. Well hidden behind a mixed facade is a Wealden Hall House, which possibly in turn clothes a timberframed building constructed on a galletted flint plinth as early as the 14th Century. Additions were made in the 16th and 18th Centuries. Internally the house is a gem, with flagstone floors, massive beams, and an inglenook fireplace. The tell-tale soot marks on the roof timbers are still there today. They remind us of the original open central hearth, with smoke rising up to filter out through the roof, in the days, before chimneys and first floors were added. However, it is the other half of the L-shaped building, angling westward towards The Street, that is the real enigma. It has defied architects, historians and other experts as to its exact age and evolution. Clearly built in two stages, its ecclesiastical style windows tell of an original purpose far grander than the agricultural uses to which it was later subjected. Whilst the left or eastern section has been 'listed' as being early 14th Century, the latest research suggests a date as early as 1220. We would not argue too strongly with this. The massive stone construction bears a remarkable resemblance to early 13th Century Manor Houses such as Boothby Pagnell in Lincolnshire, the entrance being on the first floor approached by stone steps, with an undercroft beneath. The western section is 'listed' as 15th Century, based mainly on its ornate stone window of the perpendicular style.

The name 'Parsonage' suggests that it was the original vicarage, and as we shall see later, today's vicarage is at least the third to bear that title. The vicar's tithe record book from the start of the 18th Century, contains a resume of vicarage buildings, the earliest of which is 1394. Could part of The Parsonage be this building? When Henry VIII exchanged lands with Sir Thomas Wyatt, granting him almost all of Boxley, he specifically retained The Parsonage of Boxley, together with the advowson of the vicarage (the right to appoint a vicar), to the King's own usage. We believe it most likely that it was The Parsonage that Henry gave for the use of Thomas Vicary. This appears to be confirmed by 'An abstract of all leases of lands belonging to the Cathedral Church of Rochester', which contains an entry for Boxley Parsonage stating that from 1543, The Parsonage and lands were leased to Thomas Vicary for a period of 99 years. His nephew Stephen, who inherited in 1561, appears to have disposed of the lands, but retained the house. In 1608, Margaret Vicary, widow, was described as having, "a messuage, with a garden, orchard, stable, yard and, (what appears to be a 'court' lodge, but more likely 'cart' lodge) all adjoining, and a close called Barnfield, near adjoining". (Barnfield is the field into which the graveyard is now extended, behind the church). A further record refers to her 'Mansion'. Margaret died in 1614, and the records of the Dean and Chapter of Rochester show that by 1624 The Parsonage, having reverted to their possession, was being let out to one Robert Parker, who remained the tenant until 1675, when the splendidly named Ionadab Ballam moved in for 15 years. A dynasty of Hammonds (Thomas, Elizabeth and Leonard) then held it through the next 56 years. It would appear that they never resided there themselves, as Samuel Atthawe's will of 1758 contains the statement that he had occupied The Parsonage for 48 years, and had succeeded his father there. Thus Samuel was the occupier when the Fowle family began their lease, with John Fowle, in 1753, followed by Edward in 1767. When Edward died, the remainder of the lease passed to the 'odd' William Fowle. Soon after, in 1800, Lord Romney took on the lease, subsequently sub-letting the house to his 3 spinster sisters, the Misses Marsham, whilst Richard Clifford farmed the land. Romney was incensed at the poor state of repair in which the Fowles had left the property. Repairs were said to be needed to the barns, stables, dove house, granary, and also to the chancel of the church. The tenant of The Parsonage was also responsible for the upkeep of the chancel, which was said to need retiling, the plaster to be washed and whitened, and stone buttresses and pews repaired. William denied responsibility, having never personally signed a lease, and Romney went so far as to obtain warrants for his arrest posted in more than one county. Lord Romney appears to have kept control of The Parsonage hereafter, as part of Boxley House Estate, although the names on the leases were various sets of business partners such as John Coker (the estate manager) and Samuel Gambier.

Parsonage Farm was originally known as Church Farm, and its 50 odd acres, mainly detached on the hill, included a 7 acre Coney Ground, out of which 24 rabbits were payable twice yearly as part of the rent. Terriers (complete registers of property) exist for 1637 and 1647 providing full details of the house, but that of 1698 is the most detailed. 'A messuage containing one large kitchin (sic), one washhouse or brewhouse, one buttery, one parlour, one closet with two cellars, one launder house, seven lodging rooms with seven garrets, two large barns (tyled), one large stable (thatched), wagon lodge (tyled), one dovehouse (tyled) well stocked with pigeons, two orchards and a garden'. Whilst in the tenure of the Fowles, the older stone wing was converted for use as a malthouse, a function it performed for some half a century. George Wallis's memoirs in our Victorian chapter speaks of Mr Fowle's "stone house directly opposite the present malthouse (in The Street), and nearly close to The Green". We can now the better picture those drunks of the Detling Band, lying helpless on the lawn! When Lord Romney wanted to build a new school in 1834, he applied to The Dean and Chapter to be allowed to pull down the Malthouse (i.e. the ancient stone wing), because it was dilapidated, and to utilise the materials for the school! Thankfully, permission was refused. A title deed map of 1860 still records it as the malthouse.

According to Cave-Browne, the Rev. Richards (the incumbent from 1853) purchased the Farmhouse from the ecclesiastical commissioners (probably about 1867), and converted it into 'two comfortable cottages', known initially as 'The Vicars Cottages'. When the historian E.R. Hughes visited them in 1902, the occupier of the stone wing informed him that this building was 'The Pilgrims Rest', whilst the Wealden hall was 'The Old Rectory'. The Pilgrims Rest had then just one large room with another above 'with just the appearance of a dormitory', which led Hughes to wonder whether it had once been a school. His accompanying sketches show lovely Tudor chimneys. The Old Rectory had evolved over the years, with each era leaving its architectural legacy, such as the lovely panelled study added in the Georgian period. No longer a farm, the redundant agricultural buildings were gradually pulled down. Two large barns originally fronted The Street, and a barn and stable backed on to The Green. An examination of the garden wall abutting The Street reveals evidence of doorways to these old buildings.

The once grand 'Mansion', now became the homes of gardeners and agricultural labourers. Wally Gosling appears again, because he came to live in one of 'The Vicarage Cottages' in 1907. 'Watercress Cottage', within the grounds, had been converted in the 18th Century from the large stable block. Medieval stone was re-used, with the first floor being of chalk lump, resurfaced with ashlar. The wall adjoining the cottage, and now enclosing the north east corner of the garden, is listed as medieval, constructed of galleted chalk lump with a band of flint.

After The Reverend Hale left in 1935, it seems that the new incumbent sold the premises into private hands, using the proceeds to refurbish the vicarage. The tenants had to move out, Wally Gosling went to live in one of the cottages that now comprise 'The Old House'. The new owner then put the main building back into one dwelling, as it remains today. The present owners, who are passionate in their love for the house and its history, continue to make interesting discoveries as they nurture its ancient stones. Perhaps the most exciting was when a small hole in a toilet floor led them to open it up and reveal a very deep well, with the clearest water within. Originally this well had been outside in the yard, but a later addition, probably in the 18th Century, brought it inside. The gardens still contain the two large ponds which for centuries have been fed by a number of springs, their level fluctuating with the rainfall. Other parts of the grounds have over the years been subsumed into those of the Vicarage and most of the orchard was given for construction of the school.

And was the "Pilgrim's Rest" ever used as such? The implication is that pilgrims on their way to Canterbury paused here. Because the Pilgrim's Way has become discounted as an accurate description, so the "Rest" has been scorned as a misnomer. But wait, it was Henry VIII who it is believed gave the Old Parsonage to Vicary, and it was Henry who caused Boxley Abbey to be knocked down. With all that ragstone lying around across the fields, might not some carved windows and stonework have been put to use here? Indeed, might not a whole building from the Abbey complex have been rebuilt as improvement to the Old Parsonage? The "Rest" contains some ill-assorted roof timbers which might also have come from the Abbey. Interestingly, Cave-Browne wrote of the "Rest" being a "building traditionally called the Refectory, but more probably the Old Tithe Barn".

Certainly with the demise of the Abbey, its own hospitum was converted to agricultural usage and there would have been a need for a place for pilgrims to rest and travellers to break their journey at Boxley, as they had down the ages. The 1698 inventory mentions 'seven lodging rooms with seven garrets', which could infer its use for such a purpose, but there is no documentary evidence to confirm this, whatsoever. The current owners remain unconvinced, and indeed the appellation 'Pilgrims Rest', does smack of Victorian romanticism. Make of it what you will, for it remains another puzzle of old Boxley.

Given that Park House is fully described elsewhere, we come finally to the Vicarage – now the Old Vicarage, because it has been sold into private hands. Here again, it is worth taking note of Cave-Browne who had access to the relevant records. He wrote that there was no house for the Vicar until 1394 when one was built comprising a "Hall, Chamber, Cellar, Kitchen and Stable". Cave-Browne then jumps to 1690 when there had been changes but the dwelling was still relatively modest. The great event occurred in 1704-1705, when Arch-Deacon Thomas Spratt of Rochester, pulled down all the old buildings and built a brick edifice with two wings. In 1711 and again in 1717 he acquired additional ground and made a series of canals and cascades. Successive vicars added their own touches – a barn here, a brewhouse there, bow windows and a marble chimney-piece. The wings have been demolished, but basically the Old Vicarage survives. It is a Grade II listed Queen Anne building.

The Rev. John Watt's wife Helen has left a description of the Vicarage as they found it in 1935. She ascribed the pulling down of the remaining wing to their predecessor who, it will be recalled, had funded his improvements with the sale proceeds of Parsonage Farm. A lovely Georgian curving staircase was apparently removed, together with the old fireplaces. There remained a range of stables, harness room and pig styes even. The garden, Helen Watt thought delightful, with an enormously high yew hedge which took a week to cut, superb old trees, and "Tennyson's Brook", in which grew delicious water cress.

With financial pressures upon the church, the Vicarage was sold in about 1967 and a modern substitute built close by. This prompted a more recent Vicar's daughter, Elizabeth Mortimer-Lamb, to write in the Parish magazine in memory of, "a palace standing majestically in acres of ground". She conceded that her mother probably bemoaned "a rambling mass of corridors and cobwebs galore" and that her father did not appreciate having to "haul coals for innumerable fires". But for Elizabeth – "one simply had to gaze out of the window for a moment and drink in the glorious surroundings, the church tower to the north, the centre of the village, and to the south – the brook, an orchard, flowers – the intoxicating scent of the summer jasmine and the honeysuckle, or listen to the birds singing their everlasting song. It was all so peaceful, so friendly and always such a warmth sprang from those walls".

Almost an epitaph for a lost Boxley.

Parsonage Farm, formerly known as 'The Pilgrims' Rest'.

BOXLEY PARISH

Yew Tree Farmhouse, Weavering Street.

Number 2 Boxley Cottages on the edge of the parish in Ashford Road.

CHAPTER 20

Weavering and Grove Green

The ancient hamlets of Weavering and Grove Green comprise the eastern quarter of Boxley parish. Wallenberg in his 'Place Names of Kent', suggests that the name of Weavering derives from a settlement of unstable or wandering people. Similar names in this country are normally derived from their position on a weaving or meandering stream. However, Weavering's stream, to the east of the street, runs fairly straight on its course to its rendezvous with the River Len. The stream formed the boundary between Boxley and Bearsted parish. The earliest known reference to the community was in 1189 when it was cited as 'Wavering', mainly in the possession of the Hougham family with a smaller part owned by that of the Bournes. Other documents describe it as Weverynge or Wayfering. If Boxley is named from Box or Beech trees, might Weavering's derivation be from the Wayfaring Tree, a native shrub which formerly grew in abundance locally on the chalk scrub? An infusion of its leaves and berries was used as a gargle to settle stomachs and its leaves produced a black hair dye.

No archaeological evidence of settlement prior to the Roman period is known. However, The Romans were certainly quarrying the Fullers Earth at Grove, where artefacts and coins have been unearthed. A surprising number of oyster shells appear in the area. These shellfish were highly prized by the Romans, and their presence points to a long term occupation. Both Grove Farm and nearby Well House bear anecdotal evidence of possible settlement sites, and a Roman cemetery was excavated on the Ashford Road opposite Turkey Mill. In 1274 John De Walays held 'Weveringe' in 'sergeanty' of King Edward I. This meant that in exchange for the land, he was required ...... "to attend upon the King in war – and follow his army into Wales for 40 days at his own cost, with a horse valued at 5 shillings and a sack valued at 6 pence, and a bottle". It was noted that the value of the service due to the King had been diminished by 5/- because The Abbot of Boxley refused to allow those who held Weavering (and thus their tenants) to graze animals on the common pasture of 'Pynendenne' (Penenden Heath).

A stroll up and down Weavering Street is very rewarding for its variety of ancient buildings, all of which owe their existence to agriculture, around which activity the entire area evolved. Apart from the excavation of Fullers Earth and Sand, farming provided the means of livelihood for the inhabitants for more than two thousand years, up to the 1950's. Industry did not impinge until the end of the 17th Century, when the fulling mills began to be converted for the production of paper. For more than 150 years, up to 1954, the Whatman family owned an ever increasing portion of these fertile acres. Unfortunately a disastrous fire which destroyed the title deeds to almost all of their properties has severely hampered our researches. Following painstaking detective work through every available document and rating record we have managed to reconstruct something of the story of these erstwhile rural communities, now metamorphosed into residential 'villages'.

The loss of Weavering's cultivated land had begun at the end of the 18th Century with the expansion of James Whatman's Vinters estate, and Lord Romney's park at The Mote. The construction of the new Mote House in 1795, alongside the then Ashford Road, tolled the death knell for both the road itself and a significant portion of Weavering. Romney began to agitate for the removal of the main highway, and in 1815 it was reconstructed a couple of hundred metres to the north (See Final Chapter). At this time Weavering Street was some 25% longer than it is today. Below the old houses known as Boxley Cottages, which stand today on the A20, the street zigzagged through what is now Mote Park (in true 'wavering' fashion) to its junction with the earlier Ashford Road at a point some 250 metres east of Pole Mill. This mill marked the southernmost point of Boxley parish. Opposite it on the side of the then Ashford Road, now just the narrow carriageway through Mote Park, were three cottages, and behind them a large hop garden. A further cottage with an oasthouse was in the occupation of Edward and James Oliver when Whatman exchanged the 11 acres of land with Romney in 1834. Having already purchased land left to the Overseers of the Poor of Maidstone, Romney had all the buildings levelled in order to further extend his ornamental park, and the lower end of Weavering Street reverted to grass.

Nestling in seclusion behind the walls of Mote Park, just west of the late Victorian lodge house that guards the Park entrance almost opposite Weavering Street, lies Raigersfeld House. It is a fine example of a timber-framed 15th Century hall house whose many later additions have only added to its charm. Of particular interest is the first floor latrine which projects from one end. If original, this is an almost unique survival. In 1629 John Brewer, whose family worked the Grove fulling pits, sold to John Fletcher the house together with 'a close, barn, stable, two gardens, two orchards and 34 acres of land lately in tenure of Thomas Dodd, and before that William Boorman, situated at the lower end of Weavering Street'. Having passed through the Cripps, Bix and Knight families, Brett Netter sold the farm to Lord Romney in 1714. Thomas Grimshire resided there from 1680, and in 1711 the occupant was John Swinnock the papermaker at nearby Pole Mill. Richard Bridgland and his widow farmed there from 1744 to 1792 and in 1799, when occupied by the Alman brothers, it was said to have a malthouse and $65^{1}/_{2}$ acres, which included parts of Grove. With the construction of the new Ashford Road in

1815, Romney subsumed the southern lands into Mote Park and exchanged part of the northern section with the Company of Sadlers. The then tenant George Hills junior having given up the farm, the house and garden alone were leased in 1817 to John Luke, Baron de Raigersfeld of the Holy Roman Empire, a member of the Austrian Embassy. He was confined to bed having suffered a paralytic stroke which had also resulted in his indiscriminate usage of the six different languages in which he was proficient, thus making communication difficult! For nine weeks prior to his death in 1819, his family became aware of a strange ticking from the region of the fireplace. Whilst they searched for the source, the noise would occasionally cease only to recommence shortly afterwards. His son informed the family to pay attention to the sound as he believed it was a forewarning of a death in the household. Sure enough, three days before the Baron's death, the ticking ceased altogether and was never heard again. Lord Romney gave permission for a vault to be opened in the chancel of Boxley Church. The parish poor attended the funeral and formed an avenue on each side of the walkway in the churchyard. For this they were paid one shilling per adult and sixpence per child. The Baron's son Captain Raigersfeld remained as occupier of the house. He had served as a midshipman on H.M.S. 'Victory', and was at the time a Post Captain of H.M.S. 'San Josef' (a Spanish ship captured at the Battle of St. Vincent in 1797). In 1805 Lord Romney, a family friend, had obtained for him the position of Commander of the Sea (sometimes River) Fencibles based at Maidstone. This was a body of bargees and other river workers raised to prevent an invasion by the French up the Medway. (A form of early 'Dads Army'). He remained in command throughout the existence of that force until peace brought about its disbandment in 1810. Presumably he was the inspiration for the fictional Hornblower's father who was said to have commanded The Fencibles and supposedly to have lived at the more glamorous Boxley House. Raigersfeld was created Rear Admiral seven years prior to his death at the house in 1844. His daughter Harriet married Charles Whatman, youngest son of James Whatman of Vinters. Thomas Tassell, whose company dismantled the old toll house at Allington Lock in 1833 and built the elegant lockkeeper's house which graces it today, was the next tenant before Lord Dudley North took up residence in 1851. In 1862 Colonel Meyer became the first of a succession of officers from the Maidstone Barracks to make the house their home.

Adjoining Raigersfeld House to the east, stood the former Fox and Goose Inn that Edward Hills left to The Sadlers Company, as described in 'Places of Refreshment'. When the Sadlers exchanged lands with Romney in 1818 they gave him the cottage and 5 acres of land. They received 4 pieces of land on the opposite side of the new Ashford Road totalling $9^1/_2$ acres and tenanted by Thomas Shrubsole. It would appear that Romney lost no time in demolishing the historic cottage. Half of the lands received by The Sadlers had come from Raigersfeld farmlands, and the other half from a farm based on the large ancient farmhouse that still stands today on the Ashford Road, immediately prior to the Weavering Street junction, and known as 'No. 1 Boxley Cottages'. In 1600 this was the home of Nicholas Stonehouse who had obtained it from John Burbage. In 1655 it was purchased by Thomas Usborne, whose heirs sold it to Lord Romney in 1705. Stephen Gosling was the occupant in 1680 followed by his son William, until Edward Kennard took the tenancy in 1735. By then the farm had a barn, oasthouse, outhouse, 2 orchards and 23 acres. Part of the 'Raigersfeld' farm lands were added and thus it had 57½ acres when in 1834, then in tenure of Stephen Stonham, it was purchased by James Whatman. Included in the sale was what is now 'No. 2 Boxley Cottages', then known as 'Mrs Parks Cottage', after its occupant. A laundress, Mrs Parks plied her trade there from around 1830 into the 1850's. Probably a very early conversion of a barn, it was perhaps the pair of cottages occupied in 1799 by Moses Bridgland and James Barrow. The eastern end may once have been a tack room. Jessie Killick became tenant of the farm in 1846, running the lands together with those of Vintners Farm, and the farmhouse reverted to residential use. An enormous washing machine was installed, occupying one whole room at 'No. 1', which became the laundry for the entire Whatman Estate. Various laundresses and a laundryman William Laurence resided at the premises up to about 1891, when the Pound and Hepton families occupied both cottages, remaining there up to the Second World War and beyond.

The row of 8 cottages lining the Ashford Road at the Weavering Street junction were probably constructed by William Charles junior in 1832, when he succeeded to the estate of his father. William Charles and his father-in-law William Arnold, both apothecaries in Maidstone, had purchased 'a tenement in Weavering Street divided into 2 dwellings occupied by William Clemmons and Thomas Fuller, with an oasthouse, 2 gardens and 5 acres of land' from Thomas Randall in 1769. Earlier in 1679 Stephen Gosling had obtained it from Mary Sedwicke and it remained in his family for 70 years. This land was on the east side of Weavering Street extending across today's Ashford Road. The attractively converted oasthouse that stands today by Orchard Drive is probably that mentioned in the 1769 deed, although the roundels were added later. The 'tenement .... in 2 dwellings' together with a further house were demolished in 1883 to make way for the Maidstone/Ashford railway. About this time a row of 3 cottages were constructed below the oasts. The Charles family bought more of the adjacent land on most of which they cultivated hops. In 1815 they increased their holdings further when they purchased a farmhouse and 8 acres from Romney, which had previously belonged to The Overseers of the Poor of Maidstone. Romney had purchased it in 1803 so that he could add a detached field called Weavering Well to his Mote Park Estate. This bordered the stream just east of today's refreshment kiosk. The Overseers appear to have been left the property around 1625 by the heirs of James Field. In 1800, valued at £720, it was described as having a small home and one other building on 11 acres of land. The rent was a donation made in bread to the poor. Successive Abraham and Thomas Bakers tenanted the farm for almost 150 years prior to 1815. Thus it was known as 'Bakers Farm', but today 'Weavering Grange' occupies the site. Probably constructed or enlarged by William Charles junior, today's building appears to be similar to that marked on the Tithe Map of 1844. At that time it was occupied by Stephen Lepine, the Charles' farm bailiff, his wife and 7 children. By the end of the 19th Century it had become a house suitable for gentry. Morris Ruck resided there during the first quarter of this century, followed by Walter Usmar. Although resident at Chillington Manor, now Maidstone Museum, from where they ran their felting and blanket business, the Charles family so adored their country retreat at Weavering Grange, that successive members of the family chose to take their eternal rest in the family vault in Boxley churchyard.

Walnut Tree Farm is the only property in Weavering that has managed to retain its title deeds. The farmhouse itself is 'listed' as being built towards the end of the 16th Century, but it can claim a deed as early as 1540 at which time Thomas Roger paid a quit rent to William and John Salmon, for a tenement and 4 acres. Further deeds appear to show it passing through the hands of the Cutt and Austen families, before John Dadson sold it to Robert Salmon in 1627. In 1632 John Baker sold Salmon a $3^{1}/_{2}$ acre piece of land called Longham which adjoined the farm to the west. From then on the farm remained in the Salmon family for the next 200 years. Throughout this time $7^{1}/_{2}$ acres were farmed by tenant farmers. Notable amongst them were William Dunning, there for 29 years from 1758, and William Stanford 1796-1823. Under Stanford the house was divided into two dwellings. Around 1824 the adjoining hop-kilns were added. About 1860 James Stephens purchased it, farming there to 1881 when he was replaced by Edward Bodiam. By 1886 it was the property of William Taylor and tenanted by Charles White growing mainly hops.

Vintners Way is built upon part of the farm belonging to The Worshipful Company of Vintners. When Stephen Mason, a wealthy vintner (wine merchant), died in 1560 he left to his wife and thereafter to the Vintners Company – his "mansion with a yard, stable, garden, orchard and a number of pieces of pasture and land, with a horse mill, kyle, malthouse and barns to the south and a farmhouse adjoining the mansion on the north side, in tenure of John Allen".

The house dated from the early 15th Century and may well have been known as Weavering Manor, as it is today. Only a portion of the original extensive building remains, with alterations having been made around 1620 to make it suitable for use as a farmhouse. Parts including a chapel are no longer there, although some stained glass windows remain. A succession of tenant farmers worked the 60 acres. John Burford 1694-1741, then Thomas Burwash, Thomas Allman, Richard Orum, George Luck and N.J. Luck and Golding.

William Bonny's reminiscences contain a story of a Weavering Street occupant called Golding who purchased a ton of coal from a barge at the coal wharf in Maidstone. With transport unavailable he made the journey twice daily with a wheelbarrow returning each time with a hundredweight of coal. It took him 10 days to fetch it home during which he had trundled his barrow around 120 miles! In 1833 Anthony Killick took over the farm followed by his son Jesse. Jesse took on the tenancies of other neighbouring farms, swelling his holdings by 1863. Then they included 12 cottages, and provided employment for 15 men. His son Austin T. Killick increased the acreage further to 130 by 1881, but by 1891 he had retired although aged only 46, retaining the farmhouse and 5½ acres.

Above Weavering Manor is an equally beautiful and historic dwelling - Yew Tree Farm House. A late 15th Century hall house it was described in 1954, when sold as part of The Whatman Estate, as of brick, half-timbered with 2 sitting rooms, scullery, washroom, 5 bedrooms and an outside privy, in occupation of J. Simmons. In the mid 17th Century it was the home of William Godfrey who also farmed at Newnham Court. He died in 1691 a very wealthy man with assets of £1,112. The house contained a hall, kitchen, great parlour, little parlour, buttery, brewhouse, drinkhouse, best (bed) chamber, three further chambers, a milkhouse chamber containing 4 beds, and a barn or granary with extensive stock. In 1696 it was leased to John Bills together with a barn, stable, garden, apple orchard and 24 acres of land. He and his widow occupied it for 27 years. All the farmland was detached from the house, most of it, including Crossway Field lay between Grove Green and the fields bordering the west side of Weavering Street, with other isolated fields lying to the south. In 1739 James Castreet of Grove Green purchased the farm and on his own death he willed it to his maid servant Sarah Andrews for the term of her life, and thence to his cousin James Whatman. Sarah married a Richard Bridgland and together they farmed the lands until her death in 1789. Then becoming part of the Whatman Estate it was tenanted by George and Bridgland Allman until Thomas Osmer took over in 1825, by when it had shrunk to just 13 acres of orchard and a 1½ acre vineyard. William and then John Osmer followed, gradually taking on more land, so that when John relinquished the tenancy to George Parker in 1894 there were 33½ acres. Today the house is split into two cottages, and has been so since at least 1833 when William Goldsmith a carpenter tenanted the smaller cottage. His son William was still there in 1863. In 1891 it was the residence of Francis Eden, an optician.

Between Yew Tree Farm and The Fox and Goose Pub a pair of cottages belonging to The Vintners Company had been constructed by 1844 where previously had stood farm buildings. The pub has been fully described in 'Places of Refreshment'.

The story of Stone House has been particularly difficult to unravel. One of the oldest properties in Weavering, it was partly constructed in the mid 15th Century with 16th Century and later additions. The floor in the entrance hall is of Tudor brick set in silver sand, and it has a crown post indicating an original open hall. Its age and obvious status suggests that this was the original farmhouse for the surrounding lands. The property of The Allen family in the early 17th Century, they sold it in 1738 to James Cripps together with a barn, stable, orchard and 18 acres of pasture and meadow. Richard Driver, landlord of The Running Horse Inn, purchased the farm 6 years later displacing the tenant of some 20 years, John Peckham. Robert Pope replaced Dancy Sawkins in 1772 and his family retained possession until Charles Mares, a solicitor, moved there in 1826. At some point James Whatham had become the owner. Before long he had exchanged much of the land with The Fishers Charity, but retained Stone House with a barn, stable, yard and 7½ acres. In 1846 he made a further exchange giving The Charity everything except for the house. It was probably Mares who constructed the building known as Park Farm on the land north east of the old farmhouse, and Stone House was divided into 2 dwellings, becoming the residence of farm workers. The present owner Lyn Simpson, whose reminiscences of Grove Green are quoted further on, can trace her family's occupancy of Stone House back more than 150 years. Her great great grandfather Samuel Winchester occupied the eastern half in 1841, and her grandfather Charles Upton, a freeman of the Borough of Maidstone, purchased the entire property in 1954 together with almost 4 acres including the land alongside described as a 'drying ground'. The 1844 tithe map shows that this piece of land was occupied by John Fuller the then proprietor of The Fox and Goose, and an oasthouse stood upon it. It was probably this oast which was later converted into a dairy and used as such by The Chittenden family. They occupied the other half of the house from about 1880 and later farmed at both Park Farm and Yew tree Farm. James Betts took over the tenancy of Park Farm in 1847, planting two thirds of his 15½ acres with hops and the remainder with cherries. The Victorian oasthouses to the farm were used as a livery stable in the 1960's. Stone House possibly takes its name from The Stonehouse family who owned extensive lands in Weavering in the 16th Century.

Wents Wood occupied the corner on the west side of Weavering Street where it joined the Bearsted Road. Tucked against it to the south was Prospect Cottage, now surrounded by housing rather than chestnut trees. In 1825 Josiah Wise Dawes took over the tenancy from John Joy and set up a garden nursery. About 1858 Thomas Bridgland replaced him, and by 1871 he was farming a total of 40 acres including those of Park Farm. William Bridgland and then William Dennis were followed by Daniel Coveney who farmed just 9 acres there in the 1920's and 1930's. As a part of the Whatman Estate it was sold with 3 acres in 1954.

Up until the 20th Century, the west side of Weavering Street between

Prospect Cottage and Boxley Cottages on the Ashford Road, had only 2 dwellings throughout its entire length, other than the buildings of Walnut Tree Farm. Across the road from Stone House was a cottage that in Lyn Simpson's grandfather's time sported a small shop selling sweets. It was owned by The Charles family in 1841 and occupied by John Wood, a gardener, but had been pulled down by 1931. The other cottage stood just above Walnut Tree Farm, almost opposite Weavering Manor. Owned by The Vintners Company, it was occupied through the 1840's and 1850's by William Britter a carpenter.

Turning into Bearsted Road at the cross-roads, or The Four Wents as it was known, 'Popes Wood' spread north to the Boxley boundary. Named after the family of Thomas Blisset Pope, who owned it up to 1838 when Whatman purchased it, it was originally known as 'Crow Pack Wood'. 'Gidds Hill Cottages', south of the road were built around 1892 on the site of an old uninhabited house. Beyond them, 'Sevenoaks' was built in 1833 by William Baker on land he had enclosed. He sold it to the Whatmans the following year but continued to reside there. Thereafter it was occupied by a succession of gamekeepers. The cricket field and pavilion stood alongside and behind it in the 1960's. Much of the land north of the Bearsted Road was known as Bartnolls and its ownership can be traced back to John Trindale in 1600. The first residential development in Weavering, built in the mid 1950's, was centred on the ancient trackway that had connected Grove Green to Weavering Street and which is known as Grove Green Road. The surrounding land formed part of a 22 acre farm which belonged to the Godfreys in the 17th Century. Successive Thomas Althawes farmed it from 1693 through to 1783 when the Crispe family took possession. In 1796 Richard Fowle, husband of Mary Crispe, advertised for sale by auction a farmhouse, barn, stable, oasthouse, lodge and other outbuildings which were purchased by The Vintners Company.

The area known as Gidds or Giggs was centred on a pond which lay to the north of the Bearsted Road. Much of it was owned by Stephen Mason the vintner in the late 16th Century. In 1629 John Cohlman had 'a cottage at Ghids Pond at leave of ye lord'. At his death in 1671, Alexander Fisher, the youngest son of two times Major of Maidstone, Walter Fisher (the owner of a vast acreage within Boxley), made a bequest to the poor of Maidstone. He gave to the Overseers of the Poor several houses and more than 33 acres, mostly in Boxley. Nine acres were in Sandling and at least 13 acres in Weavering. Ten of these were on the south side of the road at Gidds Pond, and became known as 'Fishers Gift'. The rents were to be used to pay the apprenticeship costs of 3 poor boys and to provide an annual sum to 4 indigent widows. In 1694 William Tuppeny replaced William Athawes senior as tenant of the 10 acres at Gidds. His son John remained there until 1758. Thereafter the tenancy was combined with that of the Charity's lands at Park Farm. In 1825 Matthew Clements took over 5½ acres from Thomas Pope together with a property known as Gidds House. He built a malthouse alongside which he worked until

1848. The house, divided into 2 dwellings, remained as accommodation for agricultural workers throughout the second half of the century. In 1846, part of the Charity's lands became the property of James Whatman by exchange. The land north of the road remained in the Mason family until 1786 when it was purchased by the Whatmans. The tenant of 20 years, Thomas Burwash, continued to farm there until the turn of the century. In 1776 John Powell and Walter Hunt had erected 'a building divided into 4 tenements at Gidds Pond' on a 3 cornered piece of land backing onto the pond. In 1797 the heirs of Samuel Giles sold the cottages to the Whatmans together with a further 2 tenements erected by Giles. Two of them were let to The Parish Officers of Boxley and another to those of Allington, as accommodation for the poor, whilst the others were let to Messrs. Froud, Weobley and Owens. Presumably the two erected by Giles were built much earlier, as in 1737 the Overseers of the Poor for Boxley were renting and repairing 'Two cottages with two large walnut trees at Ghids Pond'. The number of cottages fluctuated over the years. By 1931 the pond was no longer there and further cottages had been built westwards over the site of an old sand pit, bringing the then total to eleven. Numbers 1-3 formed part of Newnham Court Farm, and a further pair were tenanted by the farm up until the sale of the Whatman's Estate in 1954. Alf Springett sand merchant was plying his trade behind the cottages in the 1880's, and in the 1960's Hammonds Nursery reared quality fruit trees there.

As the name 'Newnham Court' implies, this was reputed to have once been a small manor in its own right. The 2 large fields to the south and east of the farm buildings are known as Great and Little Crockers and would be the 'Crokesland' recorded in 1261. By 1554 Newnham Court was part of the lands the Wyatts forfeited to the crown. At that time its 175 acres farmed by Robert Daniell was the third largest farm in all of Boxley. Queen Elizabeth I granted it to Sir John Astley in 1583 in the tenure of Thomas Cleggett. In 1638 Astley passed, to his brother-in-law Norton Knatchbull 'The Manor of Newnham Court and the fulling pits containing 223 acres in tenancy of William Hartridge and Thomas Sparlawrence'. Knatchbull sold it to Sir John Banks and it stayed part of the Aylesford Estate until 1821. In 1673 Banks recorded that he paid a quit rent for the property to The Crown (such payment released him from any other manorial service) whilst he 'quit claimed' all his other lands to the Manor of Boxley. Thus Newnham Court was held separately from the other Boxley properties. Amongst the Aylesford Estate deeds is a document of c1470 concerning the disputed tithes of 'Newnham Court Manor'. This in turn refers to a 1376 document which appears to show that the smaller manor was subsumed into the Manor of Boxley and thus had become a possession of the Abbey of Boxley. It would appear that once a major property, it gradually declined. The 1664 Hearth Tax Records show that its 9 hearths (a sign of wealth) put it 4th in all Boxley, yet by the time of the Window Tax of 1783 its meagre 13 lights had dropped it to 14th place. The Athawes family began a tenancy of almost a hundred years when Samuel Athawes inherited from William Godfrey in 1681. In 1779 Thomas Taylor took over the lease and was joined by his kinsman John Russell. He was embroiled in James Whatman's litigation with the Taylors at Pole Mill as described in the chapter on papermaking. Whatman feared that farming activity on Newnham Court lands would adversely affect the view from his new house. In 1807 Nehemiah Ford took over the tenancy from Daniel Neale who had turned to farming after retiring as landlord of The Red Lion at Sandling. Neale's tenure had not been successful and the farm was much run down. When Joseph Lee replaced Ford in 1818 the depression on 'landed produce' ruined him within 3 years. As no new tenant could be found, Whatman was invited to make an offer for the farm. A figure of £15,000 was agreed and its lands became part of the Vinters Estate for the next 133 years. Included in its 187 acres was a brick and tile kiln alongside the Detling Road, and an 'inexhaustible supply of sand' from the famed Newnham Court sand caverns. Notable tenants were Henry Barrow and his family who held the lease for some 50 years to 1880, and William Bellingham who in the 1920's and 1930's ran it together with Vinters Farm.

When the Whatman estate was sold in 1954, four years after the death of Louisa Whatman, the farm was split into 3 lots. The farm and adjoining double oast together with some 123^1/$_2$ acres and 3 farm cottages at Gidds Pond were in the tenancy of E.W. Wingrove. A farmhouse formed the second lot. It sported 6 bedrooms, a drawing room with exposed ceiling beams, 3 further reception rooms and a 1 acre garden with fruit trees. It was probably the house that the Barrows had occupied with their 6 servants. Lastly was Newnham Court (not to be confused with the Farmhouse) which lies behind today's shopping village. Described then as a modern country residence built in the Queen Anne style with a stable block including a double coach house, 2 cottages at the entrance from the main road, and the now disused sand caverns. It was built for Florence and Louisa Whatman who took up residence in 1912 and was to be where Louisa died in 1950, finally bringing to an end a magnificent era. The farmhouse itself, now incorporated into a pub/restaurant, is subject to a strange legend of Sir Henry Wyatt's cat. In the Wyatts chapter we tell of a cat which brought pigeons to help sustain Sir Henry during his incarceration in a Scottish prison. Over the years several people have witnessed and reported sightings of a ghostly cat which prowls the buildings of Newnham Court. But how anyone could tell that it was Sir Henry's cat eludes us.

Until it became surrounded by modern housing and retail developments, Grove Green was a separate hamlet nestling in rural seclusion between Weavering Street and what is now New Cut Road. Quite incredibly, of the four houses believed to have comprised the original hamlet, three are still occupied today. A tribute to the skills of their medieval builders. It exists almost like Brigadoon, a little time warp with its old buildings preserved and safeguarded

WEAVERING AND GROVE GREEN

Newnham Court Farmhouse. By the 1990's much extended as a pub-restaurant.

Grove Green Church, built about 1903 and destroyed by fire about 1966.

by their loving owners. Settlement here was almost certainly due to the discovery of the famed Fullers Earth deposits, whose industry is described in a later chapter. Indeed 'Grove' is an old word for mine. Hasted says that Grove, as it was then known, was conveyed at the start of the 15th Century by Isabel de Wavering to Thomas Burbige whose descendants, all Thomas's with the variant spellings of Burbidge or Burbage, held it for the next century. They gradually sold it off piece by piece, until finally in 1702 the remainder was sold to John Watts. He and his heirs managed the fulling pits to 1755 when his daughter Elizabeth Paris who had emigrated to Maryland sold the land to General William Belford, Colonel-Commandant of the 1st Battalion of the Royal Regiment of Artillery. The haulage carts ceased their interminable activity and the hamlet slipped into obscurity, reverting to a private farming estate with hops and pasture land. Access was via a cart track that left the Bearsted Road just after the brow of the hill beyond Gidds Pond Cottages. This was Grove Green Lane, known as Arnold's Lane in the early 1900's. The lane passed through the Fullers Earth pits, bisected the hamlet and then veered south westwards, crossing the grounds of Vinters Park to join up with Vinters Road and thence into Maidstone. A further track branched off past where the oasthouse is today, along the course of Grove Green Road to Weavering Street.

Belford owned the land to the east of the road which bisected the hamlet, together with that north of a lane later constructed, coming in from Vintners Lane (later New Cut Road) to the west. It seems likely that the northern most property Well House was actively involved in the nearby fulling industry from very early times. It is probably the 'house with a garden, orchard, stable and 4 acres of land' of which the Burbage family retained possession until finally selling to John Watts. The 'schoolhouse' building originally formed a part of the Well House premises up to the 1800's, and may well be the 'stables' referred to. Listed as being 15th Century it may well have been built a hundred years earlier or more. The present occupiers were informed that an old man with intimate knowledge of the house insisted that beneath the floor of one of the rooms were extensive Roman tiles. Perhaps some form of house upon which the fulling industry was centred has stood on this site for almost 2000 years. The house today appears truncated and almost certainly had a southern bay in earlier times. It is timber-framed with brick on the ground floor and is jettied at the north end. The interior is extensively timbered with one massive beam stretching the full width of the house. Although the beams of many cottages are said to be ex-ships timbers, those in Well House are more likely to be so than most. The ceiling timbers are all curved, being convex in one room and concave in another. Smoke blackened roof timbers indicate that an open hearth preceded the enormous inglenook with its huge bressumer beam, and this is confirmed by the presence of a beautiful crown post. A kitchen extension was built about 1750 enclosing most of the jettied end. The house takes its name from the large canopied well which would have provided the water for

WEAVERING AND GROVE GREEN

Track to Fulling Pit & Gidds Pond.

Track to New Cut

Glue Manufactury.
occ:- John Pike.
own:- J. Whatman

footpath to Weavering St.

Cottage & Garden
occ:- John S. Pike
own:- J. Whatman

Oast & Two Cottages
occ:- John Payne
own:- J. Whatman

Grove Green (pasture)
occ:- J. Avery

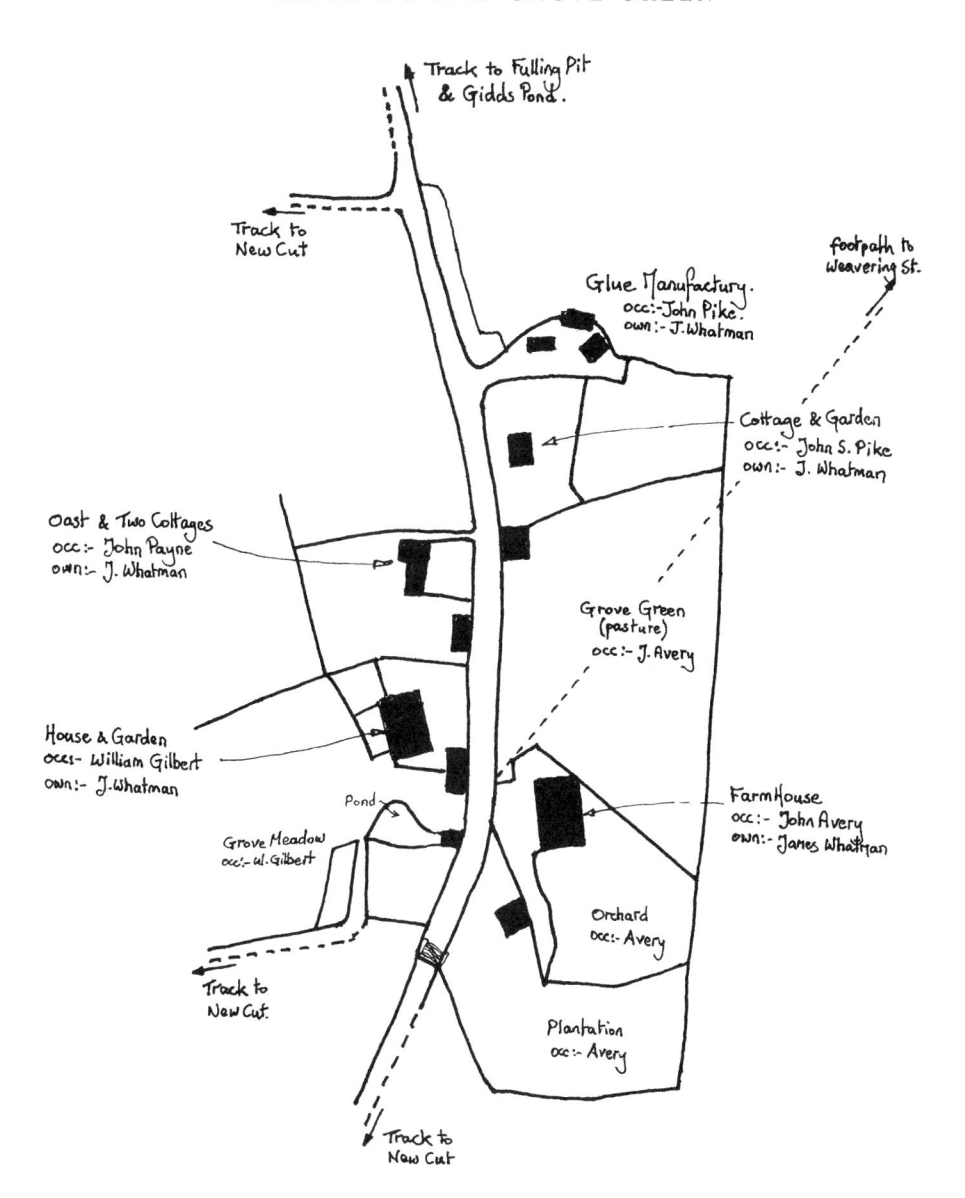

House & Garden
occ:- William Gilbert
own:- J. Whatman

Pond

Farm House
occ:- John Avery
own:- James Whatman

Grove Meadow
occ:- W. Gilbert

Orchard
occ:- Avery

Track to New Cut

Plantation
occ:- Avery

Track to New Cut

GROVE GREEN ~ 1844.

DAEVE '98

the Fullers Earth workers. There is some evidence that an earlier well existed in the garden north of the house. However the well today is very ancient with a four foot circular wheel and an original old bucket which fetched the water up from 90 feet below. It is said to be one of the deepest in Kent, having been plumbed to a depth of 400 feet overall! For some dozen years from about 1843 the house was occupied by John Pike who ran a glue manufactory from a group of outbuildings at the north end of the garden. The Poor rates appear to show that he had replaced a John Powling who ran it as a beerhouse from 1837. William Pike continued the noxious business of glue making until 1859, from where it became a small fruit farm whose 5 acres were tended by Edward Barrow and later Benjamin Goodhew and lastly by Henry Perrin. His daughter Daisy Moroney planted a rose bush as a child which flourished for many years. Just weeks after her death the rose was mysteriously found to be dead also.

Below Well House is a property now divided into two dwellings. The end facing the road has 3 bricked up archways and appears to have been a wagon lodge. Old maps show that it originally belonged to Well House. There has been a structure here for hundreds of years and it may well have housed the carts for transporting the Fullers Earth to the river. In 1864 the lodge was converted for use as a Mission Church. A house constructed at the rear was occupied by a succession of curates. The celebrant in 1895 was Edward Woollatt. He recorded that amongst the youngsters of The Bible Reading Union were 4 from Grove Green, 6 from Weavering Street and 6 from Gidds Pond. The Pound family came up from Boxley Cottages, Louisa Payne from Vinters Lodge and Daisy Relf from Mill Cottage (Sandling Paper Mill) used to make the long trek with her cousin Minnie who lived at The Forstal. Soon after its conversion to a church it began a dual use as a small school. Catherine Pierce living and teaching there in 1871, at which time it was known as The School House. In 1882 it became Grove Green Infants School catering for up to 43 children under the tutelage of Mrs Hills, utilising a single 36 feet by $18^{1}/_{2}$ feet school room. In 1903 Louisa Whatman gave to the parish of Boxley a piece of land just north of the oast upon which was built the Church of St. Michael and All Angels, which from the materials used became known as Weavering Iron Church.

Lyn Simpson who lives at Weavering has the following fond memories of the church in the early 1930's. "The route from Weavering was along a narrow footpath (now Green Lane) to a flight of stone steps (still in existence) leading to a tiny porch where the books were stacked. Mrs Hammond, the retired school mistress of Grove Green, would allocate Common Prayer and Hymns Ancient and Modern. The church was lit by the gentle glow of oil lamps suspended from the roof by chains, and I often wonder how we read the small print, but perhaps we knew most of it by heart.

A local lad tolled the single bell for some ten minutes before Evensong at 3.30 p.m. There were, on most occasions, just a handful of people in the congregation – sometimes six or eight, but at christenings, harvest thanksgiving or other festivals, the number would swell to as many as twenty-five or thirty. I remember that at such times the rafters rang with enthusiastic singing and the old tin roof was really raised! Tom Peters would cycle from Boxley to play the small harmonium and sing with great gusto, his voice booming above ours. The vicar for over twenty years was the Reverend James Hale, who also cycled from the Vicarage at Boxley, and looking back it seems to me that he was always at the service. No doubt the weather did beat him at times, but I don't remember any. Jimmy Hale, as he was always known in the parish, could regularly be seen pedalling around Weavering visiting the few houses then in the area – about eighteen in all, and he would usually join my family at teatime where he would enjoy a lightly boiled egg freshly gathered from the nest, and home-made bread and butter. Then on with the cycle clips and back to Boxley.

The Order for Evening Prayer in the Common Prayer book was strictly adhered to and I recall being called to task for inattention during many a long sermon, quite a lot of which went over my head. The stately and imposing figure of Miss Whatman (always clad in deep purple throughout Lent), terrified me as a child, long skirts brushing the undergrowth and her Victorian style hats a distinctive feature. Although Weavering is in Boxley parish, the Church of St. Mary and All Saints seemed very remote in those days when cars were few and far between. In fact I don't remember being taken there until I was old enough to walk that far".

With changing circumstances the need for services at Grove Green became less and, although many people were saddened to see it go, the church eventually closed. For a while it was used by the Wingroves at Grove Green Farm who stored agricultural machinery there, but unfortunately around 1966 it was destroyed by fire. At the same time that she gave land for construction of the church, Miss Whatman granted a new lease of the house and schoolroom to the Reverend Snape-Cadman "the same which have been used for and known as Weavering School, for the education of children and adults or children only, of the labour, manufacturing and other poorer classes, and as a residence for the teacher. The school is to be run as a National School under the criterion of The National Society for the Education of the Poor in the Principles of the Established Church". Mrs Hills continued as headmistress until 1907 when Mrs Hammond took over. Elsie Robinson came in 1908 as one of two monitors and in 1915, having obtained her qualifications, became a teacher at the school. Gradually numbers declined and at Easter 1924 the school bell rang for the last time.

Mrs Hammond continued to reside at the schoolhouse and the school room was used as a branch of the County Library until about 1950 when that moved to Weavering. It also became the parish room, utilised for Women's Institute meetings, parties and other functions until Weavering Village Hall was opened behind the Fox and Goose in 1964. The school room and wagon lodge were then converted into a dwelling.

The single kiln oasthouse now sympathetically converted for residential use was built around 1860, but is listed of architectural interest because of its unusual construction with 3 arched vaults beneath. Similarly, the schoolhouse has vaulted cellars that imitate the arches of the old wagon lodge. It is possible that the oast was raised on foundations of an earlier building which appears on a map of 1755, but of which the 1844 tithe map bears no trace. The adjacent barn contains beautiful roof timbers and likewise has taken on a new function as a residence following careful conversion. Both buildings formed a part of Grove Green Farm. Today's farmhouse with its recently added cat-slide roof is not original. The early history of the farm presents something of an enigma. The window tax records show that 'Grove House' was occupied by a Mr Brenchley in 1799, when he paid for 18 windows. Evidently some had been blocked up to reduce the tax because in 1783 a Mr Davis had paid for 23 windows. Clearly this is not the present farmhouse nor is it likely to have been Well House. Presumably therefore a large house existed but is no more. A map of Belford's lands dated 1755 apparently shows a large 'L' shaped building on the approximate site of today's farmhouse, but on a different alignment.

When General Belford purchased the property there were $34\frac{1}{2}$ acres. These included Well House and its land and would appear to be an amalgamation with a property which in 1691 Edward Godfrey granted to William Godfrey the younger on the occasion of his marriage to Elizabeth Longe. Described as 'a tenement, barn, oasthouse, and outhouses at Grove Green, now or late in tenure of James Sherborne and John Goward together with 27 acres lying on both sides of the way from Grove Green to the high road there towards Bearsted'. Watts had let this large property to Daniel Mathews and John Allen and under Belford it was occupied by John Kent and Richard Walker, and later Mr Davis. The earliest actual mention of 'Grove Farm' that we have found is when it was leased out by the Watts family in 1723. In 1804 George Luck took over from Richard Orum and farmed there for 22 years. The Belford family passed the lands to Sir Robert Wilson about 1825 and around the mid 1830's they came into the possession of the Whatmans. Stephen Stonham was their first tenant, replaced in 1846 by John Avery. His son-in-law Charles Sellen ran it into the 1880's. Henry and John Solman were followed by the Ledger family, whose 30 years occupation of the $57\frac{1}{2}$ acre farm ended in 1936. They were succeeded by the Wingrove family after whom Wingrove Drive is named. They were to remain until the land was sold for residential development. Formerly a mix of pasture, cherry orchards, arable land and hops, and now incorporating much of the old 'Raigersfeld' and 'Boxley Cottage' Farms, under the Wingroves it became a market gardening and fruit farm.

'The Cottage', to the west of the lane, dates back perhaps as early as 1440, and was originally a Yeoman's Hall House. Evidence remains of its original thatch, wattle and daub walls, and open hearth. It would appear to be the house and 6 acres of land that John Trindale owned in 1600 and passed by marriage to John Boghurst. In the mid 17th Century it came into the hands of The Fowle family. William Athawes junior was the occupant in 1691 and then John Rose up to 1738. He was a renowned breeder of fighting cocks, and representing The Widow Fowle, he took part in December 1730 in a celebrated contest. Billed as 'a great match of cocking, between the Gentlemen of Maidstone and the Gentlemen of Sandhurst, Sussex', it was held at The Royal Cockpit at the sign of the Ship in Maidstone. Each side showed 22 cocks and for a purse of 2 guineas a battle. John Holloway and then Luke Dann farmed there at the beginning of the 19th Century, when its 12$\frac{1}{2}$ acres were largely planted with hops. In 1841 the Whatmans purchased it, by which time it had converted into 3 cottages. William Gilbert took on the tenancy in 1843 through to 1865, when its land became subsumed into the lands tenanted by Austin Killick of Vintners Farm. One of the three cottages formed part of the Grove Farm tenancy, and the northern portion of the adjoining barn contained the privies for all 3 cottages. The current owner purchased them in 1966 and converted them back to a single property. The Victorian addition to the rear is believed to have been used as accommodation for young ladies attending the school.

Contiguous to the north is 'Grove Green Cottage' which in 1848, when the Whatmans bought if from the Whitley family, completed their ownership of the entire hamlet. Also originating from the 15th Century it belonged to Thomas Brewer in the 16th Century. Sold to William Dabbs in 1626 it passed into the hands of the Goldsmith family at the turn of that century. They farmed the 5 acres north of the cottage through to 1744 when Gabriel Glover commenced a tenancy of some 30 years. The Hunt family became the owners and then eventually The Whitleys. Charles Beaumont occupied it for 33 years to 1823. The 1844 tithe map shows it as divided into two cottages with a square oasthouse, in the tenancy of John Payne, farmer. William Parish replaced him in 1861 whereupon it became a single house, its agricultural connections severed until one of the Wingrove sons later took up residence there.

Today, Grove Green is a microcosm of the rural Arcadia that once epitomised Boxley parish. We can only pray that the threat of further encroachment by developers on this little enclave has now been ended for good.

Sandling Place.

CHAPTER 21

Sandling, Boarley and Tyland

The Western area of the Parish is comprised of the hamlets of Sandling and Boarley. The River Medway forms part of its boundary, but life and times 'down by the river' are dealt with in a separate chapter. With the history of Park House already told, the proper starting point has to be Sandling Place, a graceful ragstone house set in grounds adjoining Lushington's old estate. And a starting point for Sandling Place may be taken as the year 1817.

A certain Flint Stacey was proprietor of the Lower Brewery in Lower Stone Street, Maidstone, and also owned much land in Sandling. His daughter Maria married Eli Crump, who became a partner in the brewery. In 1817, whilst extending the Brewery's stock of licensed premises, Eli bought the ancient Red Lion Inn which fronted the Chatham Road, just the other side of the car park from the present Running Horse. He also bought over 7 acres of land behind the pub. Eli was not to live much longer, and in 1823 his widow Maria chose this spot to construct a large neat house on a natural eminence. With delightful understatement she named her rural retreat, Sandling Cottage.

By the time of Maria's death in 1840, the estate had swelled to 23 acres with land inherited from her father and a piece of Boxley waste land purchased from Lord Romney. Her brother, Courtenay Stacey, inherited the estate and in keeping with his status as an ex-mayor of Maidstone (as had been his father and brother), he renamed his sister's house, Sandling Place. He lived out his days here and in 1859 a banker, Richard Mercer became tenant and subsequently bought the house.

In 1890, the Stacey family sold almost all their remaining land to Richard, who gave it for the use of his brother Samuel, also a banker. The brothers were heavily involved in the conversion of Chillington Manor into the Maidstone Museum and were indeed two of its first trustees. It is probably at this time that Sandling Place was enlarged, and the old Red Lion demolished to make way for the erection of stables. The estate now included all the land on the opposite side of Chatham Road down to the river and running from the Malta Inn to Pepper Alley, as Samuel already owned Gibraltar House and its surrounding land. The estate also extended North across Sandling Lane into the woods where now stands the block of flats known as Boarley Court. For many years a delightful wrought iron foot bridge spanned Sandling Lane close by the present entrance to the flats, in order to facilitate access from the house to ornamental shrubbery and walkways and other delights that lay in this part of Cuckoo Woods. Later generations were to call it 'Squirrel Bridge', because these creatures made equal use of it to cross the road. Others called it 'Mercers' Bridge' or even 'Fairy Bridge'. Part of the supports can still be found. Alongside the stream that borders the Northern edge of the woods can still be seen the remains of a hydraulic ram. This clever invention was used by the Victorians to raise water quite considerable distances. In this case it was constructed to provide a water supply for Sandling Place.

The Mercer family were to live at Sandling Place until 1941 when Randall Mercer died there. Neither Randall, nor his sister who had shared the house with him, had any children and with Estate Duty hitting hard, their heirs sold the estate to Leonard Fawkes Wright, a haulage contractor. With the war in full swing, the house was soon taken over by the military, in whose hands it remains. Motorists leaving Maidstone on the Chatham Road can get a tantalising glimpse of the Big House.

Randall Mercer and his sister played their parts in the Church and social life of the Parish. The Reverend Hale's children remembered afternoon tea there with croquet on the lawn, and generous coinage pressed into their hands by Miss Mercer as they departed. In 1928, a little mission Church was built in Boarley Lane close by the Running Horse on land given by the Mercers. Known as St. Andrews it is some time since demolished. The Mercers' butler Henry Card was a well known character in the area.

On the Chatham Road at the end of Gibraltar Lane stands the beautiful old Kentish Hall House which once served as the local post office. Built in the 15th Century it would have been the home of a wealthy yeoman, and could possibly have been the premier house of the lost hamlet of Wilstone. It is a heavily timber-framed and studded farmhouse with a centre portion (hall), and two jettied wings, of the style often called a Wealden Hall House. This is something of a misnomer, as there is a much greater concentration of these lovely buildings around the Maidstone area, than throughout the Weald. It would appear to have lost its importance very early on, and is probably the "farm of one cottage with a garden adjoining, at Sandling in tenure of Robert Gibson", described in the Wyatt attainder record of 1554. Certainly, since the 18th Century all references described it as having no land, and indeed to be divided into two cottages, each with a garden. It remained as two cottages well into this Century. Being part of lands exchanged by Flint Stacey with Lord Romney in 1799 it devolved to his daughter Maria Crump whereupon it took the name of Sandling Cottage Farmhouse. It remained part of Sandling Place Estate until the death of Randall Mercer. In 1851, The Red Lion Inn was serving as Sandling's, and indeed Boxley's, first post office, but in 1859 it had been established at Sandling Cottage Farmhouse, where the postmaster was Henry Fullager. He and his wife Charlotte ran it into the 1880's but by the 1891 census it was occupied by Henry Mannering, postmaster and coachman, who

SANDLING c.1840

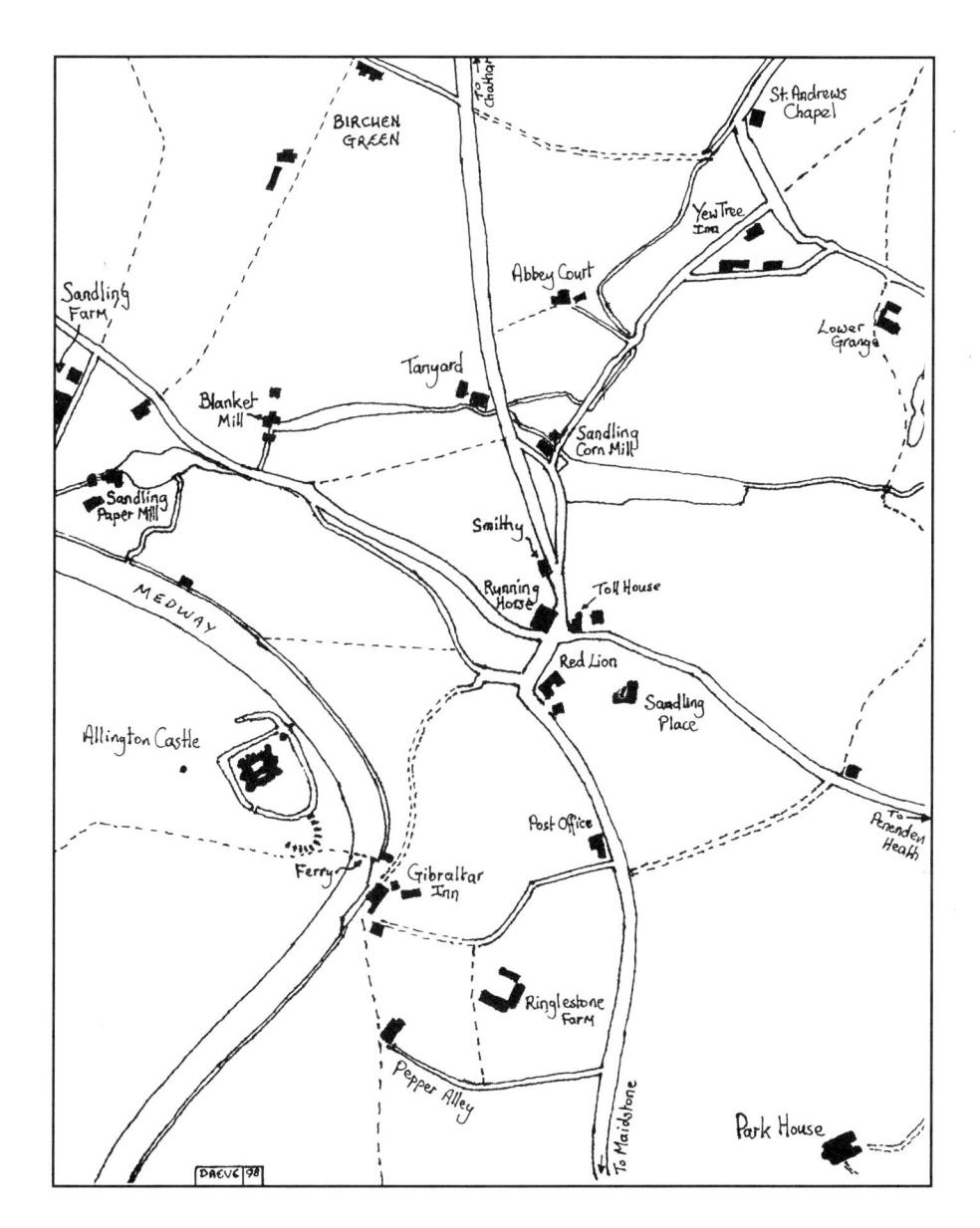

BOXLEY PARISH

The old timber-framed house on the Chatham Road, close by Gibraltar Lane. To the left are the premises of Parkes Brothers. Believed circa 1920's.

remained in that post until at least 1922. By 1930 William Fullager lived there and farmed Gibraltar Farm.

On the opposite side of Gibraltar Lane where the garage now plies its trade, stood the Parkes Brothers Wheelwrights shop, from about the turn of the Century. By 1930 they had evolved into Parkes Motor Body Builders, and then County Cellulose and Parkes Body Co. Ltd. Next to them stood a large house called Ilexholme, the home of Mrs Kitney who played the organ at St. Andrews Mission Hall.

Cuckoo Woods which lie along Sandling Lane, remain a place of beauty, and especially so when the bluebells carpet the ground. They are also an excellent Autumn venue for gathering chestnuts for roasting. They were originally known as Sandling Woods but took their present name from John Cuckow who was a gardener living in a cottage in the woods in the 1880's. Before the Water Company increased its extraction rate to meet the demands of Maidstone's growing population, the little stream running through, which variously bore the name of Moiles, Marley or Malling Stream, was of some volume. It carried trout which the local lads would catch, and there was even a small waterfall. The fields on the Northern edge would sometimes flood and the iridescent flash of kingfishers could be seen. Halcyon days indeed!

The Running Horse gained its present appearance in 1938, and for 200 years before this it was a small country pub. It is now isolated from the

SANDLING, BOARLEY AND TYLAND

Mercers' Bridge in Sandling Lane, looking towards the Running Horse.

Maidstone to Medway Towns traffic, but formally it stood at the cross-roads of the main Maidstone/Rochester Road, the road to Aylesford, and the highway to Ashford and Hythe, better known today as Sandling Lane. For some years after 1945, Sandling Lane became something of an early Maidstone By-pass for traffic coming from London towards Ashford and Folkestone. Travellers along here would include the Queen on her way to visit Mountbatten relatives near Ashford. Near the south-east corner of Cuckoo Woods stood a little cafe to provide refreshment for all those travellers.

On the opposite side of the road to Boarley stood the Turnpike Cottage, where Harriet Nye was keeper in 1841. Turnpike gates closed off the lane (then the main Maidstone/Rochester road) with a second set butting on to the other side of the Running Horse and closing off the road to Aylesford. Turnpike Trusts, which were empowered to levy tolls for the upkeep and improvement of specified stretches of highway, began in 1663 with gates erected on the Great North Road. Prior to this, major roads sometimes had a system whereby a 'pike' that formed a barrier was turned to allow access. It is probable that Boxley had such an operation in use as early as 1605 when court records refer to the presentment in court of a highway called Rayes, between Hortwashgate and Thomas Browne's house in Boxley, leading from Milton (Next Sittingbourne) to Maidstone. Horwash or Horish Wood stretched from

Boxley Abbey House (Julia Best-Shaw).

St. Andrew's Chapel, Sandling, 1911.

behind Newnham Court back to Detling, and the 'gate' or barrier probably then stood at the Boxley Parish Boundary near to Workhouse Cottage on the current A249. The highway at that time would have been further East than today's Sittingbourne Road, possibly following the alignment of the footpath that today runs from the Bearsted Road past Vinters into Huntsmans Lane. There was no Ashford Road then, and the Rayes highway would have crossed over the River Len at a bridge which is recorded as being named Ryce Bridge, (Rayes and Ryce being phonetically similar) and then veered West to the heart of Maidstone. This could possibly be the bridge at the bottom of Square Hill.

An Act of 1558 had required the annual appointment of a 'Surveyor of the Highways' for each Parish. This was unpaid and normally filled by rotation, the officer being empowered to raise local rates towards the upkeep of roads, and was answerable to the Justices of the Peace. Local people would be called upon to maintain the roads. Each householder had to provide four days (later six days) labour annually or to pay for someone else to do the work. In 1605 Richard Lea and William Betts were reported to the Justices for not having repaired the highway in Boxley leading from Maidstone to Rochester. In 1835 a new system was introduced, whereby Justices appointed surveyors for groups of Parishes. The 1861 census shows Abraham Green employed as such a Road Surveyor, and living at Tyland Gate opposite Tyland Farm, where his wife Ann was the gatekeeper. Statute labour by householders continued for all the other roads, and one of Boxley's last Overseers of the Highways was Robert Lucas, who farmed at Warren Farm and was elected to the post in 1850. In 1727, the Maidstone to Rochester road became only the third highway in Kent to be turnpiked when an act of that year approved 'An Act of Parliament to repair and enlarge the road leading from the house called the Sign of the Belles in the Parish of St. Margaret's, Rochester to Lady Taylor's Gate nearest to Maidstone'. Lady Taylor's Gate would have stood by Park House at Sandling on the boundary between Maidstone and Boxley. The Turnpike Trusts were allowed to mortgage the tolls to private individuals, to ensure that they themselves received a guaranteed annual sum upon which they could budget. Individuals would put in bids in the hope of making a good profit. In 1818 local newspapers carried an advertisement inviting bids for the letting of the Sandling Tolls (Sandling Gate and Tyland Bar) which in 1817 had raised £280.00. Later turnpike gates were erected in Boxley at the top of Sittingbourne Road – just before The Chiltern Hundreds Public House, on the Ashford Road – where it was originally joined by Huntsmans Lane (which was later diverted by a dog-leg Eastwards), and on the Sittingbourne Road level with the Queen Anne pub. (The Sittingbourne Road was further East at that time).

A walk from the Running Horse up Boarley Lane is both very interesting, and very attractive as the foot of the downs is approached. Just a few yards past the pub, Boarley Lane splits off to the right from what was the old

Maidstone/Rochester road. At this junction for more than 250 years stood a blacksmith's forge. The marriage settlement of John and Elizabeth Brewer included a smith's forge with a half acre here, purchased by his father Robert from Walter Fisher. In 1636 the smith was one John Golding or Goldwell, but his forge was eventually pulled down in 1768. Ten years later following an unsuccessful spell as landlord of The Running Horse, John Rogers erected a new forge which was reported as creating a nuisance 'by encroaching upon the King's Highway'. Nevertheless it remained, and prospered under a succession of blacksmiths, notably the Dadd family. By 1861, Levy Irvin had sufficient work for him to employ two additional smiths, but it appears to have finally extinguished its fires in the mid 1870's. A Henry Broadbridge who lived in Chatham Road, worked a forge in Sandling from at least 1891-1907. Likewise Alf Usherwood's bellows fanned the flames of his forge at Sandling from 1874 to around 1890. As well as being a blacksmith, he was also a wheelwright, probably on the site of the Parkes Bros. premises.

Down the lane on the right, the spring that rises by the Church, flowing through the grounds of Park House, and alongside Cuckoo Woods, was damned to form the long mill pond. For at least 700 years it turned the wheel of the old black and white timber mill that huddles next to its more imposing mill house. This is a very ancient mill site. It was probably already old in 1316 when it is recorded as being given by Alexander Kumba to Boxley Abbey. After the Dissolution, it became the property of the Wyatts and following their attainder it was granted in 1583 by Queen Elizabeth to Sir John Astley, at which time it was in occupation of Philip Gilberte. John Beach was the miller when in 1662 it was bought by Sir John Banks, together with Abbey Gate, Tyland and Boarley Farms. Sir John's elder daughter Elizabeth married Heneage Finch, later Baron Guernsey and Earl of Aylesford, and the mill remained part of the Aylesford Estate for more than 200 years. In 1696 Bartholomew Bewman took over as miller to the Ffisher family, creating a dynasty variously spelt Brauman, Beauman or Beaumont, which milled here for 119 years. When Robert Blinkhorn's occupation began in 1816 following John Beauman's bankruptcy, he started a Blinkhorn dynasty of his own, who tenanted the mill until its wheel finally ceased turning in 1887. The Blinkhorns also ran Penenden Heath Windmill, the treadmill at Maidstone Goal, Sandling Road smock mill (which stood behind the East Station), and they farmed at Abbey Court.

The waters of the Boarley Springs were also harnessed, in order to enable the nine foot overshot wheel to drive two pairs of stones simultaneously, but a report of 1805 notes that "there is usually only sufficient water to work one pair, and in summer they are often obliged to stand still". The construction of the water extraction works at Boarley, cutting off half its water supply, effectively sealed the doom of the corn mill. The Mill house alongside is a 17th Century building, but the mill itself is older and almost certainly that occupied by Philip Gilberte, in the 16th Century. It may originally have been taller as an 1829 description refers to step ladders to its several storeys, and in 1816 Blinkhorn had undertaken a thorough repair as it was said to be in a ruinous state.

As one stands today looking out over the peaceful mill pond with its resident water fowl there is a wonderful feeling of timelessness. It is humbling to consider that the little brook has turned the wheel here to grind corn for generations of Boxley inhabitants, probably back to Norman times, as this was almost certainly one of the three Boxley Mills of the Domesday Book survey.

For some years, the miller also farmed the adjacent land as Boxley Mill Farm. In 1805 there was only an old thatched cottage on the 16 acres, but when in 1813 Thomas Carter senior took over the tenancy he rented additional land from the Boxley Abbey Estate, extending the acreage to 56 acres. He then constructed " a very good house and offices at a cost of £1,100". In 1835 Joseph Mellin leased the farm, then called Sandling Cottage. When the Blinkhorns took over in 1839, to avoid confusion with Mrs Crump's property, they altered the name to Sandling Homestead. Subsequently the land was farmed by the Clifford family and the house became a private residence known as Abbey Court, with its man-made lake. For many years this was the home of Dr. Constant Ponder who was County Pathologist and then Medical Officer of Health for Kent. His wife Margaret used to ride a motorbike and sidecar, and they had a large family. Their barn was a happy home to some of Maidstone's musical and dramatic groups, most notably the Old Barn Orchestra. In 1916, seventy-nine freehold building sites were offered for sale on part of the land, and Abbey Court Estate evolved.

Close by, with the modern intrusion of the motorway rushing overhead, is the Yew Tree Pub, and the cluster of old cottages in the area known as Farthings. It is here that long ago, the monks were given permission to hold fairs, which probably were used for the sale of horses, goods and produce. This was probably the tenement, barn and stables leased in 1696 by William Athawes. William was heavily involved in quarrying of stone and minerals throughout Boxley, and certainly in 1738 "tile earth" was being extracted from here. Three of the cottages were owned in 1844 by Ann Constable and it is perhaps her family that first used The Yew Tree as a beerhouse. A further two cottages were owned by the Roots family of Nether Grange Farm. Farthings had formed part of that estate since at least 1554, when the farmer was John Stile.

Further on, at the junction with Grange Lane is the very ancient building which incorporated part of the old 15th Century St. Andrew's chapel, described in the chapter on Boxley Abbey. A writer in 1870 described it as being then, ' a pair of cottages occupied by a poor widow whose family had lived there as tenants of the Abbey Estate for more than a Century'. This would have been Mrs Ann Archer, who with her husband Henry had farmed the 4$^{1}/_{2}$ acres adjoining. The chapel formed part of the Boxley Abbey Estate. When Francis Austen bought the estate in 1740, the chapel was referred to as 'The

Hermitage with 4 acres in which John Macey formerly dwelt'. In 1875 Frederick Mannering took over the tenancy and ran it for many years as a grocers shop. It was still a grocers in 1913, but by 1930 The Sandling Post Office had move there, and newspapers were also being sold. It continued to trade as such, into the 1960's, throughout much of which time it appears to have been run by Jack Beer's wife. He was chauffeur/gardener to James Clifford of Abbey Farm.

The first of the row of three cottages on the left of the lane before the crossroads was originally occupied by a Mrs Webb, who with Mrs Stephens farmed 8 acres known as Abbey Street Farm. She was replaced by the Danes family, cousins of the Danes who owned the Anchor Brewery in Aylesford. In 1851 Thomas Danes rented the 3 acre field behind his house from which he ran a market gardening business. The 1871 census records him as a beerhousekeeper, perhaps retailing his cousin's beer, or more likely brewing his own and selling it in his parlour. However his was only a 'two up and two down' cottage, and it is equally possible that he could have been working for James Fullager, licensee of the Yew Tree or at the beerhouse in Abbey Gate Cottages. By 1891 his son John was living there and described as a Brewer's clerk. John set up his own brewery, behind the house, but manufactured only Ginger Beer. From at least 1895-1909 the Danes were shop proprietors. Possibly from their house, but probably succeeding Mannering at St. Andrews Cottage.

On the right of the lane is the imposing Abbey Gate Farmhouse, now a private dwelling. A grade II listed building, the oldest, left hand part is believed to date from the 1400's, and the right from the 18th Century. It is difficult to determine the chronology of tenancy of this farm. The Wyatt attainder survey of 1554 records no fewer than five farms at the Abbey Gate plus at least two others whose field names prove that they were also based there. What is certain is that the occupant of Boxley Abbey also occupied Abbey Gate Farm for many years.

The long row of attractive cottages on the left of the approach to what is now the main gate to the Abbey House, go back to monastic times and are believed to have been built to accommodate visitors and pilgrims. Originally they were only two large cottages built around the late 15th Century, and almost certainly the property described in the 1554 survey as – 'A farm of two tenements with a garden and two pieces of land:- one piece of $3\frac{1}{2}$ acres and a garden, called The Vine, and the other tenement having a piece of ground of 9 acres called Moilles, in tenure of William Dobbes. In a lease of 1536, John, the Abbot of Boxley leased to John Dobbys of Boxley, a tenement called "the signe of the Cock, together with a second tenement and a piece of land called Dobbs land, and the herbage of the wood called Tyle Wood". Intriguingly, the Abbot of Boxley was himself called John Dobbes! Was the crafty Abbot, aware that his Abbey was about to be dissolved, leasing to himself or a relative, the Abbey hostelry? If so, this could add credence to the surmise of an earlier writer who suggested that the good Abbot may have been somewhat fond of his liquor. One reason for this supposition was that when the Abbey was dissolved, the accusation was levied that the monks had spent Abbey money on gillyflowers. The common use for this plant was in the flavouring of wine. Abbot John was also the fun-loving Abbot clapped in the stocks by Sir Henry Wyatt's wife Anne, for his outrageous behaviour. In 1665, Edwin Wiat mortgaged two tenements at the Abbey Gate called The Vine and The Cocke in occupation of Ffrancis Ffryer. In 1660 a Mr Ffryer is recorded as granted a victualling licence as an innkeeper in Boxley, presumably at The Cocke. It is possible that it continued as a beerhouse for many years.

Sometime in the next 50 years, the two cottages were extended to six. The Bath family occupied one cottage for decades, James Bath keeping a beerhouse there as shown in the census of both 1851 and 1861, probably in the end cottage. Stephen Bath was later to be landlord of The George Inn by the bridge in Aylesford. By 1724, Joseph Springate's cottage had a smith's forge attached. Presumably this remained active, as between 1841 and 1881, censuses show George Dadd, blacksmith occupying one of the cottages and William Obey, blacksmith in another. Anyone walking the footpath behind these cottages after rain, will realise from the claggy mud on their boots, why the soil hereabouts was favoured by the monks and later generations, for brick and tilemaking.

The gateway to the Wiats Abbey House, once impressive, is today a ruin. From Tudor times another large cottage stood just outside the gateway on the opposite side of the road to the remaining cottages. It was possibly the 'Farm of one tenement at the Abbey Gate plus 3 acres of land adjoining the wall-late in tenure of Richard Boyerst,' recorded in the 1554 Wyatt attainder survey.

Boxley Abbey and the Abbey Estate remained in the hands of the Selyard or Seyliard family until 1740 when it was sold to Francis Austen of Sevenoaks. Sir Edward Austen died at the Abbey in 1760 and chose to be buried in Allington churchyard. He had no children and his heir was his wife's cousin, John, son of Nicholas Amherst of Barnjet, Barming. The 1774 terrier of Boxley, records John Kentennius as running the Abbey Farm for John Amherst. At Amherst's death, also childless, in 1797, the estate was split between Sir John Thomas Amhurst, William Allen, and James Allen's widow-Eleanor. Liberty Taylor a paper manufacturer of Wrotham gained a 1/3 share by his marriage to the widowed Eleanor, and then with his brother John purchased the remaining portion in 1799. In 1811 Taylor sold the Abbey and 64 acres plus further estate lands of 96½ acres to Lord Aylesford for £15000.

Henceforward the Abbey lands and Abbey Gate Farm were let out to tenants, firstly to Thomas Carter and then to George George and John Millen. As well as farming the lands Millen and George ran the Abbey Brewery based at the Great Barn (formerly the hospitum), from around 1840 until at least 1862. In 1863 James Varney took over the Boxley Abbey farm tenancy and he in turn was replaced by James Fauchon in 1885. Fauchon and his son Robert also ran Street Farm, as did their successor James Clifford.

The Abbey House was an ideal residence for relatives of Lord Aylesford. Lady Maria Finch lived there from at least 1816 to 1846. Thereafter it was let to local gentry. The Reverend Edward Balston moved there in 1852 to be replaced by Captain Colson Festing in 1863. The Balstons returned in 1871, when Richard Balston the paper manufacturer took on the lease. In 1890 the estate was put up for sale and Maudistly Best secured the Abbey House and Farm with 113 acres, for £15450.00. Since the preceding year the house had been rented by Mrs Anne Mercer, widow who remained there until 1903. Another widow, Mrs Lavinia Young sub-let the Abbey Gate farmhouse from Robert Fauchon, but James Clifford moved in when he took over the farm tenancy in 1891.

Once again occupied by its owners, the Abbey House flourishes today in the caring hands of the Best-Shaw family. Sir John Best-Shaw the elder moved there with his family in the 1950's following the deaths of the Best-Dalisons. Beautiful gardens are nurtured within the encircling walls of the old Abbey. A delightful water feature nestles within the nave of the original church, on top of whose walls grows incongruously a huge, majestic oak tree.

To the left at the crossroads, (back at the main road) runs Tyland Lane whose houses are post 1918. Further West, where the lane joins what was once the Maidstone/Rochester Road is Tyland Farmhouse, listed Grade II and said to be built in the late 16th or early 17th Century. In 1629 this was described as Tylands Manor House and farm of 85 acres in occupation of Thomas Newman, who also held Boarley Farm. A farm was certainly here in 1554 when it was 'Tilandes' with 65 acres in occupation of John Goldsmith. Passing through the tenancies of Chowning, Fowle, Kemsley and the Hatch family to 1803, when the tenant William Leigh was evicted with vast rent arrears of £700.00. Under the new tenant Edward Wickham, the farmhouse and Tyland Barn were thoroughly repaired and stables, cow lodge and other outbuildings erected. In 1811, William Hills took over the farm and it remained in his family for decades. Tyland Barn was built in the early to mid 17th Century, but the two left end bays were rebuilt this Century. It is now the headquarters of the Kent Trust for Nature Conservation and contains a wealth of information on local flora and fauna. Especially recommended is the delightful pond. Take a walk around its trails and experience a natural environment our forefathers would have known. In 1841 the census shows Carter Nye the occupant, as gatekeeper of the toll-bar. Later the simple bar was upgraded to a full turnpike gate and a separate toll-house constructed.

Continuing North up Boarley Lane from the cross-roads, the house 'Curlews' is on the right. This was the home of Biddy Foster, and where the Boxley Girl Guides under her care would spend some of their noisy time. The spring waters of Boarley were reckoned to be particularly pure, and in 1885 a group of three springs was acquired by the Maidstone Waterworks Company who also drove an adit into the hillside, and the water was collected in a covered reservoir to the east of the lane, which in 1938 was said to hold 200,000 gallons.

The attractive oast houses to the west of the road were built around 1910 by Robert Style. Hereabouts he also reared Partridges for more shooting parties. At the end of the lane, on the left stands Boarley Farm, with its land stretching West to the old Chatham Road and marking the Western extremity of the Boxley House estate. Here for some years in the early part of this Century farmed George Brooker, whilst his brother Charles had Tyland Farm. In the 1990's it is arable and grazing land whereas around 1900 it was hops and fruit that flourished here.

Boarley Farmhouse can be traced back to before 1554, having been a possession of Sir Thomas Wyatt, and farmed by John Collyns. In 1583 it formed part of the lands granted by Queen Elizabeth to John Astley. From 1670 through to the start of the 19th Century it was farmed in succession by the Mills, Apsley, Sedger, Tomlyn and Hatch families. By 1805 it was in the tenancy of Isaac Haberfield and described as 'a very old farmhouse, two barns, a stable and cart lodge, all thatched'. In 1810 it is further described as 'a very ancient structure of wood and brickwork, very slight, and gone entirely to decay'. However an interesting transformation occurred that year, when one Arthur Stone took over the tenancy. He had a large family, and struck a deal with Lord Aylesford the landlord. Stone would pay a high rent and in return his Lordship would repair and enlarge the house. The exterior walls were taken down and a new shell entirely rebuilt of red brick. The result was the handsome farmhouse we see today, cloaking a much older interior. Unfortunately for Stone, he fell foul of the depression on landed produce caused by the precipitous drop in prices of foodstuff from the high wartime levels, and by the increase in imports, following the Napoleonic Wars. Misguidingly, he had ignored Boarley's reputation as the best adapted farm in the area for sheep rearing, and ploughed up his meadows for crops. Like hundreds of farmers across the country, he was ruined, and in 1822 he quit. Boarley's fortunes were resurrected by the diligence of young William Millen, whose father was the tenant of Eccles Farm. His tenancy lasted for some 40 years and by its end he was farming 312 acres and providing employment for eleven Boxley men and two boys.

Opposite is a most attractive old timer-framed building, known as Boarley Cottage. Scheduled as being of Historic Interest it is said to date from the early 17th Century, and sports a rare moulded dragon post on its corner. It was probably built by the husband of Bridget Wainwright on a $2^1/_2$ acre field in the tenancy of John Collyns of Boarley Farm. Bridget was widowed at a young age, living alone there as a widow from at least 1629 to 1662. The premature death of her husband Francis may have been engendered by a calamity that befell them in 1593. Due to a series of poor crops they had accrued arrears of rent. An abundant harvest appeared to have solved their problems, but their landlord seized the barn laden with the entire produce before they could market it, and they were ruined. He may well have succumbed to the plague, which devastated Boxley the following year. By 1799 it had grown to 5 acres and was known as Pages Field (presumably from a previous occupant). It was now once again utilised by the occupant of Boarley Farm, and was to remain so into the 20th Century. In 1831, Lord Aylesford became its owner when he exchanged if for other land with Lord Romney, and formally added it to Boarley Farm, which he already owned.

Due West of Boarley Farm was for many years an Army Firing Range used by soldiers from their various barracks in Maidstone. In 1885 Lord Romney, and the then tenant of Boarley Farm, William Bensted, had agreed to lease the land to the War Department for £50 per annum, to set up a rifle range and camp site, and allow the soldiers access to the spring. The small-arms fire was directed towards the Pilgrims Way, where a sentry was posted with a red flag to keep walkers out of harm. However there is still the story, be it apocryphal or not, of a nanny and pram somehow getting into the line of fire and causing panic to the officer in charge. It became disused, perhaps somewhat prematurely between 1933 and 1938 and was finally used again during the Second War. Even now, spent cartridges are turned up in the fields. P.C. Ted Kirby's sons used to harvest the spent lead shot from below the Pilgrims Way for use on their fishing lines. This ploy was thwarted when spoil from the excavations for Boxley Waterworks in the late 1930's, was tipped on top.

The downland here is named Boarley Warren, from the rabbits, introduced by the Norman's, and cultivated by the monks for food. Around 1900 at harvest time, the gypsies would camp, their fires lighting up the night sky. Even allowing for the motorway and other roadwork's, Boarley remains unspoilt. If you take the ancient footpath to Boxley village, running East from the top of Boarley Lane, within minutes there is nothing but the wildlife, the wind and the sky. The final large 10 acre field that you reach, before the village, was known as Poor Field. Presumably as it invariably appears parched, its soil crazed by countless cracks and fissures. It was here, on the highest point that William Fowle built his windmill in 1802. It is doubtful whether he was personally engaged in the milling of the corn as by the 1779 will of his father Edward he had inherited Aylesford Corn Mill, which was always run by tenants. He built a little cottage attached to the windmill, which was occupied by a succession of millers including, John Clark, John Simmonds and William Killick Smith. The millers job was somewhat peripatetic, and the same names surface at different mills. Thus John Simmonds was also recorded at Sandling Mill and Dunn Street Mill, and William Killick Smith was subsequently running Penenden Heath windmill. His Boxley mill was obviously very dear to William, as he stipulated in his will that he was to be buried beneath it. A vault was to

WILLIAM FOWLE'S WINDMILL

From a sketch in the margin of an Estate map of 1837
By John Quested

be constructed and a half acre of ground adjoining fenced off with iron railings – thus creating a private burial ground. Goodsall quotes his epitaph as thus "Underneath this little mill, lies the body of poor Will, odd he lived, and odd he died, and at his burial no one cried". The nature of William's oddness, that prompted this somewhat sad memorial, must remain an enigma, but certainly he never married Mary Pattenden, the mother of his four children. In 1796 he was prosecuted unsuccessfully by Lord Romney, when he tried to enclose Marlands Bank. Twenty four locals gave evidence against him. Mary Richards relating how he threatened her whilst she was beating oak trees to collect acorns, from which she made a coffee substitute. His bastard son, William Pattenden, later took the surname of Fowle, and prospered. The Vicar of Boxley was most unhappy that William should be lying in unconsecrated ground, but his son was adamant that his father's wishes should be respected, and indeed insisted at his own death in 1839 on lying beside his father, under the mill. The Vicar subsequently had his way, and both bodies were exhumed, and re-interred in the Church yard. The mill ceased working in 1865, and sometime between 1876 and 1880 it was dismantled. Marian Foster, then of Yew Tree House, told William Coles-Finch in 1933, that the sweeps were removed and the upper part put on a 'bavin tug', and brought to the village, where it was re-erected at Street Farm and used as a granary and pigeon cote. The top section was pulled down for safety around the end of the Second World War. Several of the old grindstones are said to be in the village.

CHAPTER 22

Down by the River

The easternmost point of old Boxley parish lies on the River Medway at the Forstal, where the convergence of the stream flowing down from Cossington Springs made an ideal site for the construction of Maidstone's earliest paper mill. The Medway was the artery along which trade came and went between mid-Kent and London, bringing prosperity to the County Town. Although tidal up as far as East Farleigh, the approximate head of low-tide navigation was where Allington Lock now stands. Thus from early times wharfs were constructed at the Forstal to take advantage of uninterrupted traffic.

Much of the land in this corner formed part of first the Preston Hall Estate and then the Cobtree Manor Estate throughout the 19th and 20th Centuries. Cobtree was never a Manor, the name being a modern affectation, but certainly it was the premier farm in west Boxley from early times. Confusingly, the 1554 record of the lands forfeited to the Crown by Sir Thomas Wyatt, mentions two farms with similar names:– 'Copptree', a 70 acre farm with barns and stables in tenure of William Goodwin, and 'Coptree', an 18 acre farm and certain lands in tenure of William Smythe. Other early records show an Edward Wyatt receiving a grant of Coptre, Styles Meade and Coldeblowes in 1567, and John Astley being granted Allington Castle in 1583 together with 'Toptree tenement and 20 acres formerly in tenure of William Smythe'. Despite having been a leading supporter of Wyatt's rebellion, Smythe, also the tenant of Park House at Sandling, avoided execution and helped to reorganise the town following the withdrawal of its charter. He was elected Mayor in 1564.

Aylesford Parish Register records the burials of John Wyatt of Boxley, and his wife and son, between 1654 and 1656. It is almost certain that they lived at Cobtree, as perhaps did Sir Henry Finch, buried in Boxley Church in 1625, whose son John, the Lord Speaker of the House of Commons, married George Wyatt's daughter Elionora. Certainly Lady Anne Finch, widow, died at Cobtree in 1658. Sir Henry was a serjeant-at-law and wrote several legal works of great merit, and a book entitled 'The World's Great Restauration', which predicted a world-wide empire of the Jews. This brought him into disfavour with King James I, who considered the book libellous and suppressed it. Around the same time, Allington Parish Records show baptisms in 1657 and 1659 of children of Ursula and Andrew Lydall, gent of Coptree. Around 1680 it records baptisms of children of Richard Godwin, gent of Coptree. Clearly the similarity of names would point to Godwin being a descendent of the Goodwin who occupied Wyatt's 70 acre 'Copptree'. However if this is so he did not remain there much longer because a deed of 1700 shows the 70 acres in possession of Sarles Goatley, and had lately been in tenure of Elizabeth Collins widow. Goatley's daughter Anne, married Henry Heath, and they took possession in 1748. In 1774 it was described as 'Cobtree Hall Farm' of 72½ acres in occupation of Henry Heath. However, a few years after this, Heath found himself unable to continue repayments of a mortgage on the property arranged by Goatley in 1700. Ever watchful for an opportunity, Edward Fowle purchased the property, making it his home and it remained part of the Fowle estate until 1831 when Charles Milner purchased it and incorporated it into his estate centred on Preston Hall.

Cobtree Hall, now greatly extended from the initial 16th Century farmhouse, stood empty for a couple of years. Heath farmed its lands for a few years more, and then they were let to the Bristow family before William Randall became tenant of both house and lands in 1833. Although still there by the 1841 census, the 1844 tithe map has him replaced by Thomas Franklyn, a tanner by trade. A deed of 1848 shows the farm lands together with Forstal Farm, totalling 250 acres, let to William Hobbs. However, the 1851 census records Franklyn as living at 'Cobtree Mansion', and farming 135 acres, whilst his farm bailiff Richard Starnes occupied 'Cobtree Farm House'. The 1871 census shows Starnes still there, but Franklyn apparently having retired from farming occupied 'Cobtree Hall' as a wine merchant. Ten years later the occupant of 'Cobtree House' was W.B.P. Trousdell, a retired army officer, farming 170 acres and employing 7 men, plus 5 house servants.

Cobtree Hall was originally built astride the Allington/Boxley border, although since the boundary change of 1934 it has been wholly in Boxley. For centuries a wedge of Allington parish had remained isolated on the east bank of the Medway, a reminder that this was once part of the Allington Castle Estate. Astley's 1583 'Toptree of 20 acres', occupied much of this Allington section. By 1705 it had swelled to 83 acres, when Sir Jacob Astley let to Sarles Goatley of Cobtree, 'Cotland', late in tenure of Robert Rhodes. This second Coptree farm had apparently been renamed Cotland to differentiate it from that already occupied by Goatley. We know its lands included the Allington section, because Astley reserved the right of passage over the ford at Castle Shelf. In 1720 when the Astleys sold most of Allington Castle Estate to Dame Elizabeth Shovell, the farm was again referred to as 'Cobtree'. However, a document amongst the Romney Estate records, (Dame Elizabeth's daughter having married Lord Romney and conveyed the lands to him), confirms that 'Cottley Farm' and 40 acres had been obtained from the Astleys at that time, and was farmed by Goatley. Subsequently it was renamed 'Sandling Farm'. By 1794 the tenant was George Hills, whose family remained there as Romney's tenants to 1871. They also occupied Abbey Street Farm and Tyland Farm, and the census records show that farm bailiffs resided at Sandling Farm House. In 1841 and 1851 it was Richard Burr. When Thomas and George Ongley took on the tenancy in 1871 the farmhouse was 'very old and with a low-pitched roof'. It was decided to pull down the rear portion consisting of a sitting room, kitchen, dairy, bakehouse and storeroom, and convert the remainder into a labourer's cottage. A new farmhouse was built on higher ground to the north. Various members of the Ongley family managed the farm until 1904, when it was bought by Hugh Tyrwhitt-Drake. He had leased Cobtree Hall since 1896 and with the purchase of the house and the surrounding farms of nearly 300 acres, the Cobtree Manor Estate was formed.

Apart from Sandling Farm, the rest of the property had been part of the Preston Hall Estate, with Cobtree forming the 'home farm'. Charles Milner had sold the estate to Edward Ladd Betts in 1848 and he subsequently sold it to Henry A. Brassey, who in 1886 was Master of the Boxley Harriers. Sir Garrard Tyrwhitt-Drake inherited the Cobtree estate in 1908. He merged Tyland, Sandling and the remainder of Cobtree farms into one, and ran them himself to 1925, when he handed the reins to George Brundle who farmed them for the next 53 years. Much of the land of Cobtree farm was gradually incorporated into the grounds of the house, partly to accommodate Sir Garrard's collection of wild animals, which grew to be one of the largest private collections in the country. Occasionally exhibiting them to the public, he also used them in travelling circuses between 1919 and 1923 before running a miniature circus at the Crystal Palace until 1933. The following year he opened The Maidstone Zoological Gardens at Cobtree, which continued to be one of the major attractions in Kent up to 1959. The restored elephant house may still be seen. Sir Garrard was a member of Maidstone Borough Council for 49 years, serving a record 12 terms as Mayor. His dedication to the residents of the Maidstone area was second to none. At his death in 1965 with no heir, he bequeathed Cobtree Manor and its Park for their use. In 1984 the Museum of Kent Rural Life was opened, based on the buildings of Sandling Farm. Other buildings have been brought here from elsewhere and re-erected (including the granary from Grange Farm). One of the last remaining hop fields to be cultivated and harvested using traditional methods is flourishing; and having dropped 'Rural' from its title, the museum now celebrates all facets of an era remembered fondly by many. On other parts of the estate were opened the 130 acre municipal golf course, the Country Park, and the Kent Wildlife Trust Centre.

The Fowle family's Cobtree Estate of the 1830's, is acknowledged to be the inspiration for 'Dingley Dell' in Charles Dicken's Pickwick Papers. Not far from the Elephant House is a pond which Dickens is reputed to have had in mind for the winter skating party. The novelist knew the area well and 'Dingley' is said to be a contraction of Detling and Boxley. It is also likely that this north eastern portion of Boxley formed a part of the 'lost' Manor of Ovenhill. (See next chapter). Cobtree Estate papers, and those of the Fowles, contain references to fields known as Ovenden Hill, Little Ovenells and Ovenell Street. It would be easy to conclude that the latter refers to the road over the downs to Grange Farm and Lidsing. The Brewer family owned many of the lands in this area following the Wyatt attainder. A 1616 marriage settlement between John and Elizabeth Brewer refers to, 'a tenement, garden and lands of 18 acres called Birchens' – Birchen Green was a large common which originally occupied much of today's golf course, and was probably the land added to the 20 acre Topptree to create the 40 acre Cottley Farm.

The highest point on the Medway that craft could reach without grounding at low tide was a shallow stretch known as Castle Shelf. Here at the bottom of Lock Lane, a ford had been established for centuries. In 1792 an Act of Parliament empowered the improvement of the river for navigation purposes. Dredging and clearing was carried out but it was not until 1801 that the first lock was constructed. At Flint Stacey's inaugural speech that year as Mayor of Maidstone, he proposed a toast to 'New Lock' with the hope that 'its improved navigation may improve trade'. This first lock was a 'flash lock'. A simple device of a barrier that spanned the river, in which was set a gate. When this was removed, a surge of water would rush through, carrying barges with it. The words 'flash flood' have the same derivation. Almost immediately the new lock began to cause problems as the penned in water backed up at Church Lock/College Lock by All Saints Church, causing flooding of the mills of the River Len. The following year a new Act ordered a reduction of 18 inches in lock height and 'flash boards to work of themselves placed on the bay of the lock to prevent the inconvenience that may otherwise arise from the inattention of lock-keepers'. In 1849, Messrs. Sutton and Walters replaced the single gate with a double gated pound lock. The double pound lock we see today was created in 1884 by the addition of the third set of gates, to enable passage of vessels up to 160 feet in length, 20 foot beam and 7 foot draught. Two years later Knight and Cummings supplied cast iron sluices which were inserted in the great gates at the Lock. The Police at Maidstone would sometimes warn P.C. Ted Kirby that a suicide had jumped off the bridge and that a "stiff" was floating down the river, would he fish it out at the lock! In 1937 the river was finally tamed with the opening of the new sluice gates. In the 1960's, electrically controlled gates were installed to help prevent flooding that occurred regularly at Maidstone.

Originally barges were hauled to Maidstone by teams of 3 men known as 'trackers' or 'hufflers', with tow ropes attached to their bodies. This onerous task was made more difficult by landowners' fences, which stretched down to the water. In 1824 Messrs. Davison and Williams were hired to construct a towing path to allow horses to undertake the task, quicker and more cheaply. Local landowners were compensated for the necessary land, but William Balston demanded £700, (an enormous sum) for the narrow strip fronting his

Springfield Mill – Legal wrangling held up the construction before Balston accepted a fraction of this amount, and the work was not finished until 1826. Originally both sides of the river had been utilised by the men towing the craft, and the local tenants and landowners were required to keep the towing way and the river clear, provide and upkeep bridges, with rails where necessary and to 'brush the boughs' along their frontage. This latter duty was to lop off overhanging branches. Each year the Mayor would take part in a tradition known as 'The Mayors Court of Survey', or more colloquially as 'The Mayors Fishing'. He would be rowed down river from Maidstone to the Hawkwood Stone, during which a record would be made of every hindrance to navigation, and the occupiers of the land would be subsequently required to remedy all the problems.

Tolls were introduced for passage through the lock, and Charles Bartlett was elected as Collector, in August 1824. In April 1833 the old tollhouse was demolished and the present lock-keeper's house built incorporating a committee room for the use of the Navigation Company. The two assistant lock-keeper's cottages on the Allington side were not added until 1888. 1836 saw plans being drawn up to build stables for the horses which hitherto had found temporary refuge at an old warehouse nearby. The following year, during construction, it was decided to add a cottage to the project, for use of Company employees. Originally just a tiny building behind the stables, the cottage was extended in 1874, incorporating the end portion of the stables and building on top of it. Standing at the bottom of Lock Lane, one can see that this resulted in the stables appearing to 'grow through' the cottage. The building was used as a storehouse and assistant lock-keeper's house in later years, and today is the H.Q. for the Kent River Project. They run a mainly voluntary organisation which exists to maintain and improve the river and towpath as a leisure facility, and to conserve its wildlife. On a post by the stable door are marked various flood levels, the highest of which was in 1927. The first occupant of the cottage was Bartlett's son John who was taken on as a carpenter, and assistant to his father. In 1851 he was dismissed and erected a small house just along from his former residence. There he ran his carpentry business and began selling beer to thirsty bargees. In 1869 it became 'The Malta Inn'.

Behind the inn, the square building near the entrance lane was once Sandling Paper Mill, built in 1714, and converted to grind corn in 1844. The outline of the mill wheel can still be seen on its side wall. After production ceased some 20 years later, it was tenanted between 1867 and 1871 by a James Couper, possibly to make gunpowder. The Medway Dairy was run from the mill from 1885 to 1937, firstly by Charlotte Fullager and then by Ada Relf and her father Alf. The Relfs kept no cows themselves so presumably obtained their milk from the cows of Sandling and Ringlestone Farms. Medway Cottage on the opposite side of The Malta entranceway was built as the miller's house.

Later it was leased by the Aylesford Pottery Company to house its managers, such as William Finlay in the 1860's, Joseph Hamblett, brickmaking manager in the 1880's and 1890's and Frederick Rookwood Roberts in the 1920's. The row of cottages on the opposite side of Forstal Lane, known as Stream Cottages was built to house agricultural workers. In the 1940's Mr and Mrs Vine, the parents of Lady Tyrrwhit-Drake occupied one whilst Henry Card butler at Sandling Place had another. Alongside the cottage nearest to the Chatham Road used to stand the mill house to the Blanket Mill/Seed Mill, whose stream flowed under the road here before going on to power the paper mill. The mill itself stood some 60 yards back from the road where the stream made a right angled bend. More detail is given in the chapter on Paper Mills.

To the east of this mill, where its feeding stream ducked under the Chatham Road from Sandling Corn Mill, was Sandling Tan Yard. In 1664 it was owned by Thomas Mitchell whose son sold it to Samuel Stevenson. After it passed to William Kempston in 1703 it remained in his family into the 1750's. Subsequently owned by John Stubbersfield and then William Elgar, the owners tanning process was carried out by Thomas Salmon and then Thomas Funnell. Daniel Jarman purchased it around 1812, and by 1827 it was being run by Richard Dunk. Purchasing it a few years later, he soon sold out to George Fowle around 1832. Thomas Blinkhorn became the tenant and subsumed the land into his Ringlestone and Abbey Mill farms. Immediately north of the Tanyard buildings was erected a large house called 'Brooklyn'. It was originally named Sandling House by Edward Burton, J.P. and member of The Royal Society, who lived there from at least 1844-1861. Succeeded by his wife it became the home of successive members of the gentry before being demolished around 1970. During the next two decades the wooden cabins of Veglios Motel occupied the site.

Taking the delightful walk along the towpath from the Malta towards Maidstone one comes to Riverside Cottage. This little cottage on the very edge of the towpath was in use for 200 years as a store or 'lodge' for fullers earth, used by William Charles in his felts and blanket cleaning business which he ran from the 'Blanket Mill'. It had probably served as such for many years prior to this. A lovely pencil sketch by Charles himself shows it as a clapboard building with the same roofline as today, and a small projecting wharf in front to which is moored a barge. Later it is believed to have been used by the Navigation Company to stable their horses prior to building the stables at the lock. Subsequently it was converted into accommodation towards the middle of the 19th Century. It was occupied for some years by assistant lock-keepers. George Wynn moved in following the early death of its occupant, his brother Thomas, in 1864. In 1878, the lock-keeper Abraham Vane, (having throughout the previous seven years complained bitterly about illnesses suffered by his family, due to the unhealthy state of air caused by the filthy state of the river) requested that he be allowed to leave the lock-house. After agreeing to take a

DOWN BY THE RIVER

Riverside Cottage, early 1900's. Standing are Sarah and Rose Wynn.

The tow-path wending towards Gibraltar House from Maidstone in the early 1900's. No trees to impede the horses as they hauled the barges.

reduction in pay, he was allowed to move out, and Wynn and family moved in. In 1881, following improvements resulting from the construction of Allington Sewage Works two years earlier, Vane returned and Wynn went back to Riverside Cottage, where he also was to die prematurely. Whether this was as a result of the noxious air is not known. Resisting offers of money from the Navigation Company, if she would vacate the premises, his widow Sarah and her daughter Rose ran a shop from the downstairs rooms, selling soft drinks and confectionery. By the 1920's the cottage was home to the McCabe family.

Pat McCabe lived for many years by the river at Sandling, and kindly agreed to share her memories. Born at Riverside Cottage, Pat and her brother Nicholas were raised by their widowed mother. The cottage had no running water, and Mrs McCabe hauled buckets from a standpipe 200 yards away. In summer the youngsters would bathe in the old mill stream that entered the river beside their grounds. Their grandfather taught them to swim in the river from a very early age, using a long pole with a harness strung on the end through which they hooked their arms. Their uncle worked nearby at Parkes Brothers coachbuilders, and he made a flat bottomed rowing boat for them. They never ventured far from the house, either on foot or by boat. All the bargemen knew them and threw pennies as they passed, although most landed in the water. Pat recalls horse-drawn barges, and helping the lock-keepers to lock them through. The barges mainly carried coal and timber. Pat also recalls one Boxley Vicar making his parish calls upon them on horseback.

In 1937 the McCabes moved out, being succeeded first by their uncle Jim Rogers (who had been a blacksmith at Walderslade) and then by Kenneth Bills (wartime pilot and motorcycle champion). Mr Bills modernised the cottage and outbuildings, where he stored the overflow of his enormous collection of old motorcycles. The McCabes did not move far, just to the old Sandling Paper Mill which they renamed 'Malta Cottage'. All the mill machinery was still there, the big iron wheel being removed at the start of the war. The mill pond behind had dried up some years before, having been long cut off from the stream. During the war the Army parked some trucks on it, although Uncle Jim Rogers advised them against it as the ground was soft. Come morning and all the trucks had sunk up to their axles! Pat herself was to live on at Malta Cottage until 1982. Like so many Boxley children, she and Nick McCabe remember childhood days in the countryside as idyllic.

Pat's grandfather, and another uncle Charles Blackman, lived for a while at Gibraltar Cottage. This was a black weather-boarded home on two floors which stood to the right of Gibraltar House. It had been converted from a barn or large storehouse and was probably one of the Fullers earth stores belonging to Mrs Brewer some 350 years previously – see Chapter 25. The barrel-roofed boathouse whose entrance is spanned by a little bridge that carries the towpath, has been in situ for over 200 years. Originally it had an ornate tiled roof, and probably housed the ferryboat that ran from steps alongside and across to the other side. From there a footpath skirted the old motte of the original Norman Castle before going on to Barming.

Now an elegant family home, the lovely blue and white Gibraltar House was once the premier riverside hostelry, and has sported some 5 names. From at least 1629 it dispensed ale to bargees, when it was known as 'The Fulling Lodge'. Serving its final pint in 1874 it became a farmhouse and then for the past 80 years a private residence.

In the 1960's, the then owner Mr H. Hanbury-Brown discovered that part of the house was sinking. He obtained some strong engineering jacks to support and slightly raise the defective section and created a proper foundation. He always understood that in the old days there was stabling close by for the tow-horses. In those times, before the lock had been built, the tidal flow meant that the barges had to wait for the river level to rise, before the horses could haul them on their way. No doubt the bargees waited like the horses, but in rather more comfort inside the hostelry. Mr Hanbury-Brown experienced floods and would mark different levels on his study door! The family had a well rehearsed drill to roll up carpets and carry everything upstairs when flooding threatened. During one particular flood the roar of the waters rushing round the house was nothing less than terrifying. Alongside the towpath is the before-mentioned barrel-roofed boathouse, now overgrown, from which Mr Hanbury Brown would take his children by boat along to Maidstone for their schools.

Beyond the Gibraltar's grounds, a footpath runs up to the Ringlestone Estate. This is still known today as Pepper Alley, as it has been (occasionally Piper Alley) since at least 1670, when John Cripps farmed 6½ acres here. Passing through the Ward, Potter and Weeks families, by 1750 it was tenanted by George Post who was thrice Major of Maidstone. He combined the land with a neighbouring farm which his father John had purchased from Thomas Powell around 1726. It had been in the Powells possession since an ancestor of the same name bought 'a tenement, barn, orchard and 8 acres' from Robert Symonds in 1643.

North east of Pepper Alley was Ringlestone Farm, which in the 1840's formed part of Courtenay Stacey's Park House Estate, and was tenanted by Thomas Blinkhorn. The Dann family subsequently ran it for many years. Goodsells the builders purchased it from the Lushingtons and began constructing the Ringlestone Estate, completing Calder Road by 1934. Maidstone Council already owned the land to the south, which 9 acres had been given by Alexander Fisher in 1671, to provide aid to the poor. A day nursery was opened at Ringlestone in 1941 to allow mothers to volunteer for war work, or take jobs in local factories such as Tilling Stevens which produced munitions and aircraft parts. The accommodation on the estate was the cheapest available locally with some of the earliest flats, and was filled with families cleared-out of the slums of Padsole and Upper Stone Street. Their comparative poverty made the nursery uneconomical after the war and it was closed.

The Boxley boundary ran down what today is Monckton's Lane, named after the old paper mill. The Earl of Aylesford owned much of the land along the river and in 1861 he let the 3 acre plot of land next to the mill, to Robert W. Hazell, a chemist. He erected drying sheds, cement kilns, a chimney shaft, dock, coopers shop, engine house, packing room and cart and wagon lodge. The nature of the business he carried out has not been discovered.

A peaceful and beautiful corner of the parish, it was popular for years to promenade along the towpath from Maidstone and take refreshment at The Gibraltar and later The Malta also. The river was used greatly for rowing. Indeed, in 1869 the navigation authority were implored not to lower the river on Wednesday afternoons as this had become a general holiday in the town, it being early closing day, and boating was the chief amusement of the young men.

However the outside world did occasionally impinge on the rural charm. In 1801 some of the Boxley barges were taken into the service of the Crown. Transported to Gun Wharf in Chatham, where they were fitted with cannon,

The Gibraltar Inn – early 1800's. The buildings close by are probably Mrs. Brewer's Fullers Earth lodges.

they were converted into gun boats. Two years later with the threat of invasion by Napoleon's forces, the Maidstone Volunteer Force was formed. At the same time the bargees and wharfingers enrolled themselves in a company of 'River Fencibles', numbering 80 to 100 strong. They each carried a pike and wore a uniform of blue, with a black belt from which were suspended a cutlass and a holster for a cavalry pistol. C.S. Forester in his Hornblower novels, mentions Hornblower's father (whose fictional residence was at Boxley House), being involved in this fearsome 'Dads Army'.

CHAPTER 23

Over the Hill

The lands 'over-the-hill', covered a vast but sparsely occupied area comprising almost a third of the old Parish of Boxley. In 1611, the boundary stretched North from Lower Warren Road past Cossington Fields to Tunbury Wood and Walderslade Bottom, then East past Cowbeck Wood to Lidsing and Dunn Street, and up to take in half of Bredhurst village. Turning South it encompassed Monkdown Wood and then on to the delightful Wealden hall house of Pollyfields Farm, before bearing South West to drop down the face of the Downs just above Harpole.

The construction of the M2 motorway and the ever increasing encroachment of the residential estates of Walderslade and Lordswood, has tied the Northern reaches of the Parish far closer to the sprawling conurbation of the Medway Towns, almost divorcing them from the village of Boxley. We therefore intend to leave their history to hopefully be chronicled by local historians with better knowledge of the area than ourselves.

The steep escarpment of the North Downs presented an effective barrier to travellers for hundreds of years. When early man first trod the ridgeway, he wore a path just below the Southern crest, thus avoiding being silhouetted against the sky which might attract the attention of predators, or the prey he was hunting. The view North held little interest for him as the land was heavily wooded and almost impenetrable through gorse and blackthorn. Thus, when the Cistercians first came to Boxley, they found it to be the sort of secluded valley in which they preferred to build their religious houses. Access would have been along the branch road that left the main Roman road from Rochester to Maidstone, passing by Boarley and along Forge Lane. This was originally known as Reedstreet, probably from the Anglo Saxon 'Raed' meaning 'meeting place' and thus the way those from North West Kent would have taken to reach Penenden Heath. The plateau over the hill would have been reached along the pack-horse route which begins as Lower Warren Way and goes up the hillside and on to Westfield Sole. Now only a track, it was in 1611, known as 'the flinty-wall-way', when it formed part of the boundary of Boxley Parish, and was the main public highway between Aylesford and Lidsing.

The Romans had almost certainly established a farm by the ridgeway where now stands Harp Farm, but as late as 1829, the historian W.H. Ireland describes the land North of the Downs as 'a barren, dreary country covered in flints', which suggests that farming it must have presented great difficulties. Traces of Roman burials were found near Harp Farm in 1919.

However, this area was in early times perhaps more important than Boxley Manor itself. For here, it is believed was the 'lost" Manor of Ufanhylle, also known as Ovenhill, Ovenhall, Vuenhull and Wenhella. Historians have interpreted this as 'Overhill' although it could as easily have originally been, the hill farm of a Saxon named Uffa. We first find mention of it in the year 975 AD, in the Saxon schedule of contributory Manors for the upkeep of Rochester bridge, the premier crossing place over the Medway. Ufanhylle Manor was partly responsible for the upkeep of the fourth pier of the bridge. The bridge wardens records for 1400 show that John Grove of Boxley supplied 22 elms for repair of the fourth pier. In the Curia Regis Rolls of 1194 and 1195, Osbert de Longocampo and his wife Aveline, who lived at Allington Castle, agreed to pay some of the profits from the rent of Ovenhill and Oxenfryth to the Abbot of Boxley in exchange for prayers for the souls of their family and descendants. In 1236 their successor, William de Longchamp, held Ovenhill, which was a serjeanty of the King worth 100 shillings a year for which he had to personally attend upon the King, for a period of 40 days, whenever he went on a Welsh war, providing a horse and accoutrements at his own expense. The Manor's lands remained in the hands of owners of Allington Castle until Sir Thomas Wyatt lost everything following his rebellion. The last mention of it as a Manor, separate from that of Boxley, was in 1485. The only real attempt by a historian to place Overhill/Ufanhylle, sites it as 'near the farm of Westwold, one mile North of Boxley'. This unfortunately is unhelpful today, as no such farm now exists, but was possibly that marked on earlier maps as Lone Farm, near Westfield Sole.

The earliest remaining full description of Boxley Manor was that taken in 1554 on the attainder of Wyatt's lands. This shows a number of small tenanted farms lying 'on the Downe'. Unfortunately we cannot fully equate these with those extant today. The $125^1/_2$ acre farm, ' with all houses in a streate called Lidging', in tenure of William Henacre - is probably Abbey Court Farm, Lidsing. The 80 acre farm of Thomas Brook in 'Denne Street' is almost certainly Manor Farm, Dunn Street. James Drylands 200 acre farm at Great Westfield is presumably that at Westfield Sole. Surprisingly, neither Grange Farm nor Harp Farm are named, although we know that both farms were included in the lands given to Sir Thomas Wyatt the Elder, by Henry VIII.

Grange Farm, as the name implies, was earlier a satellite farm of the Cistercians of Boxley Abbey. Granges were normally situated too far away to be worked by brothers residing at the monastery itself. They would have normally been manned by lay brothers and have their own chapel. There is no evidence of a chapel at the farm, and the brothers would have had to trek to the Abbey for their main devotions when weather permitted, or alternatively used the ancient chapel of St Mary Magdalene that stood at Lidsing. This chapel fell into disuse some 150 years ago, and following a fire, was pulled down in 1886. On the map, Grange Farm is only 1½ miles from the Abbey as the crow flies, but as mentioned earlier, the only road that would take carts involved a circuitous route in excess of four miles, partly up a long steep incline which would have been impossible in inclement weather. Eventually there was a way up the hill from Boxley Street, passing to the East of the waterworks and Boxley Saw Mill, up what is now a bridleway to meet today's hill just below Harp Farm. Anyone who has tried traversing the footpaths over the Southern escarpment of the downs will know how impossibly muddy and rutted they become after any appreciable rainfall. This way up the hill would have been often impassable to carts and livestock. Later of course the current road was constructed and became the second road to bear the name of Boxley Hill, with the original having been renamed Bluebell Hill.

Following the Dissolution of the Abbey, Grange Farm became the property of the Wyatts and from them passed to Lord Romney. Always a large farm, it had 300 acres when leased by Edwin Wyatt to Sir Robert Wiseman in 1669 whilst in the tenure of John Wise. (His grave occupies a prominent position in front of the church door). Thus it is probable that it is the 300 acre farm referred to in the 1554 survey, described as 'a capital tenement with barns stables orchard and garden in tenure of Agnes Goodwin, widow'. By 1737, having been in tenancy of the Cooper family, the farm had grown to 470 acres when Frances Wiat leased to John Winter, 'The Grange with the pigeon house, oasthouse, wellhouse, wheat barn, corn barn, granary, stables, outhouses and gardens'. The granary was recently dismantled and re-erected at the splendid Museum of Kent Life, which now occupies Sandling Farm. Standing proud on its unscaleable staddle stones, it now contains an audio-visual display about the vermin whose depredations it was designed to frustrate. In 1842 when Richard Dawson took over the tenancy of 427 acres from William Miles, Lord Romney stipulated that the two cottages in 'Grange Lane', now known as Black Cottages, were to be used to house workmen only, and none of the buildings were to be used as a beerhouse. One can infer from this that one of the cottages had served this purpose previously. From 1838 to at least 1851, John Cheal, an agricultural labourer and his wife Elizabeth ran a beerhouse in Westfield Sole, as did Thomas Walter at Dunn Street in the 1830's and 1840's. Grange farmhouse itself, is today a listed building described as having a late eighteenth century front to a possibly earlier building. An earlier historian, in 'Round about Kits Coty' says it had a surrounding moat and bank, but there is no evidence of this today. Not far away was (perhaps still is) a tall clump of fir trees which Bob Style told his men was used as a landmark for ships off Sheerness. A tall story?!

Harp Farm house is also a listed building, said to be of sixteenth century construction or earlier with late 18th century or early 19th century cladding, and a 19th century wellhouse. The barn carries a datestone of 1806 surmounted by the initials L.R., with I.B.H. inscribed beneath. Presumably the L.R. is for Lord Romney. The tenant at the time was Robert Rugg, who also leased Grange Farm (then 546 acres), and other lands in Boxley, but the actual occupier is uncertain. Quite likely I.B.H. stands for Isaac Haberfield the tenant of Boarley Farm. The Court Baron notes George Fowle who, because of his commitments elsewhere, probably sub-let it yet again! The earliest lease found is that of 1718 when Thomas Athawes took a 16 year lease on 252 acres. However, in 1665 it was in the occupation of Abraham Backett who was also the tenant of Abbey Gate Farm. When George King relinquished the tenancy to Thomas Cooper in 1743, a full detailed field map was drawn up which included "Jossing Stone Field". The Jostling Stone was an 'Upping' or mounting block, which stood for hundreds of years at the top of the old way over the hill to enable remounting of one's horse, having led it up the steep track. A painting of the 1860's shows a more substantial five step mounting block on the green in front of the Church, but this stone on the hill was a three stepper and much older. The historian Lamprey says it bore the inscription, "Here I was set, with labour great, Judge as you please, twas for your ease", and the date 1609. It was the site of the Ordnance Survey Bench Mark and thus a landmark on all maps, and a priceless piece of our heritage which should never have been removed. It is no longer there, its removal around 1961 to the courtyard of Grange Farm, being just one small part of the catalogue of 'crimes' against our landscape, perpetrated by certain farmers over the years. The ploughing up of ancient hedgerows, to the detriment of wildlife, in order to create enormous American style 'prairies', has desecrated the downland that so many fondly remember. For many years, the Wyles family ran their corn mill which stood just to the North of the hamlet of Dunn Street. Its sails finally ceased turning around 1865. Coles-Finch thought that there had been a windmill on the escarpment, just below Harp Farm, but the better opinion is that he was completely mistaken about this.

Over the years both Grange and Harp Farm were frequently tenanted by the same farmer, and in 1899 when the Romney estate was sold, A.P. Style of Style and Winch brewery purchased them and they were subsequently run by a series of farm bailiffs.

In 1719, Sir Charles Sedley sold to Thomas Best, various woods on the Down including 120 acres of 'Munkendowne' or 'Monkton Downe Court', together with 'Walslade' and 'Great Cowback'. Monkdown wood appears to have been named because of its proximity to the Cistercians' Grange Farm, but it has also borne the name of 'Moreton Down'. In 1601, the constables of Maidstone and Eyhorne hundreds were given a royal warrant to go to Moreton Down, Boxley, where there were 30 cartloads of 'coal' (charcoal) ready to be carried to Whitehall Palace for the Queens Service. They were instructed to gather as much as they could and deliver it to the waterside where it could be conveniently transported by ship. Geoffrey Nutter, the Maidstone constable, commandeered twelve Boxley farmers to each provide a cart and men to shift the charcoal. However a 'collier' from Bredhurst, one Robert Bowman, alleging that he was the deputy of John Roam, purveyor of Charcoal to the Queens household, took 40 shillings from six of them:– John Field, George Allen, Hamon Beeching, William Beech, Christopher Goldsmith and Thomas Dane, to release them from providing their cartloads. He was subsequently prosecuted together with another local 'collier', William Mountford, who had taken bribes from the farmers of Eyhorne hundred.

BOXLEY PARISH

Cherry pickers at Vintners Farm 1917.

CHAPTER 24

The Countryside

Rather belatedly we should consider the derivation of the place-name Boxley. The traditional and obvious view is that the name comes from the Box trees that once clad the slopes of the Downs locally. Coles-Finch preferred the Saxon word "bocs" for Beeches, because he thought them much more prevalent. Either way, the village may be said to have begun as a Lea or clearing in woodland. Box is said to be partial to chalky soil and south-facing slopes. Being evergreen it does produce a very dense and dark thicket if growing in clusters, and as a further minus point is said to give off an unpleasant smell like a tom cat's urine! Lambarde, in his 1576 'Perambulation of Kent' says it comes from – "A place lying in 'umbilico' (in the midst or navel of the shire)".

The several chalk pits on the Downs are testament to extraction years ago, and these are referred to in chapter 25. The softness of chalk enables it to absorb water and store large reserves in aquifers. Water, like downland, is a feature of the area. Springwater abounds, springing out from weakspots where layers of chalk were laid down thousands of years ago. Springs at Boarley were acquired by the Maidstone Water Company in 1885, and in the 1930's attention switched to Boxley village as a new source to meet the County Town's growing needs for water. The Boxley Pumping Station was built above a well sunk for some 250 feet. Down almost that far an adit (or tunnel) was driven for about 4000 feet under the Downs. And then a borehole was sunk for some 550 feet to tap water that lay deep in the lower greensands. It was reckoned to be a model installation, and its impact upon the locality was very significant. Before the 1930's the various Boxley streams ran deep, and wells around the village never failed to supply its needs. There were trout to be caught. All this changed in 1939, and in compensation most of the village was given a free supply of water. Down at the sheepwash in Grange Lane the children restored the stream by building dams, to such an extent that it was like the seaside with scores of them paddling and splashing.

People who recall those days of the 1940's and earlier are agreed that the countryside was a paradise for children. Motor cars were a rarity and children could play in the road if they chose. There used to be a bath-chair kept by the Church for the use of the elderly. Two of Rev. Watt's children commandeered it one day and free-wheeled down the road beside Boxley House. P.C. Kirby was on hand to reprimand them, but there was little risk of them encountering a car. The Watt girls Marjorie and Mary remember the joy of wandering afar picking primroses and cowslips, with neither they nor their parents having any qualms for their safety. They still dream of a Boxley with bluebells in the beech woods and blossom in the orchards. The farmers seemed very happy for the children of the parish to have the run of the fields, so long as no mischief was done.

However, mischief was in the minds of certain suspects, and their confessions should be kept anonymous even after sixty years! They roamed Boxley around 1940 poaching rabbits in particular. Bearing nets and a couple of ferrets, they played a fine old game of hide and seek with P.C. Kirby. It must be remembered that before disease wiped out so many in the 1950's, the rabbit population was vast and an infestation. Major Best in his will even pleaded with his heirs to "keep down the rabbits which do much mischief". In the depressed days of the 1930's and the hungry war years, they were a prized food. The wild marjoram which they nibbled on the downs gave the meat a distinctive flavour. The young lads in questions would be up and around Boxley village at dawn, and over a couple of mornings they once netted 150 rabbits. P.C. Kirby would trundle around on his big old bicycle and use his binoculars to seek them out, and even leave notes for them. He was not concerned with their activities on the Downs, but all too often they were in the orchards after fruit or by the Park House lakes catching trout or even shooting rooks. At the end of their exertions they would call into "The Woodman" for refreshment. They too found the countryside a paradise.

Both Park House and Boxley House Estates had gamekeepers. Poachers from the Medway Towns were a particular nuisance. Up at the Summerhouse overlooking the Pilgrim's Way was Jesse Hodge, to be succeeded by Tom Hill. Down at Keeper's Cottage by the Maidstone to Sittingbourne road lived several generations of the Clements family, one of whom is reputed to have thrown a poacher over a five-bar gate. One Boxley keeper would go out equipped with a knuckle-duster if he was to clear gypsies off the land. Vinters Estate also had a keeper who lived in the lodge house by New Cut.

The attitude towards gypsies varied. Over the years they are recalled camping at the Sheepwash and close by Boarley Farm, and for many years on Penenden Heath. Some landowners turned them away, but for farmers like the Fosters at Court Lodge Farm they were a welcome labour force at fruit-picking time, when their colourful caravans would be parked in the orchards.

At harvest time the countryside really came alive. The memories of Mike and Ann Foster of Court Lodge Farm in the 1940's and 1950's tell of a different farming world. There was no combine harvester yet. A gang of men would be out with a Binder which cut the corn and tied it into sheaves, which were then stacked in stooks (George Wallis in the Victorian chapter called them shocks) to dry. It was hot and dusty work, and the men would tie handkerchiefs over their mouths. They slaked their thirst with cider brought out to them by the farmer's

THE COUNTRYSIDE

wife or their own wives. Once dry, the corn was built up in stacks. First a base of faggots, then a circular stack, topped with a thatch of the previous year's threshed straw. Later in the year the Threshing machine arrived on its rounds from farm to farm, coming from the Lidsing area and lumbering precariously down Boxley Hill. It was pulled by a steam engine named "Emma" which was to provide the motive power when threshing commenced. Then the men would dismantle the stacks and throw in the corn, the seed went into sacks and the job was done. Rats and mice would scamper out as the last of the stacks disappeared.

In early Victorian times the harvest was even more labour intensive. The corn was cut with sickles and tied up by hand. Threshing was done by hand in the barn and could provide a man with employment through most of the winter. Then the first threshing machines came in, and mechanical binders, and small wonder that the labourers could see their jobs disappearing and rioted and smashed the new machinery in their fear and anger. Court Lodge Farm was employing about nine men in the 1940's, which number was to steadily decline as mechanisation and tractors arrived. Until then there were three horses, including two cart-horses Prince and Major.

Then there was fruit-picking, including from tall cherry trees when two men were needed to pitch the long and heavy ladders. This was a skilled job in itself. Don Vaughan remembers lying in his bed at Park Cottage very early in the morning around 1950 and hearing the chatter of women with their children in prams who had walked all the way from Shepway on the other side of Maidstone to earn some extra money from fruit-picking. Dick Foster was then raising Sussex beef cattle and keeping breeding ewes. Come the spring and it was lambing time, and Ann Foster remembers weak lambs being put in the warming drawer of the Aga in the farmhouse kitchen for comfort. As they gained strength and began kicking the door to get out, so they were moved out into snug bushel boxes. The shepherd used to burn their tails off with a red-hot iron and also deal with certain male appendages by biting them off. This stopped the lambs from later on making amorous approaches to the ewes. One imagines that the sheep at least were glad when Shepherds like this became redundant. Wool shearing was done by several men and over several weeks using hand shears. The village children in general could all share and enjoy the sights and sounds and smells of the farming year as it progressed around them. For many years they were allowed time off school to help with the harvest and fruit-picking.

The farmlands of the Boxley House Estate are well remembered around the 1940's by stalwarts such as Amos Golding, Tommy Thompson and Stuart Murray. Like Court Lodge Farm there were work-horses, and also a cumbersome steam plough. This needed coal and water to keep it going, and up to three men to tend to its needs. In time this was replaced by an exciting motor tractor requiring one man. One day three of the men were on a tractor going down Boxley Hill when it refused to go into gear and the brakes were not responding. Just before the sharp bend at the bottom the driver managed to engage gear and regain some semblance of control, and enquire of the other two why they were getting so het up. Towards D-Day, it was not unusual to find Bren-gun carriers out on manoeuvres ending up in the field when they failed to get round that notorious bend.

Bob Style grew a lot of corn, and root crops for his animals, and also linseed. The latter was for its flax which was apparently used during the War for parachute material. He had acres of woodland which were in the care of his wood-reeve. The present Timberyard above the Pumping Station was then part of the Estate and known as Shillings Lodge. All the Estate's fencing needs were provided for from here and any fallen trees cleared away in a horse-drawn timber-tug. Bob Style employed a whole range of men, including a shepherd, at least two gamekeepers and a rabbit catcher. Soot was considered good for the swedes and was obtained from a chimney-sweep and then spread on the fields by hand – a particularly dirty job.

Hops were clearly grown in Boxley over the years, as witness the oasts still to be seen around the parish. Bob Style as a brewer as well as a landowner felt obliged to grow hops near Tyland Lane, and it was he who built the imposing oasts going up towards Boarley Farm. Several oasts are clustered around Weavering. Bagshaw's directory for 1847 refers to the parish having 200 acres of hops, whilst Kelly's directory for 1899 refers to Charles Foster at Court Lodge Farm as a farmer and hop grower. But it does not seem that Londoners came to Boxley for hop-picking.

If one recites the farms in the parish (with apologies for omissions) it becomes apparent that this was a truly rural landscape. Over the hill were chiefly Upper Grange and Harp Farms. Around Sandling were Boarley, Abbey, Tyland and Lower Grange Farms, and Sandling Farm itself towards the river. In and about Boxley village were Street, Court Lodge, Warren and Harbourland Farms. There was the Park House Home Farm. Eastwards were Newnham Court Farm and all the farmlands around Weavering and Grove Green and Vinters.

One can imagine the constant bustle and activity that there must have been in the parish in years gone by. It was estimated nation-wide that in the 1940's there were half a million farmworkers, compared with 100,000 in the 1990's. As to domestic servants, it is estimated that by the 1880's there were nearly one and a half million, mostly female and most "living-in". Boxley would certainly have reflected these numbers. And when one talks of bustle and activity, the landowners had their shooting parties and there was work for blacksmiths and wheelwrights, and there was a village school, and there was the self-made amusements of flower-shows and cricket matches and scouts and guides and all the goings-on that make up English village life. And if you were up and about early enough you might have seen sheep on market days being driven through the village and on into Maidstone, marshalled by boys and a couple of dogs.

The years approximately 1850 to 1880 are called by some the 'Golden Age' of farming. And yet, not long before, say 1800 to 1830, there had been desperate years for the farm labouring class. In our Victorian chapter we had seen how hard life was, leading to emigration for some, the Workhouse for others and even the hangman's noose for those caught burning ricks and barns. Now from about 1850 the Victorian gentry began to form a sentimental view of rural life and its "attractions". Prince Albert fostered the interest of many landowners in creating "model farms" with the most up to date facilities. Elaborate dairies were built. In Boxley, Major Best added such a Home Farm to his new Park House. Whereas the farm labourers had been looked down upon with a feudal disdain, now they began to be seen as "living engines" who needed to be properly maintained to work efficiently! Their housing began to improve dramatically, partly by the enlightenment of the landowners, partly by legislation, and not least by the landowners wishing to show off with the designs of their Estate cottages. Major Best built new cottages and re-furbished the old ones, very often adding the attractive hung-tile exteriors that are seen all around Boxley village. Architects did well, producing pattern books of designs for cottages, lodge-houses and even farm houses.

From 1850 the employment situation improved, despite increasing mechanisation. Ironically, emigration had helped those labourers left behind because there was a smaller pool of men to meet growing demands. The coming of the railway meant that produce and livestock could now be moved quickly to markets miles away.

Boxley from 1850 was now set to a pattern that was to remain essentially unchanged until 1950. Throughout the parish a few landowners ran their Estates and employed a large number of men on their farms and a large number of servants in their Houses. The farming year still moved through its seasons in much the same way in 1950 as it did in 1850, albeit with a little more mechanisation. But soon after 1950 the Boxley House, Park House and Vinters Estates were all broken up. No village school, no shops, no cricket team, no bus. For a few years a private bus would run on Fridays between Boxley village and Maidstone for the ladies to make a shopping trip and exchange gossip on the way. Mechanisation increased on the farms, the Common Agricultural Policy arrived, orchards were grubbed up and hop fields disappeared. A motorway cut a swathe through the parish east and west, whilst rush-hour traffic was to build to a crescendo through Boxley village north and south. Grove Green and other parts were to disappear under bricks and mortar.

Are we like the Victorians taking too sentimental a view of the Boxley countryside prior to 1950? We leave our readers to judge.

CHAPTER 25

Harvesting the Earth

Beneath the cloak of Boxley's thin soil lay a number of materials useful to man, which over the centuries the men of Boxley strove to recover.

The land all along the river was quarried section by section over a period of hundreds of years to extract the prized Kentish ragstone. Its hardness made it difficult to shape and thus was not widely used locally for building. Efforts to cut and shape it resulted in ragged edges – hence the name. The ease with which it could be transported by barge down river resulted in most of it being sent to London together with stone from Allington and Boughton, where the master masons used it both for paving and building. Two prime examples of the endurance of this valued limestone are the Norman built White Tower of The Tower of London, and the reconstructed St Paul's Cathedral. Between 1674 and 1700, the staggering figure of 10,884 tons of Kentish rag was hauled to and down the Medway, for use in the rebuilding of St Paul's, after the ravages of the Great Fire of London.

The birth of artillery with the invention of the bombard, provided a further use for the stone, which was shaped into cannonballs. In 1419 John Rennet, Mason of Maidstone received an order for 700 cannonballs from stone dug from local quarries. William Athawes in the 17th Century was one of the principal Boxley quarriers, as were Charles Hollands and the Bensted family in the 19th Century.

The vivid white scars on the southern scarp of the North Downs bear evidence to the extensive chalk industry, which still goes on today just beyond Boxley's border at Detling Quarry. Down the ages, Boxley men hacked out this invaluable material which, once burned in kilns, produced lime which was spread on the fields as fertiliser. For many years, the main Boxley lime kilns stood on, 'a scrubby piece of land with a small cottage', alongside the hill below Harp Farm. In 1714 it was run by John Norris and thereafter by several generations of Boghursts, having been bought by the Best family around 1750. Many readers will still remember the lime kilns which stood near the bottom of Blue Bell Hill. With industrial growth came a loss of innocence. In 1805, John Boys, in a report to The Board of Agriculture complained that each year the lime burners on the chalk ridge above Boxley appeared to use ever decreasing bushel measures so that wagons which formally brought away 200 bushels now carried as many as 300 bushels!

A particularly hard form of chalk was also quarried here, which proved invaluable in building and much of this too was floated by barge to London. However it was also used locally, the columns of the nave in Boxley Church providing testimony of its strength. It can also be seen in the walls of Watercress Cottage alongside The Green.

The earth does not give up her treasures easily. Armstrong, in 'The Economy of Kent 1640 - 1914', quotes an observer who was shocked by the life-threatening risks taken by the quarrymen. He spoke of men "with a lifeline fastened around their bodies, securely tied to an iron crowbar driven into the ground at the top, some few yards from the edge of the cliff". Thus they dangled down the cliff face, chipping away at the chalk with pickaxes. The Parish Register as early as 1606 records the death of William Stocke, killed by a fall of chalk, and perusal of any early local newspapers provides evidence of continuing local tragedies. In 1818 Nicholas Smith was digging in chalk pits on Boxley Hill when a large mass gave way nearly burying him – he died an hour later. Just four months on, Jacob Coulter was crushed to death at the same pits. Evidence that our forefathers were mining chalk in Boxley long before the quarrymen, is provided by the Deneholes which from time to time come to light. In 1998, the local paper had a story of a dog rescued from a 60 foot denehole near Harp Farm. Thought by Victorian antiquarians to be ancient hiding places, Neolithic grain stores, or animal traps, amongst other romantic notions, they are now more prosaically known to be chalk mines. They were often dug at the edge of the fields upon which the chalk marl was to be spread, thus avoiding transportation problems. Normally between 30 and 100 feet deep, a cylindrical well would be dug down to the chalk layer and then chambers excavated out from the bottom. Foot holes were dug on either side of the shaft and the chalk hauled up by means of a primitive windlass. The earliest of such holes are pre-roman and they continued to be dug up to the 15th Century. There was a revival from the 17th to the 19th Centuries, although these later holes can be identified by their larger size. The emergence of the Kentish Cement Industry in the 19th Century provided a new and continuing use for the chalk.

In the Middle Ages, the somewhat rare mineral Copperas was dug up amongst the chalk and flint of Boxley's soil. More usually found on beeches, Copperas is a mineral substance formed by the decomposition of pyrites. It is in fact a sulphate of iron and contrary to the implication of its name, contains no copper, despite being coloured bright green. Among its principal uses were the dying of wool cloths and hats, black, the tanning and dressing of leather, and making ink. It was also used extensively for dressing 'scab' in sheep. An account of 1320 records that 2 pounds of 'Copperose' was sold at Boxley for six pence, for sheep ointment.

Soon after their arrival at Boxley, the Cistercians discovered that their Abbey was perfectly sited for the reintroduction of an industry which had died with the departure of the Romans. The soil along the Boxley valley contained an abundance of clay known as 'brick earth', well-suited for the production of tiles. The name Tyland, which was frequently written as Tileland is almost certainly derived from the tile earth found beneath its fields. After the Romans, thatch or wooden shingles had become the preferred substances for roofing. However as towns and cities grew, and houses became crowded together, the risk of fire increased considerably. In the 12th Century the citizens of London banned the use of thatch and the Cistercian's fledgling tile industry really took off. In 1362 their tile yards at Boxley sold 5,000 flat tiles @ 6 shillings and eight pence, plus 2,000 at ten shillings - the thousand. The Victoria County History recounts that the Boxley tile labourers were paid between one shilling and six pence and two shillings per week. Later in 1424 the Steward of the Corpus Christi Fraternity, whose ancient buildings later housed the town Grammar school, and still look out over the Medway at Maidstone, purchased 4,000 tiles from John Brode of Boxley, for the Maidstone College. Tiles were not only used for roofing, but also became very popular as baked clay floor tiles. Tiles from Boxley are believed to have been used for the mosaic floors at Canterbury Cathedral, Rochester Cathedral and Leeds Priory.

A medieval tile kiln was discovered in the grounds of Abbey Farm, a half mile from the Abbey. It was built of broken tiles which contained the impressed declaration that "Guillelmus de Dudis me fecit "– William Dodes made me. In 1637 a William Dodes was churchwarden of Boxley Church. Either a descendant, or the kiln was not medieval, but Stuart. A large pan was contained within the kiln, bearing traces of metals, thus suggesting a possible use for smelting. The present owner of Parsonage Farm frequently comes across Crystallised Iron Nodules whilst digging his gardens. One wonders whether the kiln was perhaps used for extracting iron from these as a side product?

Tile production continued in Boxley for some 700 years. In 1554 Nicholas Porter was tenant of 5 acres with a 'tile host' – (tile oast, or kiln). This was probably the kiln which stood many years at Cookes Cottage on the high point of Grange Lane. In 1841 Henry Jarrett and William Hook were producing tiles here, as later did the Finnis family. By 1861 there were three occupied houses here, and in 1867 Henry Towsley advertised himself as a brick, tile and drainpipe manufacturer. Whilst the Maidstone by-pass was being constructed, a 16th Century kiln was discovered at Beulah Wood near the Detling Road, close by the lake which nestles alongside the North Western end of the now vast "Newnham Court' roundabout. Now only frequented by a fishing club, this little lake, presumably then larger, was known in 1554 as 'The Great Lake of Boxley'. John Warcoppe had been the tenant of 9 acres and a tile host adjoining to the Great Lake of Boxley, when he swapped his tools for the accoutrements of war and followed his lord, Sir Thomas Wyatt on his ill-fated uprising. Poor John was one of Wyatt's followers actually to be prosecuted for high treason. Happily he kept his head, and although eventually pardoned, he was fined and his tenancy revoked and given to one Richard Bryst. Probably the very kiln discovered centuries later by the road builders. It was described as being just over twenty feet long, consisting of two arched tunnels of brick tapering into one at the Northern end, where there was a stokehole.

Another kiln close by, belonged to Newnham Court and was in 1697 in occupation of Samuel Athawes, whose table tomb lies in the Churchyard. Yet more kilns were sited on the other side of the motorway in Park Wood. The ordnance survey maps show that the wood bordering the North side of the motorway is called Kiln Wood, a living memorial to the long gone workhouse yard and kiln, which stood to the East of Sandy Lane next to Stone House.

In 1850, the Fowle family sold the paper mill and 9 acres at the Forstall to Edward Ladd Betts. Betts erected a large scale pottery and brickyard there, providing employment for generations of Boxley locals, and rendering the small local kilns economically unviable. The Abbey kiln in Grange Lane was probably the last to cease production when it closed in the mid 1870's. Several people with Boxley connections are still proud to own old bricks stamped "Boxley " as souvenirs of this local industry.

Of the three different types of clay found in the Boxley valley, the most impressively named was 'terra porcellana phlogistica aliisque heterogeneis minima portione mixta', more prosaically known as pipe-clay, from which tobacco pipes were manufactured in Maidstone. The famous Midlands potter Josiah Wedgwood, was invited to examine the clay for possible use in porcelain making.

The abundance of woods provided the woodsmen with labour, both in coppicing and charcoal making, as well as the cutting of mature trees. When, in 1400, John Grove of Boxley supplied 22 elms for repair of Rochester Bridge, they were said to be so large that, "three or four trees were all that 4 men with 9 horses could bring". John Mason who owned the Nether Grange Estate (now Lower Grange Farm), became in the 1660's and 1670's, the most important supplier of hardwood timber to the shipbuilding docks of Chatham. In addition the woodland craft of coppicing remained in constant demand. Cants of chestnut and ash were planted out by the 17th Century, to supply hop poles. The hop growers were said to prefer poles grown on the poorer soil of the Downs which grew slower and thus stronger and more sinewy. The best poles were used for hop poles and then others for thatching, hurdlemaking, timber for the wheelwrights, piles and props for the quarrying industries, and to make the tenter frames used for drying the cloth outside fulling mills. Nothing was wasted, for what remained was cut for 'bavins', for the tile, brick and oast kilns. 'Bavins' were bundles of brushwood used for the initial kindling. Daniel Defoe wrote in 1724 of 'small light bavins, made in North West Kent, which are used in taverns in London to light their faggots', thus providing evidence of yet another local commodity export. It was a local 'bavin tug', (probably similar to a hay sledge or slide car) which was used to haul the upper part of William Fowle's mill to Street Farm for its recycled use as a granary.

'Coaling', the wood, by charring it to produce charcoal was normally done in-situ. The charcoal burner, or 'collier', would dig pits alongside the coppice, the wood once stacked inside would be covered with soil or turf and burned slowly. The end product at Boxley was of such quality that it was not only sent to the Weald to fuel the iron furnaces, but was also required for the royal household in London.

In 1802, the local newspaper reported that a group of woodmen from Boxley Hill, zealous to imitate their superiors, gathered at the Upper Blue Bell Inn where they 'turned out' a marten cat, (presumably a pine marten). The creature had 15 minutes grace before being pursued by 3 couple and a $\frac{1}{2}$ beagles (7). After affording an exciting run of $2\frac{1}{2}$ hours, it was taken in a tree with great difficulty, and the organisers intended to turn it out again on the following Friday morning.

And so we move to two materials below the soil of Boxley Parish which brought it most fame – Fullers Earth and Glass Sand.

Fullers Earth is a rare, highly valued clay-like substance, with a waxy appearance, varying in colour from dark or blue-grey to pale grey and yellow, which rapidly crumbles apart when immersed in water. It occurs naturally in seams between the local Sandgate Beds. At Grove Green and to the north of Vinters Park, seams were discovered lying about 30' deep and being 7' in thickness. They were mainly of the most valuable blue-grey variety and considered second only in quality to the outcrop at Nutfield in Surrey. Their proximity to the surface allowed them to be quarried rather than mined, wide vertical shafts being dug down and then opened into pits which left characteristic bowls and depressions over much of the area.

Of its many properties, the one that made it so highly prized was its ability to remove natural oils from sheep's fleece, more quickly and efficiently than by any other method. The earth was added to water, the wool immersed in the resultant slurry and then trodden underfoot by men known as waulkers – hence the surname 'Walker' – until the grease was sufficiently removed. The cloth was then stretched on hooks across a wooden frame of poles called a tenter, to dry. This gave us the expression of 'being on tenterhooks', when one is in a state of suspense or tension. In the 14th Century, a new mechanical process was introduced to England by Flemish immigrants. Small mills were constructed on streams and the water power harnessed by a wheel to raise and lower large wooden hammers to pound the cloth. Although Leeds Castle is known to have had a fulling mill as early as 1368, the first known mill of this kind in Boxley was Pole or Mote Mill, which stood on the River Len a few hundred yards from where Turkey Mill now stands. The earliest reference to it was in 1518, when Hugh Waram leased this fulling mill to John Alphne.

By then, fullers earth had been extracted in Boxley for perhaps two hundred years, and maybe even since Roman times. In 1345 Roger Vinter owned a famous fullers earth estate, which in 1554 was forfeited to The State by Sir Henry Isley for his part in the Wyatt rebellion. Passing through the hands of Cavaliere Mayeot, and the Covert, Tufton and Ongley families to James Whatman of papermaking fame. The other famed estate – The Grove, was according to the historian Hasted, conveyed around 1405 by Isabel de Wavering to Thomas Burbige, whose descendants, confusingly all called Thomas, owned it until 1702 when it was bought by John Watts under whom it flourished until 1757. When his heirs sold it to General William Belford in 1782 it became a purely residential estate.

The extracted earth, was hauled by cart along Sandling Lane then down a track behind where Sandling Place now stands, to the Maidstone/Rochester Road opposite Gibraltar Lane, proceeding down that lane to the river at Wilstone Wharf, where it was stored in clapboard storehouses (or lodges) to await transport to Rochester.

Wilstone or Wilston was once a thriving hamlet that has long since disappeared from the map. In 1540 Henry VIII exchanged various properties with Sir Thomas Wyatt the elder of Allington Castle. Sir Thomas gained the Abbey of Boxley and the farms and lands belonging to it, including Upper Grange, plus a number of local villages and hamlets including 'Sandelying' and Wilston. Following his son's ill-fated rebellion and the subsequent forfeiture of the Wyatt lands to The Crown, Queen Mary granted to George Clarke several parcels of land in Boxley, previously part of the Wyatt estate, including the Nether (lower) Grange. In 1579 his son alienated this land totalling 340 acres to Robert Bruer (Brewer), which land included the hamlet of Wilstone. In 1608, Robert Brewer was paying tithes for a piece of land called Wilstone fulling lodges and by 1629 at least, his son Thomas, was paying for the storehouses and also for The Fulling Lodge, an inn later to become The Gibraltar.

From 1627-1640 Thomas Brewer, a leading figure of religious radicalism and pioneer Congregationalist, was imprisoned for sedition. His wife together with a Richard Roades continued to run the fullers earth trade. By the beginning of the 17th Century, The State's cloth industry, whose products constituted two thirds of the entire nation's exports, was coming under stiff opposition from a growing European industry. In order to maintain an advantage, The Government imposed a prohibition on the export of the valuable fullers earth, which could only be found in marketable quantities in England.

However, they reckoned without the long established Kentish tradition of smuggling. The 'owlers', as they were known, had been smuggling wool to the continent for some 200 years, in order to obtain a fair price for their wares, which in England were subject to a fixed price, and punitive taxes. Already experiencing deep resentment, engendered by the harsh suppression of her religious beliefs and the incarceration of her husband, it is not surprising that Mrs Brewer was soon heavily involved in smuggling. In 1630, John Ray, a London merchant was sentenced to a £200.00 fine, whipping in the pillory, and imprisonment for smuggling 76 loads of fullers earth purchased from Richard Rods (Roades).

The prohibition was obviously ineffective, and thus on 5/5/1639 The Government imposed a complete ban on the transportation of fullers earth by water. That same year the clothiers of Surrey and Essex petitioned The King's Council, asking for a licence to 'ship 300 chauldrons now lying drying near Maidstone', to Manningtree and Maldon in Essex. A chauldron was the largest measure of volume of the time, and equivalent to 36 bushels or 288 gallons.

In 1640, Mrs Brewer and Roades were accused of 'sending fullers earth to the waterside, where she has three houses on the shore, where she stores it 'till the tide serves to bring up boats in which it is carried to Rochester and then in greater vessels beyond seas". Roades was in court again in 1662 together with Mr or Mrs Brewer, accused of smuggling 450 loads and 75 loads respectively, but both were acquitted. Previous historians have incorrectly sited the storehouses in Maidstone. In fact Boxley was the centre of both the digging and the export of fullers earth.

The rise of the papermaking industry produced another Boxley business for which the fullers earth remained essential. Part of the papermaking process required the newly made sheets to be stocked in a press in order that all the water could be squeezed out. Each sheet needed to be separated from its neighbour by a woollen blanket known as a 'felt'. In the final quarter of the 18th Century, Dr William Charles entered into a felt making and blanket cleaning business in partnership with Walter Harris of Gabriels Hill, Maidstone, and later his son Robert. The fulling mill at Sandling which belonged to the doctor's father-in-law, furnished the necessary equipment and later in 1801, he purchased Chillington Manor, now Maidstone Museum, whose hall and attached buildings provided room for expansion. An advert of 1797 reveals an earlier outlet for their wares – "Messrs. Charles and Harris having made this season a variety of handsome coatings on an improved plan from our own Kentish wool .... will be sold on very moderate terms, either in cloths or coats, at Mr R Harris's, Draper, near the Corn-market, High Street, Maidstone". It is doubtful whether William was particularly involved in the felts production, as throughout his life he remained a practising surgeon and general practitioner, with a large practice mainly in Allington. Likewise, Harris was essentially a draper. James Whatman's accounts show that he purchased his felts from a John Balcombe. Our research has uncovered a John Balcomb feltsman, living in Stone Street (near the Harris family) at the time. As William Charles was described in The Paper Trade Review of 1826 as 'practically the only maker of felts', we believe that Balcomb probably ran Charles' mill.

The sight of yards of thick, compressed material hanging on tenterhooks to dry, was obviously too great a temptation for at least one poor local, perhaps needing to make winter coats for his family. In 1809 posters were put up advertising a 5 guinea reward for the apprehension of the person or persons responsible for – "cutting out of the rack in the tenter ground adjoining to Mr Charles mill in Sandling – 13 yards of felting cloth, 1 yard 2 inches wide, Kersey wove, the wool raised on one side, and plain on the other. Also 2 new quarter – blankets with blue borders at each end". The business was later run as 'Stacey and Charles', obviously a partnership with local landowners the Staceys who also ran the Lower Brewery in Maidstone, before being sold to Messrs. Whitehead & Bros of Oldham in 1840.

Gradually the main Boxley pits became uneconomical to work, although the precious earth was still dug from smaller workings. With the decline in the English wool industry and scientific advances in cleansing, the Fullers Earth Industry slowly subsided, although the wonderful absorbent qualities of the earth remained prized for other uses. Fulling Mills across the country ceased to work from the 1680's to the 1750's, some of them being converted to seed crushing, or grinding corn. In Boxley, and all along the River Len from Hollingbourne to Maidstone, a far more profitable use for the redundant mills was found – that of papermaking.

Fullers earth is still used today in the production of cosmetics for skin care, in cat litter, and to absorb the agents used in chemical warfare. In 1954 The Fullers Earth Union acquired the extraction rights to the Vinters estate as a reserve, and the Boxley industry effectively ceased.

In 1741, the historian Newton writing of the Maidstone area, stated that "by the hoys going from hence is London supplied with a fine white sand for the glass-houses, which is reckoned the best in England for melting into Flint Glass and looking glass plates, and much used for writing sand". By that time, the wharves of Boxley had been exporting sand, dug from throughout the area between Aylesford and Hollingbourne, for at least a hundred years. The glass furnaces at Greenwich and Woolwich were almost solely dependant on this silver sand, which was completely free from impurities, and thus capable of producing the clearest glass for creating fine drinking vessels and mirrors.

The main Boxley pits were at Newnham Court, where a vast labyrinth of caverns were excavated by mining down to where the sand lay beneath the Folkestone Beds. Other worked outcrops in the parish were at Popes Wood against the Detling boundary, Sandling Wood (now Cuckoo Wood), Sandling Bank by the Forstal Road motorway bridge, and on the southern part of Penenden Heath. This latter pit was by the site of the old gallows which had been erected on a large mound of sand on the Maidstone/Boxley boundary. In 1817, the sand was extracted and much of it taken to build the new county gaol in Maidstone, thus levelling the land, during which operation were discovered more than 300 skeletons of those unfortunates who had fallen foul of a harsh penal system. Lord Romney donated profits from this sand to the relief of the poor. Discovering that much sand was being removed improperly for personal gain, Romney prosecuted the prison's architect, Daniel Alexander, who had previously built Mote House for his lordship. That mining was used here as well as quarrying was evidenced by the sudden subsidence in 1976 at nearby Norman Close, where a fifteen foot crater appeared with an apparently enormous cavern below.

Slightly less pure sand was excavated at Sandling from the area between The Malta Inn and Gibraltar House, possibly only for local use, but its proximity to the river suggests the probability of wider distribution. The historian E.R. Hughes believed that sand from here was used in the construction of Allington Castle, which stands on the opposite side of the Medway. If Sandling's name was, as is claimed, derived from these very pits, then excavation must certainly have been going on from an early date.

Apart from its use as mortar, sand was used for strewing on floors prior to floorboards, and also on interior brick or tiled floors to soak up spilled grease. Spittoons were filled with it, where sawdust was unavailable, and its capacity to smother flames made it invaluable for dealing with fires. The fine sand had a further most important use in early times for sprinkling over written work to absorb extraneous ink.

Once excavated, the sand from Bearsted, Hollingbourne and Boxley, was hauled along Sandling Lane to the public wharf where The Malta now stands, and the wharf at Cobtree. In the 1840's, William Colegate took thousands of tons of sand from Newnham Court, and by Bearsted station, transporting it to Sandling. From there he shipped it to London in barges which he had constructed himself at Leeds and launched at Cobtree.

With the emergence of the vast Aylesford sand pits, the distribution point moved to the Forstall, and around the 1850's Newnham Court mine ceased working. By then it had become a tourist attraction, with visitors coming from far and wide to explore the maze of interconnecting passageways with their caverns and soaring buttresses. Writing around this time, Hasted gave the following description – "We visited the remarkable sand caverns at Newnham Court Farm, and really they are worthy of notice. These subterranean passages are so long and intricate as to render the assistance of a guide necessary. The boy who conducted us said that the length of the various pits exceeded half a mile, and that formerly their extent was much greater, more than half part of them having been filled up by the falling in of the earth above".

So whilst the vast majority of the old parish was composed of a conglomeration of farms and individual smallholdings, Boxley can lay claim to a substantial industrial past.

CHAPTER 26

Boxley Paper Mills

English papermaking began in earnest in 1588, with John Spilman's erection of a paper mill at Dartford. Within 150 years the abundance of pure streams in the Maidstone area had elevated it to the premier district for the making of paper in the country. The sleepy parish of Boxley may justifiably lay claim to being the cradle of papermaking in the Maidstone area.

Probate records show that in 1640 Thomas Taylor, papermaker of Maidstone, died a wealthy man. The earliest documentary reference to an actual paper mill in the Maidstone area is in a deed of 1665, which refers to a mill in Boxley belonging to the Duke family of Cossington and occupied by a Thomas Taylor. One could therefore presume that the earlier Thomas was his father and worked the same mill, which by later deeds is identified as Forstal Mill. This stood on the Aylesford to Sandling Road (Forstal Road) in the south west corner of Boxley parish, by the Aylesford boundary. The earliest definite date we have for this as a paper mill is 1671 when Thomas Willard was the papermaker. However it is quite likely to have been making paper for at least 40 years prior to this date, and was possibly a fulling mill before that. That the mill was there in 1661 could be inferred from the following intriguing snippet. In that year were buried in Aylesford, Henry Gorham, a bricklayer, and John Allen, carpenter's apprentice, who went into the river at 'Jermans Forstall' to wash and were drowned. Were these artisans altering or possibly building Forstal Mill? Indeed it is just possible that paper was being produced here almost 100 years earlier. In 1567, serjeant-at-law Nicolas Barham (whose family certainly later had connections with Boxley) received authority from Queen Elizabeth to bring foreign artisans into Maidstone from Europe. Among them were both white and brown papermakers. Unfortunately no records exist to confirm whether such papermakers set up production around Maidstone. However, at least one of the families who emigrated here at that time, namely The Callants, became domiciled in Boxley, but there is no evidence of their involvement in papermaking.

For years the mill was known as 'Russell's Mill', after the family who from 1725 for almost a century, provided a succession of papermakers there. It is possible that the opening in January 1807 of the mighty Springfield Mill, where was installed one of the first Boulton-Watt steam engines, marked the beginning of the end for the handmade paper at the Sandling Mills. In 1816

BOXLEY PARISH

Clement Taylor Russell, occupier of Forstal Mill, was made bankrupt. It would appear that he continued to remain involved, sub-letting it to other papermakers. In 1826, the Gill family, owners of the mill since about 1716, sold it to George Fowle, 'for the use of Clement Taylor Russell'. The actual occupant up until George's death in 1840 was John Lavender. John Mason then ran if for a year followed by Edward Fowle, until in 1844 Thomas Compere took on a year's lease of half of the mill and one of its two cottages, signing a 21 year lease the following year. In 1850 the Fowles sold the mill to Edward Ladd Betts, and on most of its 9 acres rose the sprawling brick and tile works, later to become known as Aylesford Pottery. The Boxley Poor rates appear to show that the half of a papermill continued in production, with Isaac's and Company taking over in 1853. The following year they also began producing their millboard at Pratling Street Mill. This mill stood astride the Boxley/Aylesford border, on the same stream that fed Forstal, and at the north end of the Forstal site. It had first begun producing paper in 1810, when John Young and John Pett converted an old mill previously occupied by William Plum. In 1813 Young was replaced by Thomas Stroud and his son Thomas, until 1821 when Charles Wise took over. He was also the proprietor at Forstal and Cobtree Mills as well as at Padsole Mill in Maidstone. Papermaking at the smaller mills appears to have been a precarious business resulting in many bankruptcies, and the mills often standing empty. At such times their excise general licences were surrendered and re-issued to other mills, thus causing confusion in attempts by historians to follow the succession of tenants at individual mills. In 1824 Wise went bankrupt, and just 15 years after its opening the mill stood empty for a year. A number of papermakers attempted to succeed here thereafter, with the mill lying empty between tenants. John Lavender from 1825-1829, William and Joseph Moreton 1831-1834, John Clarke in 1836, John Mason 1837-1842, and Timothy Healey from late 1843 to 1844. This is probably when actual papermaking ended here. The Aylesford Poor Rate shows that the mill stood empty for the next 5 years. However when in 1848 the landowner Charles Milner sold the 2$\frac{1}{2}$ acre site to Edward Ladd Betts, the deeds stated that Compere and Company had taken out a lease in 1847. They produced millboard and corrugated paper only, but they too went bankrupt in 1851.

It is almost certain that the original Forstal Mill stood on the banks of the Medway, and surprisingly is still there today, albeit in disguise. The small bungalow almost opposite what was The Pottery Arms in Forstal Road, holds a secret. Its walls are some 21 inches thick. In 1892 it was said that some ten years earlier the upper two stories of the mill were removed, a roof added and a residence created. The true history of the mill remains an enigma. The mill by the river was said to have only one wheel whereas there are many documentary references to Forstal Mill having wheels. There are also references to more than one papermaker working on the site at the same time.

This leads us to suggest the following hypothesis. Possibly there were two mills on the site, the northern one by Pratling Street, both going under the umbrella of Forstal Mill. The southern one may well have finished production around 1844. That to the north continued, producing board rather than paper, and often run in tandem by tenants of Pratling Street Mill, with whose name it gradually became associated. Mills often stood empty, and thus this could well be the 'New Mill at Sandling' opened by William Peters and Thomas Chaplin in 1819, which ran to 1825 only. An existing mill revived, and given a new excise general licence number.

What is certain is that Isaac's & Co, later under the names of John Skelton Isaac, and Warwick Isaac & Co, continued at one or both mills to make millboard and other patent composition boards, artists boards, coach panels, and later panels for railway carriages into the 1880's. They also had a saddle and harness making business in Maidstone High Street.

The most famous mill in Boxley, once described as the largest and most prestigious in the entire country, was Turkey Mill on the River Len. We believe that this mill was first built in 1536, when Thomas Hartredge, a Maidstone tailor, agreed to repair the existing 'Motte Mylles' (Moat Mills) – later known as Pole Mill – and construct two additional overshot mills. Hartredge, together with Thomas Sparlawrence had the tenancy of the nearby fulling pits at Grove Green, and constructed his new mills just a couple of hundred yards west of Pole Mill upon a plot of land which also contained a rich supply of fullers earth. The mills probably remained in the occupation of a succession of Hartridges, Hartrups or Hartnuppes (as the name was variously spelt), into the next century.

In 1640, Simon Smythe of Tenterden, whose family had lived at Great Buckland in Maidstone, now the site of The Girl's Grammar School, sold what was now known as 'The Overloppe Fulling Mills with 10 acres', to John Fletcher, for £493. At this time it was in the occupation of Thomas Tolherst. Fletcher's son Richard conveyed the freehold to John Cripps in 1657, when the latter married Richard's daughter Katherine. The fulling mill then had 15 acres following the purchase in 1646 of the 5 acre Savours or Sawyers Croft. Tolherst's widow Joane was now the proprietor together with her son Thomas, and remained there to around 1675. Soon thereafter came a new tenant, who was to raise the profile of this unassuming little mill, and sow the seeds of a papermaking concern that would bring Turkey Mill and Boxley to national prominence.

George Gill had served an apprenticeship under John Spilman at his Dartford No.1 mill, and following his 1676 marriage to Susanna Cox, came to Boxley. The first documented record of his presence in the parish is in the tithe records for 1680 when Dorothy Cripps paid a tithe for a messuage and two mills in occupation of Gill. The description of 'two mills' refers to the mill having two water wheels. One of Gill's first improvements on converting the old fulling mill to papermaking was to install an additional wheel, thus making it a 3-wheel mill, and a large concern indeed. Soon he was making high quality white paper, and had established himself as a leading light of the national grouping known as The Ancient Paper Makers, and was one of the foremost master papermakers in the country. An indenture of 1695 shows that George had a partner in Turkey Mill, one James Brooke, a London stationer, whose affluence was to prove invaluable through the ensuing years.

George's son William married Brooke's favourite niece, Elizabeth Lawrence in 1713, and, probably with her uncle's backing, embarked on a meteoric rise as an entrepreneur. Having built Sandling Mill in 1714, he went on to purchase Forstal Mill two years later and to take over the running of Turkey Mill. The rapid expansion of his business empire into Brewing and the management of pubs, required more cash. Although Brooke was happy to back ventures in the papermaking industry, it appears that he did not approve of William's other business activities. These also appear to have caused an estrangement with his father, who virtually excluded his son from his will. William mortgaged Turkey Mill for £400 in 1723 and took on the tenancy of Pole Mill in 1728. This was a step too far and he was made bankrupt the following year. Brooke cleared the mortgage on Turkey Mill, temporarily bailing William out. However his financial position was too precarious and in 1731 he was bankrupted for good. His possessions at this time included The Upper Brewery in what is now Brewer Street, Maidstone, which he owned in partnership with Edward Bedwell. Joseph Cordwell took on a lease of the mill, followed by Peter Musgrave until 1736, when Richard Harris arrived, ushering in the Whatman era. We have, of course, devoted a separate chapter to the Whatmans.

When James Whatman the Younger retired in 1794 he sold the business to the Hollingworth brothers and Thomas Balston. Its three 8 foot overshot wheels together with the Whatman expertise and business acumen had built a thriving business that provided employment for a large number of Boxley residents. (By 'overshot' wheels we mean that the water to power the wheels was carried in a trough above them, and flowed over them in order to propel them around. It is believed that 'Overloppe Mill' means overshot). In 1805 Balston dissolved the partnership, leaving to set up a new mill at Springfield which would rival and finally usurp the position of Turkey Mill as the premier local mill. The Hollingworths created an empire of their own having an interest in many other paper mills.

Although Springfield continues in production today, mainly through diversification into chemical filter papers and other products, Turkey Mill finally ran down the curtain on Boxley's papermaking industry when it ceased production in 1976. Today the lovely walled gardens of Turkey Court remain, as for the moment do the many attractive old buildings. Presumably somewhere in their future they have a date with the developer's bulldozer as, strangely, none are 'listed'. It seems somewhat incongruous that the railway viaduct spanning the entrance is listed, as is the screen wall with its circular cut-outs, built to prevent sparks and soot from the steam trains, drifting on to the hand-made paper as it lay drying in the louvered drying sheds. Although another theory is that the brickwork screened the railway from the eyes of Whatman as he looked across from his mansion at Vinters.

It was probably the introduction in 1712 and 1714 of new and much heavier Excise Duties on the importing of foreign paper that inspired William Gill to set out on a course of expansion. In June 1714 William applied to Sir Jacob Astley who owned the Allington Castle Estate, for permission to build a new mill on 5 acres of former quarry ground on the east bank of the Medway where the Boxley streams flowed into the river. William agreed to build at his own expense within one year "a watermill for grinding corn, or for the making of paper or paste board, to carry 3 troughs and beaters at the least". Astley reserved the right to fish in any millponds created, and Gill agreed not to dig any stone or to suffer any fullers earth to be loaded or shipped from the premises. The discharge stream for the mill ran across what is now the pub car park, entering the river just before Lock Lane. Later it was diverted under the lane, and the sluicegate controlling its flow can still be seen from the steps up to the river sluice.

The first papermaker was David Dean, and the mill remained in the Dean family occupancy until his grandson died in 1781, whereupon his granddaughter Fanny Dean inherited. The mill was run by her husband William Thomas up to 1812. Previous historians have identified this mill as 'Cobtree Mill'. However in every title deed, and also in the Rate Books, it is only ever referred to as 'Sandling Paper Mill', 'Sandling Mill', and on one occasion 'Allington Lower Mill'. This latter name derives from it belonging to Allington Castle until 1720 when Astley sold the Castle Estate land on the Boxley side of the river to Dame Elizabeth Shovell. She was the widow of the famous Rear-Admiral Sir Cloudesley Shovell, who drowned in 1707 when his flagship went down. Her daughter Elizabeth married Sir Robert Marsham, later made the first Baron Romney, and the mill was absorbed into the Romney Estate. In 1799, the 2nd Baron, exchanged it with Flint Stacey the brewer, 'in occupation of William Thomas, as tenant to Mr Gill'. Thomas was later in partnership with John Pine at Lower Tovil Mill, and Basted Mill, and it is possible that he sub-let Sandling for part of the time.

As previously mentioned, these mills would stand empty for short periods whilst awaiting take over by a new papermaker. This resulted in the belief by previous researchers that mills had shut down for good, and thus in their placing known papermakers at incorrect sites. The Rate Books and Land Tax Records show that Stacey Wise took over from Thomas in 1813, followed by his brother Charles, until his bankruptcy in 1824. Probably a combination of overstretching his resources in too many mills coupled with the success of

Springfield and Turkey Mill. The ten vats of Springfield, more than that of any mill in the country, together with the use of up-to-the minute technology, including stream power, could produce paper far quicker, more economically and of better quality than the small Sandling Mills. Gradually they slid into decline.

According to tax records, Henry Alnut and John Wilson took over, superseded by John Lavender in 1827 and 1828, with Henry Alnut returning until 1831. Lavender was also running Pratling Street Mill from 1824-1829, and it is possible that he was the supervising papermaker for both mills throughout. The mill ceased production and lay empty from 1832 to 1838, when William and Reuben Hunt reopened it. Their papermaking venture here proved short-lived, as was that of their successor Moses Clark, who likewise ran it for just two years. From 1842 the mill lay still, its papermaking duties over for good. Its machinery was converted, millstones were installed, and in 1844 Robert Spratt, miller, began to grind corn there. This new lease of life continued under John Large and then George Larking, until 1865 when Larking stopped work both there and at Fowle's windmill behind the Abbey. Its milling days over, the mill became primarily residential. Later it and its land were put to various commercial activities which are described in the chapter –'Down by the River'.

In the south-east corner of the parish, in Weavering ward, the waters of the River Len have for centuries been harnessed, firstly for fulling and then for papermaking. The mill, historically termed Poll or Pole Mill was known as Mote Mill in 1518 when Hugh Waram leased it to John Alphne, shearman of Maidstone, as a fulling mill. In 1534, William Warham leased it to John Stennett, blacksmith of Maidstone. At this time it was described as a 'stedle', meaning it was raised on supports above the stream. Alphne agreed to build an additional wheel for turning grindstones. Two years later, when Thomas Hartredge contracted to repair the two Mote mills they were described as having one wheel turning a grindstone for corn, and a second wheel activating the fulling stocks, all under one roof. The site of Pole Mill is now partly beneath the waters of Mote Park Lake alongside the old stone boathouse, and within a couple of hundred yards of Turkey Mill. Hartredge also agreed to build an additional two mills (or wheels) which would have made Pole Mill an unwieldy 4-wheel mill. As earlier stated, these new mills were most likely Turkey Mill. Certainly The Mote Mills continued with just two waterwheels, let in 1537 by William Tylden draper to William Bassock fuller and John Bassock miller. Tylden was a steadfast advocate of Wyatt's revolt and was responsible for 'raising the downland' in support. The Wyatt attainder survey of 1554 shows that John Collins had a 31 year indenture of the fulling mill, now called Pole Mill, with a stable and two acres. Collins was a farmer and tenant of Boarley Farm and Sandling Corn Mill, and is again recorded at Pole Mill in 1583, by when the land had been granted to John Astley. It is highly likely that the occupant of the mill at this time was called Powell and that 'Poll' is a corruption of his name. By 1629 the occupant was Stephen Geery, who was still there in 1638 when Astley passed it to his brother-in-law, Norton Knatchbull. In 1662 he sold the land to Sir John Banks and the mill, let to widow Giles and with 30$^1/_2$ acres of additional mill land, became part of the Aylesford Estate. By 1670 the tenant was John Mapilsden with William Baseden as his sub-tenant. He was replaced in 1676 by Ed Savery. It is possible that Tolhersts, the tenant of Turkey Mill, leased it at some time as it is referred to in later deeds of adjoining land, as 'Powells Mill, later Tolhersts'. This has caused confusion and led previous researchers to believe that Turkey Mill previously bore these names. However, the succession of occupants also detailed in the deeds make clear that this was Pole Mill.

In 1718, John Swinnock, who had been fulling there for at least a decade, was granted £300 by Lord Guernsey to construct a papermill in place of the existing mills. The change of occupation to papermaking did not sit well with Swinnock who went bankrupt in 1727. He was replaced by the equally unfortunate William Gill and, on his bankruptcy, brothers William and Joseph Cordwell took over, managing to turn the papermill into a profitable concern over their 24 year tenure. The Fearon family ran it for the next 5 years until Clement Taylor senior arrived in 1761. He was the patriarch of a papermaking family and together with his 4 sons was to run 5 mills in the local area. His first move appears to have been to introduce new technology, in the form of an engine to beat to a pulp the rags which were used as the basis for making paper. A number of the occupants of Boxley scratched a living by collecting rags of fibrous material from every possible source, to feed the insatiable appetites of the paper mills.

Essentially, the art of hand papermaking involved breaking down fibrous materials (in fact anything of vegetable origin) into separate fibres, initially by beating them for hours with huge wooden hammers powered by the water wheel. The resultant pulp was heated and then gathered in shallow trays with a fine gauze base, through which the excess water escaped. The sheets thus produced were than stacked one upon another, separated by woollen 'felts', and placed in a huge press which removed almost all remaining water. They were then hung out to dry. Locally, rope was easily available from yards along the river. Its collection giving rise to the saying – 'money for old rope'.

Taylor's sons James and George took on the tenancy at his death, and were the papermakers when James Whatman, owner of the successful Turkey Mill, purchased it from Lord Aylesford in 1785. Believing the mill to be in a poor state of repair, Whatman sought new terms for the tenancy, only to be dumbfounded when the Taylors produced their father's will. This purported that he had not been an annual tenant but in fact held a long lease which he had left to James, and thus the terms could not be changed. The will apparently also stated that virtually all the fixtures and fittings and equipment within the mill belonged to the Taylors. During the next 2 years the affair became very acrimonious. James Taylor, in partnership with his brother-in-law John Russell, was also tenant of Newnham Court Farm, part of which lands bordered Vinters House to the east. The kinsmen refused to allow Whatman to cross their land in order to build an access road from Vinters to the Bearsted Road. Whatman took them to court in 1787 and was able to prove that there had never been a lease, and that Clement Taylor senior's beating engine was all that they owned. The Taylors were evicted and Whatman built his road. After 1815 he extended it to the newly constructed Ashford Road, and it is known today as New Cut Road. Thereafter Whatman ran the mill himself until October 1794 when he retired from business and sold both Pole Mill and Turkey Mill to Finch and Thomas Hollingworth. They ran it until at least 1824, after which it may have continued making paper, but certainly for a time it was occupied by a bleacher.

In 1836 there was a severe flood on the River Len, and a landslide swept away the twin water wheels. Shortly after the mill was demolished, and its site partially disappeared when the valley was flooded to increase in size the ornamental lake for the new Mote House.

The last paper mill to be built in Boxley was known as Medway Paper Mill, (down Moncktons Lane) and erected in 1858 by Uriah Macey and his partner Elves. It was born of an experiment that brown paper could be made from the sugar beet root, after the sugar had been extracted. A wonderful idea financially, yielding a double source of income. Unfortunately it failed to produce paper! However, ships cables, tarpaulins and old sacks did produce paper (all easily available from Chatham Docks) and the mill prospered. This coarse material could only produce brown paper, and the partnership found their niche in creating the wrapping paper required by all the local mills.

By 1872 the mill had been taken over by Walter Monckton, after whom both the mill and the lane alongside became known. The boundary line between Maidstone and Boxley ran down this lane and then followed the course of the river as far as the Forstal. A circular store for chemicals stood on the river bank with a tramline running from it straight into the mill, worked by a patented steam hoist with automatic stopping gear. It continued to produce coloured paper for packaging into this century, employing 40 people who turned out 12 tons of wrapping paper per week with the aid of 3 powerful steam engines, working night and day. About 1902 it was purchased by R.J. Balston, owner of the neighbouring Springfield Mill. The reason for the purchase has been said to be because the Balstons did not take kindly to the continuous pall of smoke from its chimney drifting across Springfield House, the family home. Within a couple of years it was closed down, its buildings being finally demolished just a couple of years ago, for residential development.

The story of one final Boxley mill remains to be told, possible the oldest of all. Centuries ago, the Boxley or Marley Stream was diverted after it left the site of Sandling Corn Mill. A channel was cut along the top of a bank creating a narrow mill pond. At the far end a fulling mill was constructed and then the water sent at right angles back down to the original channel, thence beneath the Aylesford/Sandling Road and on to discharge into the Medway. Its site can still be found some 100 feet back from Forstal Road, alongside Stream Cottages. This was Sandling Mill, also known locally as 'The Blanket Mill' and 'Cuddy Mill'. The appelation 'Cuddy', together with its position, leads us to believe that this is the very mill referred to in the Curia Regis Rolls of 1196. Osbert de Longocampo and his wife Aveline, who lived at Allington Castle, agreed to give to the Abbot of Boxley in frankalmoign (that is – in return for prayers for the souls of the donors and their families) two shillings rent in the mill of Cuciddemille in Boxley. It has been suggested that the name was mistranslated, and should read Cucittemille i.e. a mill sited on an artificial cutting, or channel – just as is Sandling Mill. It stood in the wedge of Allington parish that lay on the east bank of the Medway, and was almost certainly the 'half-mill' credited to Allington in the Domesday Book, for which no site has ever been found in today's Allington parish.

In the last quarter of the 18th Century it was owned by William Arnold, a Maidstone apothecary. William's daughter Mary married her cousin William Charles, also a doctor, and in 1784 he took over his father-in-law's properties. He ran a blanket cleaning and felts business from the mill as described in the previous chapter, and from this it took the name 'Blanket Mill'.

When the business was sold in 1840, it appears to have quickly ceased production, for in 1844 the mill and land were sold to Stephen Kelcey junior and converted to 'a mill for sifting seeds'. In Bagshawes directory of 1847 Kelcey is described as a seedcrusher and it is almost certain that he was pressing linseed to produce linseed oil. He continued in production up to 1861, and thereafter in partnership with a John Daniel or Donaldson up to 1869. For the following 7 years a James Driscoll paid the Poor Rate for the mill, The historian E.R. Hughes visited the site in 1884 and made a delightful sketch showing extensive clapboard drying sheds erected astride the stream between the mill and the road. He wrote that the extended mill buildings were – 'for some process, paper or board making, which did not succeed'. Watermill expert Bob Spain also heard a rumour of it once being used to produce gunpowder. By the time of the survey for The Ordnance Survey Map of 1897 the mill was dismantled.

We trust that the reader will forgive the somewhat pedantic attention to detail accorded to the succession of occupants in the various mills. The history of the sites and occupants of the Sandling Mills in particular have frustrated the efforts of all historians, and this is the first real attempt to sort them out in print. We have used J.N. Balston's deeply researched tomes on The Elder James Whatman as a base and from much personal research have concocted as near to the true story as we think has yet been divined.

CHAPTER 27

Famous Connections

The Abbey and its notorious mechanical 'miracles', and later the exploits of Sir Thomas Wyatt, thrust sleepy Boxley into the national limelight. Over the years, other characters with strong connections to the parish also strutted the national stage. One such Boxley luminary, who has been sadly neglected by historians, is deserving of far greater celebrity – namely **Thomas Vicary**.

The story has it that in 1525, whilst staying at Allington Castle, King Henry VIII was suffering excruciating agony from gout. Thomas Vicar or Vicary, a minor local practitioner, was summoned and was so successful in alleviating the problem that the King took him into his service. Referred to as 'of Maidstone' it is quite probable that Vicary was in fact from Boxley. Allington at the time had only one dwelling in addition to the castle, and even when it did begin to grow, its local medical practitioner was for centuries based in Boxley. What is certain is that when Henry decided to reward Vicary, it was with a grant of lands in Boxley. It was probably not gout for which Henry was treated. He appears to have suffered from an ulcerative condition in first one and then both of his legs. Some have suggested that this was a product of syphilis, but this is very doubtful. Henry's biographer, Swarbrick, suggests they were varicose ulcers developed from inadequate care of varicose veins. Another possibility is that osteomyelitis was the cause. This is a chronic septic infection of the bone. It is considered by Henry's biographers that it was not until 1528 that he began to be afflicted with any problem with his leg, and indeed it was in that year that Vicary was made surgeon to the King at an annual salary of 20 shillings. The story may therefore be correct, but the year wrong.

However, in 1525 Vicary was made Third Warden of the Barbers Company, a prestigious appointment for an obscure surgeon. The red and white pole which traditionally hung outside barbers' shops until very recent times, represented bandages and blood, signifying that originally surgery could also be obtained within. In 1528 Vicary became Upper Warden, and in 1530 achieved the position of Master. In 1540 the Barbers Company and the Surgeons Company were united by an Act of Parliament and Vicary became the first Master of the Royal Company of Surgeons. Hans Holbein, court painter to Henry VIII, was employed to paint a picture showing Henry seated on his throne presenting the Act (which is painted with a royal seal as if it were a charter) to Vicary, who heads a line of fourteen kneeling Barbers and Surgeons.

As proof of the esteem in which he was held by his fellow practitioners, he was elected Master on a total of four occasions, a frequency not rivalled by any thereafter. In 1530 Vicary found further favour with his sovereign and received the promise of the office of serjeant-surgeon to the King as soon as the then incumbent died. Thus within a few short years he had been propelled from obscurity to the threshold of the most eminent medical position in the land. He succeeded to the post in 1536 and held that office until his death 25 years later, having also served Edward IV, Queen Mary and Queen Elizabeth.

His ties with Boxley were cemented in 1539 when Henry granted him 'The tithes of grain, glebelands, and chief house of the rectory of Boxley', together with 10 pieces of land totalling 101 acres, excepting all woods and big trees, and the advowson of Boxley parish church (i.e. – the right to select a Vicar). The lands concerned stretched back eastwards from the church and rectory. They were comprised of, Great and Little Harpoule (backing onto Harpole Farm), Blacklands (still shown on modern maps), The four Wheatparks, The Hayle (bounded by The Street to the west and the old road by Park House to the south), Rushetts (to the east of the Hayle), Haytons Meadow, Boxleyfield, Squires Croft and Carters Croft. This was not an outright gift, but rather a 21 year tenancy at the rent of £40 per annum. This was quite a lot for the time, but presumably reflected the quality of the lands. The cost was cushioned by the absolution from any other charges, such as tithes. In 1541, Thomas and his son William were granted the posts of 'Bailiffs of Boxley Manor, and all other manors lately belonging to Boxley Abbey', for the full period of whichever of them lived the longest. With this came a further 68 acres of land comprised of the 40 acre farm of Polhill Field, Copphill, Little Meadow, Little Squiers Croft and The Straike and pond, totalling 15½ acres in all, 3 parcels called Church Croft of 6 acres, 4 acres in Shepeland, 2 acres in Barnecroft, and 2 gardens containing 3 rods. These were granted on a 60 year lease. Vicary was regranted the office of bailiff by King Philip and Queen Mary in 1555. Historians are divided over which building was 'the chief house of the Rectory of Boxley'! Hitherto, the consensus of opinion appeared to be in favour of Court Lodge Farm. However our own research has led us to believe that perhaps The Parsonage has the better claim. Within 'An abstract of all leases of lands belonging to the cathedral church of Rochester', there is a complete list of tenants of The Parsonage commencing with Robert Parker in May 1624. It is recorded therein that prior to this, Thomas Vicary had held a series of leases of The Parsonage totalling 99 years. It is also noted that William Vicary had been the lessee of a portion of tithes called Vinters. These had formerly belonged to the Priory of Leeds, and were described as 'all tithes of corn, wool and hay, and all profits of lands belonging to Vintners'. These tithes always formed a part of The Parsonage lease in subsequent years. There is no evidence that Court Lodge ever belonged to the church (indeed its position suggests it was the early manor house), whereas The Parsonage obviously did.

Further eminence came in 1548 when Vicary was appointed to the post of Governor of St. Bartholomew's Hospital. At the time, London was served by five Royal Hospitals, each dedicated to a different branch of care, such as the insane, or the poor. St. Barts catered for the care of the sick. He held the position until 1552 when he was made 'one of the assistants of this house for the term of his life'. He lived in a house within the precincts of the hospital which was maintained for him free of charge. The beauty of the gardens in which it stood resulted in the area being known as 'Paradise'. In addition he received an annual grant of livery of – 'fyne new colour of four yards at 12 shillings a yard'. As he was required to reside in London to be close to the King, it is probable that his son dwelt at The Parsonage.

Vicary was in the forefront of research into the workings of the human body, utilising the corpses of those hanged on Tyburn Hill, in his dissection work. One wonders whether when in Boxley, he would carry out a little 'homework' on the poor felons executed on Penenden Heath! In 1548 he wrote, 'A Profitable Treatise on the Anatomie of Mans Body'. Modern study of this work has concluded that much of it is a transcript of a 14th Century manuscript in English, which itself was based on the writings of Lanfranc and Henri de Mandeville, together with a few original passages. His main obsession was the attempt to discover the mysteries of the circulation of blood. The physician William Harvey, finally credited with this discovery, was born in Folkestone in 1578. One imagines that the young William may well have been inspired by the meteoric rise to eminence of his fellow Kentishman. Harvey too, lived at St. Barts from 1609 and would have had access to his forebear's research. He was acclaimed for his knowledge of previous research into the subject and one wonders how much influence Vicary, the unsung hero, may have had on Harvey's celebrated treatise of 1628.

That Vicary was obviously well thought of in the parish can be surmised from the will of Stephen Mason, the vintner of Weavering Manor. At his death in 1560 he left to 'Thomas Vicars, surgeon of London – a ring of gold'. We can obtain a glimpse of the affluent and elegant figure that Vicary became from his own will, proved after his death at the end of the following year. In it he bequeathed – 'To my brother Dunkyn', (Thomas Dunkyn was the bother of Vicary's first wife), 'my gown furred with white lambe, my great ring of gold, and my velvet 'bagges' with the gilt fringe'. Two of the three 'first surgeons of the land', also received bequests. To Thomas Bailey he left a gown of brown, blue lined, and faced with black budge, a cassock of black satin, his best 'plaister-box', a silver salvatory box and all his silver instruments. George Vaughan received a doublet of crimson satin. Having outlived his own son William, he left – 'To Stephen Vicarye, son of William, late of Boxley, all my house and land being next to Boxley Church, the which I late purchased off John Joyce. Also all my right, title, interest, and tenure in the lands I obtained from Sir Thomas Wyatt, for farm by indenture'. He also left to the poor householders dwelling within the parish of Boxley – 'The yearly farme of Polhill Fielde', (now Pollyfields Farm to the north of Detling), 'which is 40/- per annum, in occupation of Richard Gouldsmyth and Jane his wife, to be given by advice and direction of the vicar'. He left 'The yearley farme of 4 acres lying in Shepeland and 2 acres in Barnecrofte now in the tenure of William Boote, which is 13/- per year'. The churchwardens were to employ this about the most needful reparations of the same parish of Boxley. Despite his high status he obviously retained a great fondness for Boxley, its occupants and its church.

Vicary's description of 'house and land purchased off James Joyce' could be construed to refer to Court Lodge. He never owned 'the chief house of the rectory of Boxley', merely held it at the King's discretion, and thus it is possible that both Court Lodge and The Parsonage were occupied by Vicary and his family. What is certain is that the lands that came to comprise Court Lodge Farm were originally Vicary's. In 1528 Stephen Vicary assigned to Ralph Pettye – 'All the lands in tenure of Sir Henry Cutte, Robert Brewer and John Ffuller, which were leased by indenture from Sir Thomas Wyatt'. However no mention is made of a house. In the chapter entitled 'The Village', we mention Margaret Vicary's house of 1608. The church registers record her death in 1614, but confusingly in 1629 one Margaret Vicary paid a tithe for a 'mansion house and sundry piece of land'. It is possible that either these records simply failed to acknowledge her death or that this is a later Margaret, possibly the daughter of John Vicarye, son of Stephen, who married Johanna Atkin in 1613. They were both interred in Boxley Church in 1630. In 1631, a 'Dionisian' Vicary married a Richard Gouldsmith (possibly a descendent of the Pollyfields, Gouldsmyths), and the final record of Vicarys that we have found in Boxley, was in the vicar's notebook, which recorded a John Vicary – 'near ye Upper Grange', paying tithes between 1722-28. Thus the name of Vicary disappeared from local knowledge. Hopefully this book will go some way to resurrecting a prominent man of his time, in the minds of the present and future occupants of the parish he loved.

William Alexander

In the chapter entitled 'The Village', we mention various members of The Alexander family, who played an important part in the life of 18th Century Boxley. They produced a landlord of the Kings Arms, a wheelwright, a shopkeeper, and successive tenants of Street Farm. More importantly, they also produced an artist of national importance.

Harry Alexander was a wheelwright and coach builder and had learned his trade in the workshop of his father William Alexander, in the building now known as 'The Old House', in Boxley Street. He and his brother Thomas, both Boxley born, moved their families to Week Street in Maidstone, to set up separate coach building businesses. It was there in 1767 that Henry's son, William Alexander was born.

After attending Maidstone Grammar School, William was admitted to the Royal Academy Schools in 1784, as a 'painter'. In 1792, he obtained the post of draughtsman to Lord Macartney's embassy to the Chinese Empire. The purpose behind this expedition was to facilitate trade with China, and to promote British goods by direct contact with the emperor in Peking. Following their return two years later, Alexander spent the next 14 years converting his numerous sketches into finished water-colours, which were exhibited at the Royal Academy. In 1802 he obtained the position of the first Master of Landscape Drawing, at the new Royal Military College, in Great Marlow, Bucks, – a post previously offered to, and eventually rejected by, John Constable. Six years later he left to join the British Museum, where he took the newly created position of Keeper of Prints and Drawings. In 1816, after suffering for sometime with rheumatic gout, he became seriously ill and was sent from London to his Uncle Thomas's house, in the hope that the fresher air would aid a recovery. Thomas Alexander had risen to be a prominent citizen of Maidstone. He was a churchwarden and one-time Overseer of the Poor, and now resided in a comfortable property in Rocky Hill. Unfortunately, the hoped-for improvement in his health was not forthcoming, and he died a few days later, of 'brain fever'.

His legacy to his countrymen, was his provision of the first authentic, composite picture of China. The paintings published in his 'Authentic Account' of the expedition, and in 'The Costume of China', created a revival of interest in chinoiserie. Views and motifs from these works were borrowed by many artists and craftsmen, and inspired interior decoration in many Great Houses. Not least among these is the fantasy interior of The Royal Pavilion at Brighton, where painted glass windows and scarlet and gold paintings on linen wall-hangings, are taken directly from Alexander's work. A tablet was erected in Boxley Church, which attests to his "mild and engaging manners, active benevolence, and unsullied integrity".

William of Ypres, the founder of Boxley Abbey, was not 'Earl of Kent' as claimed by Cave-Browne amongst other historians. The son of the Count of Flanders, William supported Stephen Count of Blois in his successful attempt to usurp the throne of England from his cousin Matilda, following the death of her father Henry I in 1135. Matilda was also known as The Empress Maud, from her first marriage to Henry V, Emperor of Germany, and The Holy Roman Emperor.

The land seethed in a constant state of insurrection as differing parts of the country rose in support of placing Matilda on the throne. Amidst the death and destruction, no hand was more bloody than that of William of Ypres, chief confidant to the King. In 1139, Stephen and William carried out a successful siege on Leeds Castle in Kent, which was owned by Matilda's half-brother Robert of Gloucester. It is quite likely that much of Boxley was also under Robert's dominion, whilst William de Warrenne, Earl of Surrey, held sway over the western portion from his stronghold at Allington Castle. It was possibly during this campaign that William of Ypres first laid eyes on the secluded vale in which he was later to found his abbey.

In February, two years later, disaster befell Stephen at the Battle of Lincoln. As the wife of Geoffrey Plantagenet, Count of Anjou, Matilda had the backing of a vast French army. However, it was Welsh auxiliaries in the pay of the Empress who broke through the ranks of the King's followers and surrounded him. Contemporary accounts state that Stephen fought until he was the last man standing, before he was captured. William, who held the position of joint second-in-command, was isolated on another part of the battlefield, and realising it would be futile to try and aid the King, he fled with his men. Returning to the Queen in Kent, he helped to raise fresh forces, perhaps rallying on Penenden Heath. Taking the field once more, in September he defeated and captured Robert of Gloucester. In November, Stephen was exchanged for Robert, bringing Matilda's seven month reign to an end. Considering himself indebted to William, Stephen granted him substantial lands in Kent, including the Manor of Boxley. Although the civil-war continued for a further five years, Matilda's husband Geoffrey became increasingly involved in conflict within France, thus stretching their resources. In 1144 he conquered Normandy.

Stephen and William embarked on an orgy of retribution against those who had opposed him. William became notorious for his ruthlessness, and he was described by a contemporary as 'a fear and terror to all England'. A particular focus of his wrath were the monasteries, who had exerted a great influence over public opinion. Perhaps this invoked a Divine intervention, because suddenly William was struck blind. He repented his sins and, as his contemporary wrote, 'God enlightened his heart'. In exchange for the Manor of Boxley and the founding of the Cistercian Abbey, he received absolution. Throughout the following years he donated much of his wealth to ecclesiastical causes, before retiring to France in 1158. The next seven years, preceding his death in 1165, were spent in seclusion at the Monastery of St. Peter, at Loo, to whom he was a great benefactor.

Another notorious inhabitant of Boxley was **Sir Thomas Bourghchier** or Bourchier. He was the nephew of Archbishop Thomas Bourchier who was ordained as Archbishop of Canterbury in 1454, holding the premier ecclesiastical post for more than 30 years. During this time he crowned Edward IV, Henry VI, Richard III, and Henry VII. As Archbishop he built up a large holding of lands in Kent, including Knole at Sevenoaks, which he presented to the See of Canterbury for the use of future archbishops.

Like many of his contemporaries, Sir Thomas was heavily involved in the 'Wars of the Roses'. His family, which included the Earl of Essex, were highly placed at court, and he supported Richard III when he deposed his nephew Edward V. However by 1485, Sir Thomas had seen which way the wind was blowing. Richard suspected him of treachery, and on the eve of The Battle of Bosworth, he sent men to keep a watch on his tent. The duplicitous Thomas was too cunning, and eluding the watchers, he slipped away. The next morning, he fought under the banner of 'The Duke of Richmond', helping to bring defeat and death to his former liege. Thus the turncoat ensured that he remained in high favour at court after his uncle placed the crown of England on Richmond's head and created him the seventh King Henry.

Sir Thomas inherited much of his uncle's lands in Kent, and was described as being 'of Boxley', when in 1512 he donated £100 to each of the universities of Oxford and Cambridge in fulfilment of a bequest from his late uncle. He made generous donations to the Abbey of Boxley, expressing the desire to be buried in the cemetery there. Whether Sir Thomas lies beneath Boxley's soil is unknown. Neither is it known where exactly he lived, but presumably it must have been at one of the great mansions, either one of the Park Houses or Boxley House.

The Yew Tree public house, Sandling.

CHAPTER 28

Places of Refreshment

Most rural parishes had hardly any inns until well into the 18th Century. The thirst of their inhabitants was catered for by just a few alehouses, with most 'serious' drinkers preferring to frequent the larger establishments in towns. With three of the main arterial highways in the area traversing its soil, plus the traditional county meeting place and execution site at Penenden Heath, and with the main trade route of the Medway forming one boundary, Boxley was more amply served than most.

The earliest record of inns in Boxley is from 1510 when there were said to be two, trading under the signs of The Bull and The Lion, plus another at the Abbey Gate. This latter establishment appears to have served as an inn only until soon after the dissolution of the Abbey when, without extraneous custom, it reverted to the more humble role of a beerhouse. Neither of the other inns survived into the 20th Century. Today there are ten public houses within the parish, almost the same number as 260 years ago, despite the vast increase in population.

Ale was the universal drink of every strata of society, and both genders, from early times. An accompaniment to almost every meal, it was often more beneficial than the dubious quality of some drinking water. Known as 'the Englishman's vice', drunkenness became a national pastime. Most households would brew their own ale, sufficient for their needs, but in the 13th Century it became common for some to sell their surplus to neighbours. Thus the alehouse was born. Normally the sale of ale merely supplemented the family's income, and would be carried out by the wife, whilst the husband continued his own occupation. A system of licensing began in 1495 but it was not until an Act of 1552 that any real restraint began to be enforced. These early places of refreshment were known as 'tippling houses' and their proprietors as 'tipplers'.

In 1599, an application was made for a licence to allow one George Grymsey to continue running an alehouse at Sandling "which place has been used as an alehouse long tyme, even tyme out of memory". Descriptions of it in various applications refer to its proximity to the Ashford to London Road (at that time that was Sandling Lane) and to a place for the shipping away of Fullers Earth, and also to a river crossing. These tend to suggest that it may well have been the forerunner of the Gibraltar Inn, as the only other candidate, The Red Lion, was already an inn and stood on the Maidstone to Rochester Road.

BOXLEY PARISH

In 1583 Queen Elizabeth I granted to John Astley Allington Castle and Manor, including lands in Boxley. One property of 3 acres in Sandling, in the tenure of Richard Bryse, was very likely The Red Lion Inn, and also The Lion Inn of 1510. Richard Bryst is recorded as occupying it in 1554 when the Wyatts lost their lands. The earliest known title deeds for the inn, dated 1646, describe it also as a property of 3 acres, then in tenure of George Charlton. Thomas Brook owned it, having inherited it from Elizabeth Brewer, the widow of John Brewer. Passing into the possession of Robert Saunders, the inn became the property of Mary Selyard of Boxley Abbey, after Saunders defaulted on repayments of a mortgage. By 1699 it was leased to Thomas Bliss, the proprietor of the Lower Brewery, in Maidstone. He was elected to Parliament as M.P. for Maidstone in 1701. His popularity was said by his adversaries to be largely due to generous drinks being provided to prospective supporters by the major inns he had tied to his brewery. Bliss purchased the inn in 1712 and it passed via his widow to William Horsmonden Turner, her new husband, who also twice represented the town in Parliament.

The earliest confirmed landlord was Richard Sheeres in 1688. He probably replaced William Rowles who ran it from at least 1670 to 1683. The first 20 years of the 18th Century saw a succession of short term landlords until John Eastland, who at his death in 1763 had been 'mine host' for more than 40 years. Although relatively small, the Red Lion was a coaching inn, and obviously a profitable one, as illustrated by the unusual length of its tenancies. Robert Packham held it for the next 20 years before Daniel Neale took over in 1773. He relinquished the tenancy to William Rayfield in 1796, retiring to farm, somewhat unsuccessfully, at Newnham Court Farm.

In 1799, William Baldwin left The Lower Brewery to set up his own Medway Brewery, by Maidstone Bridge, which was later to become Style and Winch and eventually Courages. He succeeded in obtaining The Red Lion and tying it to his own fledgling brewery with whom it stayed until its demise. Curiously, the last five lessees of the rectorial tithes of Maidstone, from 1714 to their expiry in the tenure of William Baldwin junior in 1877, were also all owners of The Red Lion.

That the popularity of the neighbouring Running Horse and Gibraltar Inns were beginning to adversely affect trade at The Red Lion, may be indicated by the fate of Michael Whyman, who took over in 1818, but lasted only a year. He was unable to sustain sufficient custom, and his willingness to allow regulars to obtain drink on credit, perhaps contributed to his downfall. In 1820 he was committed to Maidstone Prison for debt. The only assets of himself, his wife, and his daughter were clothing worth £15-4-3d, and the one shilling he had in his pocket. In addition he was still owed about £2 for beer and spirits by Mr Dadd, the Sandling blacksmith, plus sums by 3 other regulars who also had not cleared their slates. His successor, James Tester (1819-1822), perceived that the inn must change to survive, and in 1820 applied to William Baldwin to dig up the bowling green that lay behind the pub, to enable construction of an extension. He received the following reply – "Mr Baldwin acquaints Mr Tester, that so far from consenting to his request for digging up the bowling green, he warns him of in any way injuring its present state from becoming a resort for 'Company' to enjoy bowling or otherwise. Although one tenant may not be calculated to entertain the kind of Company that used to frequent the green, another will be found to give encouragement to a superior class of society, to whom it used to prove a pleasurable resort, and such a tenant there will be no difficulty in finding, even at an advanced rent!". A few years later Baldwin leased the premises to William Manwaring.

1836, saw Thomas Ongley take over as licensed victualler, passing the licence to his son Thomas in 1852. Over the next 5 years, Thomas junior concentrated on the family wheelwright's business which he ran from premises adjoining the inn to the east. The Sandling Post Office was also being run from the pub at the time of the 1851 census.

For some time, a flourishing beerhouse by the lock had succeeded in further diminishing custom at the Red Lion, and the former's elevation to a pub in 1868 sealed its doom. The then landlord Thomas Bennett, declining to apply for renewal of his licence that year. It appears that no time was wasted in demolishing it. The land was subsumed into the Sandling Place grounds and the owner Richard Mercer erected stables on the site. In 1890, Thomas Francklyn of Cobtree House informed the historian E.R. Hughes that locals believed The Red Lion to be the inspiration for Charles Dickens's 'Blue Lion', which the novelist described as 'a little roadside public house with 2 elm trees, a horse trough, and a signpost in front'. Hughes himself recalled it as 'having a long timber, or timber and plaster frontage which doubled the corner, so that some rooms looked west and some north'. William Baldwin's estate book describes it as being very old and thatched. Our map of Sandling shows its exact position opposite the south eastern tip of the car park that now fronts the Running Horse Inn.

The Running Horse

In 1732, after having spent four years as landlord of The Plough (a long-lost Sandling Inn), Richard Driver, a saddler by trade, erected, "a messuage or tenement, to make a victualling house for the entertainment of travellers, being a large structure consisting of a cellar, lofts, shop, chambers and stable adjoining". The building was said to be next to the Sandling turnpike gate, and aptly was first registered as 'The Turnpike Gate'. This name did not last long and by 1737 it was known as 'The George'. Between 1738 and 1752 it is strangely absent from the victualling lists, cropping up just once with the space for the inn name left blank, but doubtless it continued to ply its trade.

In 1733, Richard was reported at the Court Baron for causing a nuisance –

BOXLEY PARISH

The Running Horse circa 1909, beside the old road then leading to Chatham. Rebuilt in 1938 to its more familiar style, and later by-passed by a new road to Chatham. The old Red Lion pub stood close by the white posts seen in the foreground.

"by setting up and continuing a frame of nine pins, which greatly annoys and frightens the horses of passengers travelling the highway, to the great endangering of the lives of his majesty's subjects". This was perhaps sour grapes from John Eastland the landlord of the neighbouring Red Lion, who no doubt found his trade reduced by the close competition – there being less than 100 yards between them.

It is not until 1753 that the victualling licence registers record the inn as 'The Running Horse', landlord John Cook, and owned by Samuel Athawes. The name is believed to refer to the runaway horse, said to have carried the image of St Runwald to the doors of Boxley Abbey. (See Boxley Abbey Chapter). In 1775 John Rogers who ran the blacksmith's forge down the lane behind the pub, was landlord for a year between landlords Forster Whitebread and Thomas Soper. By this time the inn had become the property of the Fowle family, and in Edward Fowle's will of 1780 he refers to it as 'The Horse and Groom'. This is probably colloquial, perhaps derived from the inn-sign, as it was always registered as 'The Running Horse'.

Six landlords spanned the next 74 years, during 27 of which it was occupied by Robert and Sarah Pattenden. William Green, the landlord from 1813-1821, also ran a butchers shop from the premises. When George Streitfield handed over to Samuel Bodkin in 1835 he gave him a written inventory of the entire contents of the pub, which makes fascinating reading. There was a parlour containing a stove, 2 tables, 10 chairs and 26 feet of seating-stuffed and carpeted, plus 10 iron spittoons. A bar containing a stove with irons and hooks, two tobacco dishes, a pipe box and pipes, a lead tobacco pot, a weather glass, 7 spirit measures, and 11 'rummers'. (A drinking glass, often used for drinking toasts, having an ovoid bowl on a short stem). The Tap Room sported a grate with a copper tea kettle, two circular settles and two iron-bound tables. There was a kitchen with a range, and a list of equipment from candle boxes to sugar nippers (used to snip off chunks of sugar from a solid, normally conical, sugar loaf), and a large pantry. Outside was a wash house containing a copper with a lid and an ironwork oven door, together with 3 washtubs and a clothes horse. In the garden stood a four-corner-frame, 9 pins and a ball, (presumably the very same set up by Richard Driver, and now a century old), and in front of the house, benches and tables. Upstairs there were 3 bedrooms, a lumber room and a small tent room containing a tent bedstead. By this time, the inn was a tied-house belonging to The Lower Brewery of Lower Stone Street, Maidstone. The Fowles had sold it in 1806 to Stephen Page Seager of the Upper Brewery, Maidstone, who in turn sold to Atkins and Co. in 1810, before being bought by the Brenchley family of The Lower Brewery in 1821.

William Grover succeeded Bodkin in 1838, and kept the inn with his wife Ann, for the next 25 years. Another long serving landlord was William Ward who plied his trade for 26 years from 1865. Towards the end of his tenure he was immortalised in a photograph which became a popular post-card. The

The Malta Inn circa 1950.

The Hunt gathers outside The King's Arms pre-1914.

premises were by then owned by Lord Romney, who in 1835 leased them to Messrs. Wriothesley Baldwin and Henry Godden of The Medway Brewery, Maidstone, as one of their earliest tied pubs. This brewery later became Style and Winch and then Courage and Barclay, who in 1938 pulled down the 200 year old building, and replaced it with a mock-Tudor style Norfolk reed-thatched, pub under a new landlord, Edward Charles Dickens. In 1987, this was refurbished as the Harvester steak house of today.

The Kings Arms

The Kings Arms situated as it is facing Boxley church and the remains of the green, appears to be the quintessential English village inn. It is easy to imagine our forebears patronising the establishment down the centuries from the time when it was perhaps a simple wood and thatch hovel, with a bush hanging outside to proclaim that weary travellers might purchase ale. The 'historical' notes and list of innkeepers back to 1545 which for many years have been displayed on the walls, can be dismissed as no more than a romanticised invention. It was never a coaching inn (the highway didn't originally even pass the door) nor a Customs and Excise Post House, and probably could not even call itself an inn until the 18th Century, when enlargement enabled it to provide accommodation. It is quite likely that the innkeepers maintained a couple of horses in the stable, hiring them out to assist carriages that did attempt the long haul 'over-the-hill'. Emulating, albeit on a much smaller scale, The Detling Cock Inn, whose name derives from the 'cock' or lead horse, utilised to facilitate the arduous climb up Detling Hill.

We have traced the premises back as far as 1608 when they appear in the Court Baron records as a messuage stable and piece of land which Thomas Kemsley had just inherited from his father, John. The earliest title deed known, is dated 1616, when Thomas Short sold his messuage or tenement with one acre of land to Richard Hayward and his son, John Hayward. Over the next thirteen years, the Haywards mortgaged the property on no less than three occasions. In 1630 Willliam Hayward is recorded as occupying a house and one acre in Boxley Street called 'ye Sunne'. The following year, having failed to repay a mortgage on time, William forfeited the property to Caleb Banks, thrice Mayor of Maidstone, and ancestor of the Earls of Aylesford.

In 1634 the premises were bought by an affluent Maidstone brewer, Thomas Rasell and his daughter Barbara. He died four years later leaving almost £1000. A considerable sum. That The Sun was at that time a somewhat insignificant property can be inferred from his probate inventory. The pub is neither named nor is its trade mentioned when he left Barbara "the sum of £50 and my tenement with the appurtenances, standing in Boxley". In contrast his son Thomas received The Swan Inn at Maidstone. Within the next fifty years Rasells were landlords of The Two Horseshoes (forerunner of the Fox and

Goose) in Boxley parish, perhaps moving there when in 1653 Barbara leased and then sold The Sun to William Godden. His son was later to farm at the neighbouring Street Farm. In 1680 Robert Barrett purchased, "a messuage called The Signe of the Sun, with stable, garden and one acre planted with cherries, then or late in occupation of John Hills, late Luddens".

The oldest part of the building is the southern section, with the lowest roof-line, and this small building stood on the edge of the village green which originally extended across where is now The Street and up what is now Forge Lane. It was built in the late 16th Century, probably as an ordinary thatched dwelling, possibly with connections to the church, and then became a shop and alehouse. There is no sign today of any earlier building, certainly not one as old as 1195, as proclaimed inside. But quite possibly the site was indeed occupied that far back, standing as it did alongside the old Roman road that ran through Boarley and on past the church, to Detling and beyond. The claimed dates that additions to the original building were made, in 1651, 1698, 1740 and 1787, are however possibly correct. We would guess that the centre section, which is of 17th Century date, was probably built around 1651 and extended in 1698 when Edward Tufnell took over from the widow Boswell, whose husband Thomas Bosvill or Boswell was first recorded there a decade earlier.

At his death in 1693, Boswell was described as a tailor and thus the alehouse was probably run by his wife. The inventory of his possessions provides a unique insight into the composition of the premises at that time. The kitchen contained amongst other items – 6 brass kettles, 46 pewter plates and 15 quart pots made of pewter. In the Hall, where drinkers would have sat, were 2 forms, 3 joined stools, a board and end table, 6 chairs, 2 other tables and a chest. The accommodation was completed by 3 chambers containing a total of 6 bedsteads with 1 feather and 5 flock mattresses. An attached brewhouse had a mash tub, Tun tub, brine tub, water tub and 4 small pails. Almost a third of the total value of Boswell's possessions was comprised of the contents of his cellars:- 8 hogsheads, 10 barrels, 3 small casks, some glass bottles, a flour tub, plus 13 barrels and 13 gallons of strong beer. Outdoors were a gelding, with bridle and saddle, and a sow with 5 pigs. Although his total wealth of £52 and 12 shillings affirmed him as a man of some substance, he had only £3 and 7 shillings in coins and his only other items of value were a silver tankard and a silver dram cup, worth £4 and 10 shillings.

The Poor Rate Register provides the succession of landlords through to 1707, when it first appears in the Licensed Victuallers Records bearing the name, 'The Kings Arms'. John Medhurst ran it from 1713 to 1738, and according to the licence records, altered its name in 1714 to The Queens Arms. Presumably as a memorial to Queen Anne who died that year. By the time of the next surviving licence records of 1720 it had reverted to the Kings Arms. About 1722 Samuel Hollister, who already owned The Bull on the Heath, purchased the property from Hester Barrett, together with a stable, garden and a piece of land of one acre planted with cherry trees. It was probably Hollister who further extended the pub, erecting the main part of the present building (the northern block), bordering onto Forge Lane, around 1740. In 1745 he sold the inn to Abraham King. He shortly sold it to John Broomfield, from whom Richard Bennett purchased it in 1749. Bennett removed the landlord, Matthew Wheeler who also traded as a weaver, taking over himself as owner/landlord. By 1761 he was also the owner of The Harrow at Lidsing, where William Bennett was the landlord. Richard Bennett the younger took over from his father at The Kings Arms in 1771. His wife Frances, was the daughter of Joseph Cordwell, the papermaker at Poll Mill from whom she inherited the cottages 100 yards further up The Street. In 1793 Flint Stacey and George May of the Lower Brewery bought it from the widow Bennett, installing Edmund Alexander as landlord. George Mortimer followed him before William Mannering purchased it in 1806, and ran it until 1820.

Long serving landlords included John and Judith Martin from 1821-1847 and John and Harriet Hickmott from 1854-1887. The latter were followed by their son William, whose brother Ned was a renowned local cricketer, and purveyor of appliances for cricket and lawn tennis, perhaps from the attached shop. Since at least 1840, until William Draper became landlord in 1907, the tenants ran a grocers shop from the lowest roofed section, which today is an extension to the lounge bar. Draper and the successive landlords, Lesley Slawson, J.C. Hadlow and Alf Paterson almost certainly ran some sort of shop there. Ethelbert Hollands, landlord in 1938, was definitely running a confectionery shop there as well as housing the village post office.

On the fictitious 'history' of the pub, displayed inside, is recorded that in 1635, Josias Gent was appointed 'ale taster' to the parish of Boxley. We have been unable to verify this, but certainly the perhaps enviable occupation of ale taster, or 'ale conner', was carried out for decades, in order to ensure that the ale or beer served in the smallest beerhouses to the largest coaching inns was of a sufficient standard. The conner had an alternative method to just tasting the product, which helped to prevent the impediment of inebriety which one imagines would have been a drawback to the job. Uniformly, he would wear leather breeches, and having poured a pool of beer on a seat he would sit there for a half hour. Bad, sugary beer, would stick his breeches to the seat, whereas good beer allowed him to stand freely. The penalty for selling bad beer was normally the pillory or the ducking stool.

The Gibraltar

A beerhouse probably stood alongside the river here as early as the 16th Century. Certainly from at least 1629 an inn known as 'The Fulling Lodge' dispensed ale to bargees and fullers earth workers. In 1650, Thomas Brewer sold The Fulling Lodge to Andrew Brewer and Thankful Hebdon. The latter's name was typical of those chosen by strictly pious families, who were opposed to the fripperies currently in vogue in the Church of England. When Andrew Brewer mortgaged the inn in 1685, its name had changed to 'The Three Straws', and was in the tenure of William Rowles. There is some evidence that this early building forms part of the rear section of today's house, which has a low cat-slide roof. About 1716 the name changed again to 'The Three Salmons' under landlord John Dreyman or Drummond. However, it was not to carry this name for long, although the stretch of river from the pub to the next bend upstream long retained the name of Three Salmons Reach. When William Beauman took over as landlord from William Dale, in 1739, he renamed it 'The Portobello Castle', promptly reduced to 'The Portobello', when John Stephens replaced him 2 years later. This name-change was inspired by the sacking of Portobello by the fleet commanded by Admiral Vernon, who was married to Sarah Best of the brewing family of Boxley. John Akers ran it from 1750 to 1776. Throughout his tenancy the inn name remained the same, but in 1757 Akers altered his own name to Oldacre!

Many of the external features of the house appear to date to the early 18th Century. The inn's omission from the victualling licence records between 1712-1714 would appear to point to its construction at that time. However the lack of true symmetry in the facade points towards a conversion of an earlier building.

Sir Francis Withins purchased the pub in 1688, and it became part of the Nether Grange Estate. Thomas Burwash inherited it from his father Thomas, and in 1784 sold it to Flint Stacey, proprietor of The Lower Brewery. By this time Thomas Pierce, had been 'mine host' for 8 years. He was the first in a dynasty of 5 Pierces or Pearces, who held the licence for almost three quarters of a century until Henry Pearce passed the reins to Daniel Cook in 1854. In 1785 the inn underwent its final name change, when it became 'The Gibraltar'. Once again this was in patriotic commemoration of another British Military victory involving members of the Best family. Namely, the lifting of the 5 year Spanish siege of Gibraltar.

The decision in 1823 to switch to another, smaller brewery, ultimately helped to bring about its demise a half century later. With the firm of Isherwood Foster and Stacey nearing its end, Sophia Catty, who had received The Gibraltar as part of a wedding present from her father, Flint Stacey, leased it to William Randall. He ran a small brewery in Boughton Monchelsea with his partner William Newman. At that time it had stables, cowhouse, piggery, dairy, workshop, woodhouse, yard, garden, a 1½ acre meadow, and the wharf alongside known as Wilsons or Wilstone Wharf.

From the mid 18th to the mid 19th Centuries, the inn was enormously popular. It became fashionable for townsfolk and soldiers to promenade along the towpath from Maidstone, or to arrive via the increasingly popular pastime of rowing, and then indulge in a game on the bowling green at the back. The inn was famous for its cuisine, especially its 'pudding pies', and was a popular venue for meetings. The Navigation Company Meetings were held there, as frequently, were the Court Barons. The Commonalty Society (a Tory political organisation) would stop off on their river cruises and also held fetes in the adjoining meadow. At the end of the 18th Century a group of some of the most prominent men in Maidstone met there twice yearly, as The Gibraltar Society. Flint Stacey would send his boat to collect them from Masons Wharf, because amazingly the inn had achieved its popularity despite its only public access being by towpath, river, or a footpath that runs down from opposite the site of The Red Lion.

Like The Red Lion, The Gibraltar's trade suffered badly from the success of The Malta. The introduction in 1872 of licensing laws, restricting opening to 11 p.m. weekdays and 10 p.m. on Sundays, caused riots around the country and sounded the death knell for The Gibraltar, for whom Sunday was its most popular day. Landlord, Frank Hemmings called the final 'time gentlemen please', in 1874.

The Bull

From quite early times, an inn stood on the corner of Sandling Lane and Penenden Heath, some 150 yards south west of today's Bull Inn. An ideal site, positioned on the main road from Hythe, through Ashford, to London, and also on the Heath, the venue for countless county assemblies down the centuries. Probably the very first house of refreshment in Boxley, it was possibly that Bull Inn recorded in Boxley in 1510. Amongst title deeds of Sir John Astley in 1638 was a dwelling called The Bull, in Boxley, Maidstone or Aylesford, with almost 37 acres, in tenure of George Payne. However by 1692 it was trading under the name of 'The Woolpack', in which year the Poor Rate Records contain an entry of money 'spent at ye Woolpack, agoing after Sanders'. (A Boxley inhabitant who had deserted his wife and family). A deed of 1717 refers to The Woolpack Inn, owned by the heirs of Mr Cripps, which the landowner, Lord Aylesford, leased to Lord Romney. John Cripps' ownership can be traced back as far as 1670 in Lord Aylesford's estate records.

When exactly the Woolpack ceased trading, is uncertain. In 1715 a Thomas Reynolds was granted a victualling licence for 'The Bull Inn on Penenden Heath'. Parish records show that he had succeeded William Baker there, and that in 1716 he was replaced by John Beale, all three of them being tenants of a Mr Oliver. By 1720, the Maidstone brewer, Samuel Hollister, had purchased from Thomas Oliver – 'a cottage with barn, stable, outhouses, yards, garden and a half acre orchard, in tenure of John Beale'. The available records are confusing but it would appear that at this point the ancient Woolpack Inn closed down, and Hollister renamed Oliver's cottage as 'The Woolpack'. The victualling licences show Jeremiah Parker at The Woolpack in 1720 and 1723, and widow Ann Beale in 1728. From 1735, Parker was landlord of 'The Bull and Woolpack', which reverted to 'The Bull' in about 1747, at the time that it was purchased by John Terry. The Terry family sold it to Stephen Page Seager in 1799. Thus the current inn has certainly been quenching thirsts on its current site since at least 1714. Parker remained there until 1754. Long-serving landlords were William Homan (1758-1770) and John and Martha West (1780-1798). In 1806 the premises were purchased by William Manwaring, who also bought The Kings Arms. He installed John Craute as landlord, and he continued to serve until his death in 1837. In 1823, Penenden Heath Grove alongside The Bull, was said to have been 'appropriated to a skittle ground, much resorted to by gentlemen from Maidstone'. Further prominent names over the door were Tapley Simmons (1841-1852) and Thomas Barney (1860-1875). The latter retired to farm at Warren Farm. He was succeeded by Egbert Punnett until about 1890 when Sarah Pettit commenced a tenancy of some 26 years. There is further mention of her in the chapter on Penenden Heath.

The Fox and Goose

The Fox and Goose is the second pub of that name to have catered for the thirst of the weary agricultural workers of Weavering Street. In 1687, The Company of Saddlers leased to John Rasell and Alice his wife a tenement called 'Lees Yoke', formerly the sign of 'The Horseshoe' and since 'The Flying Hog'. One document appears to infer that this property was in Roseacre Lane, Bearsted, but certainly by the 1690's the Rasells were running the Saddlers' Weavering Street pub 'The Sugar Loaf', and by the time John died in 1715, it bore the name 'The Two Horseshoes'. His widow ran it with the aid of a landlord, Joseph Lott, until she sold the lease in 1723 to George Curteis. He was a pillar of the community, three times Mayor of Maidstone, and also owned The Artichoke Inn. The Two Horseshoes was renamed 'The Fox and Goose', under new landlord Walter Mills and then his son Anthony. Thomas Baker, who took over in 1729, ran it until it finally closed its doors in 1756.

The Saddlers had originally come into possession of the building through the will of Edward Hill, a saddler, who died in 1645. He bequeathed it to his cousin Stephen March for the term of his life, and thereafter to The Saddlers Company. However there were conditions attached. Stephen must provide – 'to the Master, warden, and assistants of the Art and Mystery of The Company of Saddlers in London, – four gowns, whose cloth should cost 8 pence a yard, plus 4 pairs of shoes and 4 pairs of stockings which shall cost 20 shillings, for them to bestow upon 4 poor decayed men, free of the said Company. Two of the men to be saddlers and two, – harness-makers'. Once the property passed into the possession of The Company, they were required to utilise some of the profits each Christmas to provide similar apparel for eight such men.

Thomas Baker was foremost a farmer and it is likely that the inn was managed by landlords. By 1761, the former Fox and Goose, with a barn, stable, orchard, close, garden and 6½ acres of land, was being leased by Josiah Fuller. William Richards, a blacksmith from Bearsted, took over the lease from Abraham Baker in 1802 and was still there in 1818 when The Saddlers exchanged the property with Lord Romney. (See Weavering Chapter).

The earliest evidence of a building on the site of the current pub, comes from the 1720 marriage agreement of John Weekes. At the marriage of his daughter Joanna to John Austen in 1759 it is described as a 'tenement with a barn, stable, lodge, close, garden and 5 pieces of land containing 14 acres, 7 acres of which are planted with hops, formerly occupied by Thomas Baker, since by James Mills, then widow Figg and now John Bigg'. In 1799, the property was leased to Thomas Jessop yeoman, and John Hughes victualler, who subsequently purchased it. It is likely that they first started a beerhouse there. Edward Kennard bought it, and left it to his kinsmen – William Parkins, and Thomas and James Bridgland, by which time it had been converted into three dwellings. By 1838 we have proof that William Parkins was running 'The Weavering Street Beerhouse', from one of them. When in 1864 the heirs of the Bridglands sold the premises to Alexander Chambers, there were now 5 dwellings, one being a beerhouse with 6 rooms, an oven, and a well in the garden, in occupation of Philo T. Bridgland, beerseller. It is in 1871, whilst being run by naval pensioner James Wheeler, that we first find mention of its taking on the name of The Fox and Goose Beerhouse. Charles Arkcoll of the Lion Brewery in Chatham, bought the site in 1879. There were now 6 cottages, occupied by Messrs. Winchester , Creasey, Bridgland, Parkins, Edwards, and Jonathan Stanford, who ran the beershop for 20 years.

In 1909 William Larkin followed W. Hope as licensee of the beerhouse. He was succeeded by his widow Eliza who ran it herself into the 1930's when she married a drayman named Harwood. She is remembered as dressing somewhat severely, in the style of Queen Mary, and being afflicted with Parkinson's Disease. The youngsters of her day recall her at the side door of the pub, selling for one penny Sharps toffees in cones of paper. Their son Leonard Harwood had the licence when Weavering Village Hall was built behind the pub in 1964. Arkcolls brewery was taken over by Style and Winch and when they in turn were purchased by Barclay Perkins in 1929, the Fox and Goose premises were extended and became a public house. The current building probably includes three of the original six cottages, the other three which had all been let to employees of Style and Winch, being demolished for construction of the car park.

BOXLEY PARISH

The Chiltern Hundreds

In 1799, Robert Rugg of Detling, bought a cottage lately erected by Stephen Tucker at a cross-roads, on a piece of land that he had enclosed out of Penenden Heath. Tucker himself occupied the Detling Road Turnpike Cottage that stood diametrically opposite, on the south west quadrant of the cross-roads. In 1834, Rugg's son Robert sold the cottage to Joseph Mannering Britter, a victualler. Britter then erected a beerhouse, described as 'a substantial brick built tenement with offices', on part of the land. Five years later Britter obtained his first full licence and the beerhouse was upgraded to a public house under the name of 'The Chiltern Hundreds Inn'. However, the venture does not appear to have prospered because just 3 years on the Inn was put up for sale. The property contained 8 bedrooms, a bar parlour, and 2 back parlours, all with fireplaces. A tap or porter room, kitchen, washroom, and a cellar. A 140 foot deep well had been sunk at the back and Tucker's original small timber built cottage and half acre of garden was also included. A further attraction was a vein of white sand 'for which with the flints dug therewith, there is a constant demand, affording a source of daily profit'. Attractive as it sounds, there appear to have been no buyers. Britter persevered and in 1849 mortgaged the property to James Whatman. Possibly he was unable to meet the repayments, for in 1852, Whatman took possession and installed John Munn as landlord. Munn combined his duties behind the bar with that of his plumbing business, until Prentice Lines took over in 1857. Two years later, Whatman let the inn to the brewers Style and Company and John Hayward assumed the position of landlord, holding it for the next 40 years.

Under Hayward, the inn flourished, developing its trade from travellers on the road to Sittingbourne or Sheppey. Later it was to became a popular venue for cycling clubs who wished to avoid the inherent dangers of town traffic. In 1887, ownership passed from the hands of the Whatmans to Charles Arkcoll and eventually Style and Winch. The first quarter of this century saw a succession of some 6 landlords, none of whom remained more than 6 years, until Hargrave Walters took over in 1923.

Today, Britter's once unfavoured inn has been transformed internally beyond recognition. Reinvented for the 1990's , with all the cosy charm of a much older establishment, and now more restaurant than pub.

The Malta

In June 1850, John Bartlett, the assistant lock-keeper at Allington Lock was abruptly sacked, and evicted from his tied cottage. It appears likely that he had been using the Navigation Company's premises to sell and possibly brew beer. Undaunted, by January the following year he had almost completed the erection of a brick and timber building in the grounds of the old paper mill, just yards from his former home. From there he ran his carpentry business, and opened a beerhouse. Soon it was attracting quite a custom and in September 1852 he was forced to apply for permission to erect a 50 foot long, post-and-rail fence on the side of the towing path, to prevent inebriated clients from wandering into the river! In 1862 he sold the beerhouse to William Marchant, and when the Sills family, who ran the quarries across the river, bought it in 1866, it was named The Malta Beerhouse. The name appears to have been given by soldiers from Maidstone Barracks who had been accustomed to traverse the towpath to the Gibralter Inn. Mindful of their postings in the Mediterranean, when Malta was the next port-of-call after Gibralter, their second 'port-of-call' on an evening's drinking became 'The Malta'. In 1869 Elizabeth Sills became the first licensee of The Malta Inn, remaining so until 1883 when retired lockkeeper Abraham Vane took the reins. Eight landlords came and went over the next 36 years, until following an 8 year stint by Charles Chafer, Joseph Longhurst became the licensee in 1930. As the barge traffic decreased, over the 25 years of his tenure, Joe saw his trade decrease to a few regulars.

The popularity of today's lively establishment evolved from the vision of a new tenant, John Percy, who arrived in 1955. Since it became a pub, The Malta had been tied to The Lower Brewery of Isherwood, Foster and Stacey. This is unsurprising as the Stacey family owned the land on which it stood, together with most of Sandling. In 1929 Fremlins Ltd absorbed the brewery, and in 1952 injected some capital to smarten up the pub, adding a small restaurant on the western end. Mr Percy, certain of the potential of such attractively sited premises, applied to have further improvements made. His plans were refused, but in the true spirit of his predecessor Bartlett, he gained permission to construct a large bar extension, with a restaurant above, at his own expense! The extension more than quadrupled the bar space and, together with its popular restaurant, the pub soon became one of the busiest in the area. Bands played in both bar and restaurant, and the latter even boasted a small revolving floor. In 1979, five years after Percy's retirement, Whitbreads, who had taken over Fremlins, extended slightly further, adding the mock oast roundels.

1998 has seen the opening of its motel, but despite its sprawling growth, Bartlett's little premises remain today, as the little verandah fronted eastern section.

The Yew Tree

The story of The Yew Tree commences with the Constable family, of whom there is more in the Sandling chapter. They occupied 4 cottages at Farthings from at least 1826, one of which was to become the beerhouse. When exactly they commenced purveying beer is uncertain, but one imagines that it probably coincided with the establishment of the Abbey Brewery just a few hundred yards away in the early 1840's. The 1841 census shows that John Constable and his wife Hester had a 'female servant' living in. It is possible that she was employed behind the bar, and certainly by 1851, John was described as a 'landlord'. By 1865, George Constable the younger, was running an alehouse there for which the 1871 census first records the name The Yew Tree Beerhouse.

The following year, John Richardson began a 10 year spell in charge. In 1874 he fell foul of the increasingly draconian legislation aimed at reducing the popularity of the 'beer and gin culture'. His premises were inspected, and two quart measures were found to be incorrect, not surprisingly in his favour. Fined 10 shillings with an additional 9 shillings costs, he was lucky not to have been closed down. James Fullager followed him, seeing the beerhouse into the 20th Century. It was probably under Jarvis Jarett who ran it through to about 1930, that it finally attained the status of a public house.

Originally tied to Edward Mason's brewery of the Waterside, Maidstone, it became a Shepherd Neame pub when they took over Masons in 1956. By that time the now thriving little establishment was being run by the second generation of the Sear family who had arrived more than 20 years earlier and remained well into the 1960's. Despite the realignment of the road in front and the loss of its pastoral view, the quaint inn survived the desecration to the valley caused by the construction of the M20 which today overshadows it.

The Pottery Arms

Shortly after purchasing Forstal Paper Mill on the road to Aylesford in 1828, George Fowle erected a couple of cottages on part of the site, one of which was utilised as a beerhouse for the workers at Pratling and Forstal Mills, and the adjoining wharf.

One of the first beersellers was a character known as 'Fish' Belton, who was a cricketer of some renown. The 1851 census contains the tantalising snippet that Elizabeth Belton and her 4 children were living in one of the cottages, her husband (presumably 'Fish'), having been transported to Australia. When Ann Fowle, widow, sold the property to Edward Ladd Betts in 1850, the occupier was John Millen junior, whose father ran the Abbey Brewery at the great barn. Betts had erected the Aylesford Pottery next door the previous year and the beerhouse was to later take its name from this. James Wire, a sawyer, and his wife Sarah, ran it from about 1854 to 1870. The 1861 census shows there were 5 adults and 8 children crammed into the tiny living quarters, above and behind the room in which beer was dispensed!

Throughout the 1870's the beerhouse keeper was Jabez Katt. The first mention of the name "The Pottery Arms' that we have found is in 1882, by which time it had become a pub under landlord Charles Gilbert. It was probably at this time that it was extended by converting into one the two end

PLACES OF REFRESHMENT

cottages of what was now a substantial row. By this time the pub was part of H.A. Brassey's Preston Hall Estate. It had been tied to The Lower Brewery and remained so until 1888 when Style and Winch purchased it from the Brassey family. Following short-lived tenancies by Edgar Figgis and George Cheeseman, Henry Beddow took over in 1905. His family were to remain into the 1960's. Unable to compete with the current vogue of theme pubs and bars it closed in the mid 1990's. Despite two abortive attempts to reopen under new names, it has become a guest house.

We have come across many references to licensed victuallers and innkeepers of Boxley whom we cannot allocate to any specific inn. The earliest known Boxley licences were granted in 1602 to Stephen Scott, and the widow Martin. Presumably they occupied ye Lion and ye Bull. There are also inns we know existed, but that we cannot place. William Rowles landlord of The Gibraltar at the end of the 17th Century was also landlord at the Red Lion in 1707 and 1710 taking over for a year whilst the pub was in between landlords. In 1709 he obtained a licence for his own inn called 'The Three Cups', which establishment also figures in the licensing records for 1712 and 1713. He died the following year, and his widow Margaret was granted a licence for 'The Bottle and Glass'. Between 1719 and 1728 at least, she was landlady of 'The Plough'. Whether these establishments were one and the same is not known. They were all in Sandling, and the archives contain a title deed for a house built in 1708 by William Rowles which was owned by The Lower Brewery. It was demolished in 1768 after having served as a smithy. It stood about 100 yards west of The Running Horse. Between 1691 and 1693 at least, a Mrs Williams was running 'The Ship' in Friday Street in Boxley parish, late Mr Balls. Isaac Jones and his widow were the proprietors from 1705 to 1735. The pub or beerhouse disappears from the records in 1757 whilst in the occupation of Henry Lamb. We have been unable to trace the location of Friday Street.

Various alehouses are also known to have existed, which never became pubs. In addition to those mentioned in other chapters, Thomas Walter ran one between 1839 and 1842 and Filmer Day (1843-47). In 1615 Richard Gilbert was indicted for keeping a victualling house in Boxley without a licence, where he sold bread and beer. It is just possible that this was The Fulling Lodge. We know that from at least 1629 Stephen Gilbert was miller at Sandling Corn Mill. The discovery of an extra-large bread oven in the chimney of the oldest part of Gibraltar House suggests a scenario of the Sandling miller supplying his brother with flour to provide sustenance for hungry workers at the adjacent wharf.

Three further pubs, 'The Huntsman', 'The Artichoke' and 'The Woodman' are described in other chapters.

Site of the 'Great Lake of Boxley' close to the Detling Road. Now a fishing lake.

Weavering House

CHAPTER 29

Odds and Ends

Our final chapter contains observations on properties at the further bounds of the parish that have failed to find a mention elsewhere in the book, together with information on several roads and certain enigmas.

Snuggled in a fold of land beneath the Downs to the west of the A249 lie the delightful cluster of buildings that compose Harpole Farm. Harpole may lay claim to being one of the oldest settlements in Boxley. Although the parish boundary with Detling now runs through the farm, it has formed a major part of the Manor of Boxley for centuries. Originally 'Horepole', the name derives from the Anglo Saxon for 'filthy pool' or 'dark pool', which may refer to 'The Great Lake of Boxley' which still exists in somewhat shrunken form on the south-western boundary of the farm close by where the A249 and M20 join. The lily-covered, sylvan beauty of the lake today would hardly justify such a slur.

In 1197 the occupiers were Vital de Horepole and his brother Ernulph who rented 20 acres from Walter de Pierrepoint. By 1554 there appear to have been three separate farms in the area:– 'A farm of certain lands called Harpolle and the Dyhouse of 8 acres in tenure of Alexander Fisher' (fined for his involvement in Wyatt's uprising). 'A farm of 4 pieces called Dihouse (3 acres), Oxenlease (16 acres), Three Cornered Croft (2 acres) and Filket Hole (2 acres) in tenure of William Webb' Lastly, 'the fields of Great and Little Harpoule' which formed part of Thomas Vicary's lands. 'Dihouse' may refer to Workhouse Cottage which stands alongside the A249 nearer Maidstone. This was once part of the Park House Estate, and various domestic work was carried out there. This may well have included the dyeing of fabric. Certainly the raw materials of coloured dyes such as madder and saffron are recorded as being harvested in neighbouring fields. The Webb family appear to have taken over Fisher's farm, William and Thomas Webb being recorded there in 1641. By 1678 it was certainly just one farm in tenure of John Field. Sir John Banks owned it in 1681 with William Lane as his tenant. When in 1750 John Green took over from the Athawes family, starting a dynasty that was to last for some 85 years, the farm formed part of the Aylesford Estate and 43% of its lands lay in Boxley. In 1804 the oasthouse was repaired and annexed to form a home for William Green junior. When he took over the 181 acre farm 6 years later, he further enlarged the house, and in 1818 constructed a new barn followed by a stable for 7 horses. Stephen Stonham became the tenant in 1835 and was still there in 1860 when the farm was purchased by Maudistley Best. Soon thereafter Charles Foster became the tenant, running it together with the adjoining Court Lodge Farm, until he was replaced by John Jones and Alfred and Horace Betts. Worthy of mention is East Lodge in Harple Lane, which lay on the eastern extremity of the Park House Estate. It has modern additions to the original Victorian Lodge, and is an interesting marker of the wide extent of the Estate.

Horish or Horwash Wood behind Newnham Court is also ancient. In 1191 it was known as Horwessesland when an agreement as to ownership was reached between the Abbot of Boxley and the Prior of Leeds (witnesses included William Chempe whose family remained in Boxley into the 19th Century, and Humfrey the crossbowman). By 1281 it had become Horish when John son of Joce de Horwesse was required to pay to Leeds Priory, '41 pence annual rent which the Master of the New Work in Maidstone used to pay him for wood and ground he held of him at Horish' (The New Work or Newark was the hospital which stood by St. Peter's Church). Horish Wood itself was said to have been purchased in 1261 by the Monks of Boxley.

It is surprising to discover how far the south west corner of Boxley impinged onto Maidstone Town. The boundary followed the centre of the River Len to Square Hill where stood Christian's Mill. This had been a fulling mill since at least 1567 and in 1608 was owned by Luce Barrington and in tenure of John Westerby. In 1656 the mill was included in the settlement made by Lady Colepeper of Preston Hall on the marriage of her daughter Frances to John Alchorne. By then it had been converted and was described as, 'a wheat mill and malt mill' (presumably it therefore had 2 wheels), plus 2 acres in occupation of John Lambe, miller. In 1710 it was sold by John Savage to William Perlis. William Gill, the papermaker and brewer, bought the property together with a barn and stable in 1718, probably with the original intention of converting it to papermaking. However, two years later he pulled it down and erected 6 tenements on the 2 acre plot, which were known as The Square. Old Square Hill, in which The British Queen pub stands, bordered the Square after which it was named, and formed the parish boundary.

Above The Square, and just south of today's Ashford Road, stood The Artichoke Public House. One of Boxley's oldest pubs, it dispensed ale from the 16th Century through to 1769 when its then landlord Thomas Smith closed its doors. Originally named 'The Greybrother', from 1700 it bore the appellation 'The Hartichoke'. Then under Thomas Brown and his wife it was 'The Cape Artichoke' followed by 'The Hop Garden Man' until in 1752 under Henry Parks it became 'The Artichoke'. Following its closure it was bought by Edward Ellis who converted it into his country house. By 1791 the property was in the tenancy of James Whatman and was probably being run as a beerhouse for the use of his workers at Turkey Mill. In 1816 it was once again licensed as a public house under landlord William Masters, and in 1821 Whatman purchased it. Michael Field took over in 1840, becoming both its longest serving and final

ODDS AND ENDS

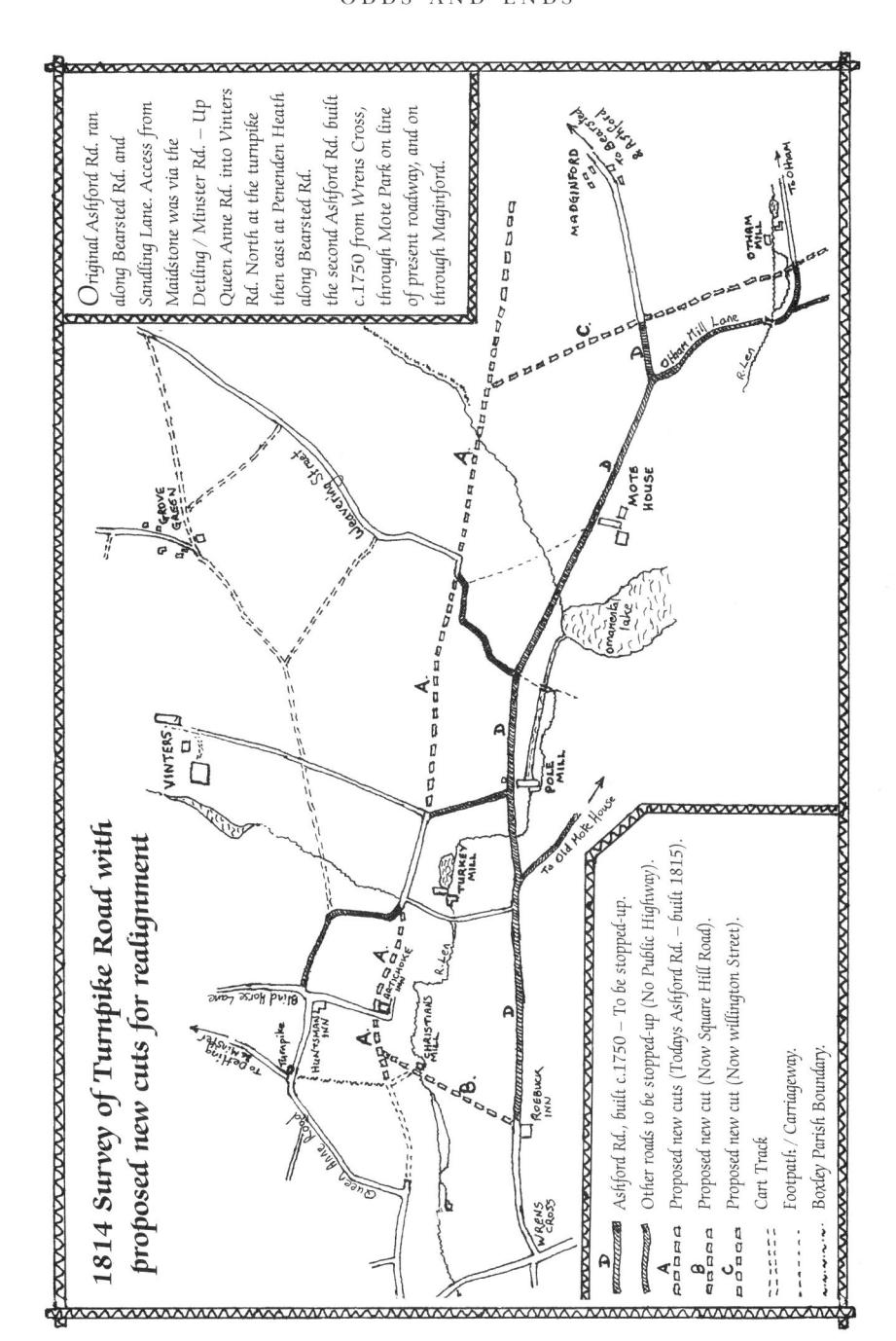

1814 Survey of Turnpike Road with proposed new cuts for realignment

Original Ashford Rd. ran along Bearsted Rd. and Sandling Lane. Access from Maidstone was via the Detling / Minster Rd. – Up Queen Anne Rd. into Vinters Rd. North at the turnpike then east at Penenden Heath along Bearsted Rd. the second Ashford Rd. built c.1750 from Wrens Cross, through Mote Park on line of present roadway, and on through Maginford.

- ▭ Ashford Rd., built c.1750 – To be stopped-up.
- ▱ Other roads to be stopped-up (No Public Highway).
- A Proposed new cuts (Todays Ashford Rd. – built 1815).
- B Proposed new cut (Now Square Hill Road).
- C Proposed new cut (Now Willington Street).
- ═══ Cart Track
- ----- Footpath / Carriageway.
- ─ · ─ Boxley Parish Boundary.

253

publican. In 1883 the proposed railway extension from Maidstone to Ashford Road sealed its fate, or rather the intransigence of the last James Whatman did. A glance at a map will show that after passing beneath the Sittingbourne Road the line loops down and then back up under Weavering Street to Ware Street, before bearing east. The reason for this is that Whatman vehemently opposed the straight line that would have taken the track through Vinters Park. The alternative loop through the southern borders of his land necessitated the demolition of The Artichoke to enable the construction of the viaduct over the Ashford Road.

The Ashford Road as we know it in the 1990's was not constructed until 1815. Originally King Street ended at a 5 bar gate by Queen Anne Road and a footpath continued to where The Artichoke stood amongst hop fields. To get to Ashford one could take two different routes. From Wrens Cross a carriageway ran through Mote Park approximately along the line of the road that today borders the pitch-and-putt course. Where the metalled road now ends were the gates to Old Mote House, and the carriageway bore sharp east here following the ridge above the Len. It crossed at a ford where now is a bridge and then went north east through Madginford to Bearsted. Alternatively the traveller went up Queen Anne Road, past the pub of that name. There was no Sittingbourne Road and Queen Anne Road continued eastward into Vinters Road. Two hundred yards on from the Queen Anne was a turnpike gate. Here the main highway branched off north to Detling and ultimately to Sittingbourne and Minster. Where it crossed the Bearsted Road from Penenden Heath one could branch eastwards to Ashford. Hasted's map of 1800 still shows this as the main route to Ashford. This however is an error. In 1793 an Act of Parliament was passed for amending and improving and keeping in repair the highway to Ashford (the southern route) which was said to be in a bad state of repair and in places narrow and meandering. A new road was constructed from Wrens Cross, past the Roebuck Inn, which stood opposite where now is Square Hill Road, and on past Pole Mill. It then went immediately north of where the present Mote House was built and straight on to Madginford. The route is preserved today in Mote Road and the roadway that continues through the park north of the lake. A survey of 1804 prompted by Lord Romney suggested the present line of the road, which took it away from his new house. The Highway Trustees advocated the construction of Square Hill Road to adjoin the new road to the old road from Wrens Cross, thus avoiding the town centre. However there was considerable support for extending King Street or East Lane as it was then called. The new route was put to public referendum and despite the survey describing the route through East Lane as 'a wanton expenditure of public money', it was this way that was chosen. Notwithstanding, the Trustees constructed Square Hill Road as well, knocking down most of The Square in the process. Today a block of flats adorns the spot. With the construction of the new Ashford Road a turnpike was erected across the road, opposite the Artichoke. The turnpike cottage remains today, being the first house on the north of the road after the railway viaduct. The houses adjoining known as Prospect Place were then erected on a piece of land called Jewry Hop Garden. In 1882 one then housed an Academy run by Andrew Crawford, probably the house that took the name 'Ions', after John Ions, the manager of Turkey Mill papermill in the 1890's. During the same period Geo Brooker occupied a house here with a 10 acre fruit farm.

Huntsman Lane originally ran north east from The Artichoke, and then sharply west along what is now Vinters Lane. It took its name from The Hunstman pub which stood on the corner. Probably a beerhouse, for some years earlier it received its first licence in 1712 and its landlord Walter Read gave it the name 'The Huntsman and Hounds'. Three years later he altered the name to 'The Green Man'. Probably because its sign depicted a huntsman clothed in green, but possibly named after the fabled spirit of nature often depicted with a visage composed of foliage. When William Rowles junior took over in 1731 it took on the name of 'The Huntsman'. It was probably always tied to the Lower Brewery in Lower Stone Street, as its successive owners Saunders, Smalvell, Brenchley and Stacey were all proprietors of that brewery. Prominent landlords included Thomas Logan 1748-62, and John Saltmarsh 1767-82. It was purchased by James Whatman in 1821, who set up George Styles as licensee and he remained as 'mine host' until its closure in 1852. His son Edward was a painter and the inn soon became a favourite haunt of artists. The 1841 census records that 9 were staying there. Next to the pub on the Ashford Road side was Huntsman House. William Bolton occupied this and the adjoining oasthouse from at least 1841 through to the 1870's. Originally a poulterer, by 1861 he was described as a pig dealer and butcher. Maryland House stood on the west side of the pub. It was also owned by the Whatmans and over the years was leased to minor gentry such as army officers and barristers. For some time in the 1880's-90's it appears to have served as a language school. Mrs Trousdell lived there in 1933. The whole area along to where Sittingbourne Road was constructed was known as Maryland Point. In 1782 The Square and Maryland Point had 50 inhabitants occupying 14 dwellings. During the 1860's another residence in the lane housed The Boxley Female Home for Discharged Prisoners under its superintendent Maria Lathangue. This may well have been the property known as Virginia House. By the Sittingboure Road, where the attractive Church has recently been constructed, George Russell ran his plumbers and glaziers shop in the middle of the 19th Century. On the opposite side of the lane where now is the school, Thomas Wicks farmer and cornfactor occupied a farmhouse and oasts. Also here was the Turnpike Cottage. The road to Detling branched off north east from here until it reached a large farm which stood where Commodore Road is today. Originally known as Callants Farm, it was occupied by Jesse Green in 1826, and was known as Queen Anne Farm when George Green farmed there in the 1840's-50's. James Oliver was Whatman's tenant at another 18½ acre farm, just to the south where he had hopgardens and a triple kiln oast. By 1871 Green had combined the two farms and with additional land was farming some 130 acres which were called Vinters Farm. In 1881 Ezekias Sanders was farming 26 acres of a reduced Vinters Farm with Mark Lane tenant of a further 24 acres. William Bellingham ran it together with Newnham Court Farm in the 1920's-30's. The Detling Road turned eastwards above the farm, skirting the edge of Vinters Stone Quarry until it reached the grounds of Vinters House where it turned north following the park boundary to the Bearsted Road. For many years this part of the road had been known as Blind Horse Lane. With the construction of the Sittingbourne Road the lane was little used and soon developed a bad reputation. It crossed James Whatman's land, and he pressed for it to be closed. The Vicar of Boxley wrote to him in 1822 and expressed his support for the proposal, describing Blind Horse Lane "as a general nuisance to the neighbourhood, from its situation rendering it a favourable harbour for idle and evil disposed persons; and there are so many other more convenient avenues to the Ashford Road". And duly closed it was. Now Huntsman Lane from Sittingbourne Road became Vinters Road, and the name Huntsman Lane switched to the length of the road north from the Huntsman Inn past Vinters Farm.

On the Ashford Road, just beyond where Huntsman Lane now joins it, was the South Lodge to Vinters House. An earlier South Lodge had stood just east of Turkey Mill during the time that the entrance carriageway to the house ran north from there. Opposite this prior to construction of the A20, the road went south to Pole Mill. In 1801 there was a gate or bar across the highway here. Every wagon, cart and carriage was halted and weighed on a weighing engine. They were charged the sum of 20 shillings for every hundredweight by which they exceeded specified weight limits. On the eastern corner of New Cut Lane and Ashford Road the imposing Weavering House was built by the Whatmans in the 1870's. By 1881 it was being leased to Miss Louisa Style who occupied it for some years together with Lady Margaret Marsham. Leslie Caldecott resided there in the 1920's.

The Vicar Rev. Bradshaw brought to our notice an intriguing Boxley tale of the 13th Century. Amongst the stained glass panels in one of the 'miracle windows' of Canterbury Cathedral is depicted the story of two crippled daughters of one Godbold of Boxley. Both lame from birth they had apparently made their laborious pilgrimage on foot with the aid of crutches. Whilst the elder sister slept, the younger prayed at the tomb of Saint Thomas Becket. She is said to have asked that if God had only one blessing, that it should fall on her. Come morning the elder daughter had been cured, reducing her egoistic sister to tears. After giving thanks for the miracle they set off for home. However, God took pity on the younger girl and cured her also. Unfortunately we have been unable to discover where in the parish they dwelt.

Another mystery concerns a building that once stood in front of the Church on the site now occupied by the war memorial. In 1900 the historian E.R. Hughes copied a water-colour executed some years earlier by Edward Pretty, first curator of Maidstone Museum. It depicts a large ancient looking house with stone mullioned windows. A later print shows another building in the same position but much smaller, and this also appears on the 1844 tithe map. Major Best confirmed to Hughes that the large building had stood there within his lifetime. We have been unable to unearth any information about it. The temptation to link it with Thomas Vicary was scotched when we discovered that it did not appear on a 1743 map of Court Lodge Farm.

A reference in P. Clarke's 'English Provincial Society' instigated a fruitless search for further information on the following subject. He mentions that a colony of 'Diggers' were believed to have been founded near Boxley around 1650. Oliver Cromwell's Commonwealth had been a political revolution but not one based on socialist ethics. The Diggers sect under their leader Winstanley believed that all land should belong to the people. They argued that Christian principles required the cultivation of all crown property and common land with the spade. Hence 'Diggers'. For years prior to this Boxley inhabitants had a reputation for radical puritan beliefs. From the late 14th Century they were 'Lollards', following the teachings of John Wycliffe who attacked abuses within the church. Then in the 1580's as 'Brownists' they became part of the earliest Puritan sect followed by Robert Browne. Under the influence of Thomas Brewer, Boxley became a 'separatist' church, preaching religious freedom. John Turner, a radical preacher from Sutton Valence, frequently preached there and from 1627 to 1640 he and Brewer were imprisoned for their faith. However for a time in 1637 Brewer escaped, and was to be found in Maidstone and the Medway Towns whipping up religious fervour against the persecutions of Archbishop Laud. It was not therefore surprising that when John Crump was ousted as minister at All Saints Maidstone in 1662 for refusing to give up his puritanic sympathies of Nonconformity, he should find a welcome in the pulpit at Boxley Church.

And so our story of Boxley Parish comes to an end. As it closes, so comes a dramatic change to its landscape as the groundwork begins in 1999 for the High Speed Rail Link. What would Rev. Cave-Browne have thought had he seen that and the motorway in his crystal ball, whilst writing his own Parish History in 1892? And what might the next hundred years bring?